The Foundations of Nature

VERITAS
Series Introduction

"... the truth will set you free" (John 8:32)

In much contemporary discourse, Pilate's question has been taken to mark the absolute boundary of human thought. Beyond this boundary, it is often suggested, is an intellectual hinterland into which we must not venture. This terrain is an agnosticism of thought: because truth cannot be possessed, it must not be spoken. Thus, it is argued that the defenders of "truth" in our day are often traffickers in ideology, merchants of counterfeits, or anti-liberal. They are, because it is somewhat taken for granted that Nietzsche's word is final: truth is the domain of tyranny.

Is this indeed the case, or might another vision of truth offer itself? The ancient Greeks named the love of wisdom as *philia*, or friendship. The one who would become wise, they argued, would be a "friend of truth." For both philosophy and theology might be conceived as schools in the friendship of truth, as a kind of relation. For like friendship, truth is as much discovered as it is made. If truth is then so elusive, if its domain is *terra incognita*, perhaps this is because it arrives to us—unannounced—as gift, as a person, and not some thing.

The aim of the Veritas book series is to publish incisive and original current scholarly work that inhabits "the between" and "the beyond" of theology and philosophy. These volumes will all share a common aspiration to transcend the institutional divorce in which these two disciplines often find themselves, and to engage questions of pressing concern to both philosophers and theologians in such a way as to reinvigorate both disciplines with a kind of interdisciplinary desire, often so absent in contemporary academe. In a word, these volumes represent collective efforts in the befriending of truth, doing so beyond the simulacra of pretend tolerance, the violent, yet insipid reasoning of liberalism that asks with Pilate, "What is truth?"—expecting a consensus of non-commitment; one that encourages the commodification of the mind, now sedated by the civil service of career, ministered by the frightened patrons of position.

The series will therefore consist of two "wings": (1) original monographs; and (2) essay collections on a range of topics in theology and philosophy. The latter will principally be the products of the annual conferences of the Centre of Theology and Philosophy (www.theologyphilosophycentre.co.uk).

Conor Cunningham and Eric Austin Lee, *Series editors*

"Taylor has performed three services in one in this work. First he offers us a comprehensive exposition of the best that trinitarian metaphysics has offered in the past century, secondly he has done this with a great deal of literary panache, and thirdly he has shown how a metaphysics of gift is required to underpin bioethical practices which will actually foster freedom and respect human dignity. This work belongs to a new generation of bioethics that goes beyond and beneath the tired old protocols that acknowledge nothing higher than technology."
—Tracey Rowland, St. John Paul II Chair of Theology, University of Notre Dame, Australia

"Taylor's use of 'integral ecology' reasserts the fact that 'nature' comprehends the entire created universe and, for this reason, includes both human bioethics and ecological ethics in the same worldview that gazes upon the manifold gift of existence. . . . The book's clarity and precision make it an invaluable contribution to the future of ethical debate, especially regarding the environment, technology, and medicine."
—Pablo Martínez de Anguita, Professor of Forestry and Rural Development, Rey Juan Carlos University, Madrid

"Dr. Michael Taylor's work offers a profound Christian vision of the real. He seeks honestly to gaze on the whole in all of its depth through the aid of figures such as Ferdinand Ulrich, Hans Urs von Balthasar, and Pope Benedict XVI among others. At the interface of metaphysics and trinitarian theology, this book ranges from the mystical into the ecological and back again."
—Aaron Riches, author of *Ecce Homo: On the Divine Unity of Christ*

"Taylor's book takes a matter that concerns all of us at some level, namely, the meaning of nature, and opens it up to depths far beyond the limits modern ecology often sets for itself. It not only lets a new light into the field, but it does so in a way that allows us to avoid all the usual tired reductions. Those seeking orientation in this field will benefit greatly from his wise insights."
—D. C. Schindler, Professor of Metaphysics and Anthropology, Pontifical John Paul II Institute at The Catholic University of America

Not available from Cascade

Deane-Peter Baker	*Tayloring Reformed Epistemology: The Challenge to Christian Belief.*
P. Candler & C. Cunningham (eds.)	*Belief and Metaphysics.*
Marcus Pound	*Theology, Psychoanalysis, and Trauma.*
Espen Dahl	*Phenomenology and the Holy.*
C. Cunningham et al. (eds.)	*Grandeur of Reason: Religion, Tradition, and Universalism.*
A. Pabst & A. Paddison (eds.)	*The Pope and Jesus of Nazareth: Christ, Scripture, and the Church.*
J. P. Moreland	*Recalcitrant Imago Dei: Human Persons and the Failure of Naturalism.*

Available from Cascade Books

[Nathan Kerr	*Christ, History, and Apocalyptic: The Politics of Christian Mission.*][1]
Anthony D. Baker	*Diagonal Advance: Perfection in Christian Theology.*
D. C. Schindler	*The Perfection of Freedom: Schiller, Schelling, and Hegel between the Ancients and the Moderns.*
Rustin Brian	*Covering Up Luther: How Barth's Christology Challenged the* Deus Absconditus *that Haunts Modernity.*
Timothy Stanley	*Protestant Metaphysics After Karl Barth and Martin Heidegger.*
Christopher Ben Simpson	*The Truth Is the Way: Kierkegaard's* Theologia Viatorum.
Richard H. Bell	*Wagner's Parsifal: An Appreciation in the Light of His Theological Journey.*
Antonio Lopez	*Gift and the Unity of Being.*
Toyohiko Kagawa	*Cosmic Purpose.* Translated and introduced by Thomas John Hastings.
Nigel Zimmerman	*Facing the Other: John Paul II, Levinas, and the Body.*
Conor Sweeney	*Sacramental Presence after Heidegger: Onto-theology, Sacraments, and the Mother's Smile.*
John Behr et al. (eds.)	*The Role of Death in Life: A Multidisciplinary Examination of the Relation between Life and Death.*

---

1. Note: Nathan Kerr, *Christ, History, and Apocalyptic*, although volume 3 of the original SCM Veritas series, is available from Cascade as part of the Theopolitical Visions series.

Eric Austin Lee et al. (eds.)	*The Resounding Soul: Reflection on the Metaphysics and Vivacity of the Human Person.*
Orion Edgar	*Things Seen and Unseen: The Logic of Incarnation in Merleau-Ponty's Metaphysics of Flesh.*
Duncan B. Reyburn	*Seeing Things as They Are: G. K. Chesterton and the Drama of Meaning.*
Lyndon Shakespeare	*Being the Body of Christ in the Age of Management.*
Michael V. Di Fuccia	*Owen Barfield: Philosophy, Poetry, and Theology.*
John McNerney	*Wealth of Persons: Economics with a Human Face.*
Norm Klassen	*The Fellowship of the Beatific Vision: Chaucer on Overcoming Tyranny and Becoming Ourselves.*
Donald Wallenfang	*Human and Divine Being: A Study of the Theological Anthropology of Edith Stein.*
Sotiris Mitralexis	*Ever-Moving Repose: A Contemporary Reading of Maximus the Confessor's Theory of Time.*
Sotiris Mitralexis et al. (eds.)	*Maximus the Confessor as a European Philosopher.*
Kevin Corrigan	*Love, Friendship, Beauty, and the Good: Plato, Aristotle, and the Later Tradition.*
Andrew Brower Latz	*The Social Philosophy of Gillian Rose.*
D. C. Schindler	*Love and the Postmodern Predicament: Rediscovering the Real in Beauty, Goodness, and Truth.*
Stephen Kampowski	*Embracing Our Finitude: Exercises in a Christian Anthropology between Dependence and Gratitude.*
William Desmond	*The Gift of Beauty and the Passion of Being: On the Threshold between the Aesthetic and the Religious.*
Charles Péguy	*Notes on Bergson and Descartes.*
David Alcalde	*Cosmology without God: The Problematic Theology Inherent in Modern Cosmology.*
Benson P. Fraser	*Hide and Seek: The Sacred Art of Indirect Communication.*
Philip John Paul Gonzales	*Exorcising Philosophical Modernity: Cyril O'Regan and Christian Discourse after Modernity.*
Caitlin Smith Gilson	*Subordinated Ethics: Natural Law and Moral Miscellany in Aquinas and Dostoyevsky.*

The Foundations of Nature

Metaphysics of Gift for an Integral Ecological Ethic

MICHAEL DOMINIC TAYLOR
Foreword by LARRY CHAPP

CASCADE *Books* • Eugene, Oregon

THE FOUNDATIONS OF NATURE
Metaphysics of Gift for an Integral Ecological Ethic

Veritas

Copyright © 2020 Michael Dominic Taylor. All rights reserved. Except for brief quotations in critical publications or reviews, no part of this book may be reproduced in any manner without prior written permission from the publisher. Write: Permissions, Wipf and Stock Publishers, 199 W. 8th Ave., Suite 3, Eugene, OR 97401.

Cascade Books
An Imprint of Wipf and Stock Publishers
199 W. 8th Ave., Suite 3
Eugene, OR 97401

www.wipfandstock.com

PAPERBACK ISBN: 978-1-7252-6497-7
HARDCOVER ISBN: 978-1-7252-6498-4
EBOOK ISBN: 978-1-7252-6499-1

Cataloguing-in-Publication data:

Names: Taylor, Michael Dominic. | Chapp, Larry S., 1958–, foreword.

Title: The foundations of nature : metaphysics of gift for an integral ecological ethic / Michael Dominic Taylor ; foreword by Larry Chapp.

Description: Eugene, OR : Cascade Books, 2020 | Series: Veritas | Includes bibliographical references.

Identifiers: ISBN 978-1-7252-6497-7 (paperback) | ISBN 978-1-7252-6498-4 (hardcover) | ISBN 978-1-7252-6499-1 (ebook)

Subjects: LCSH: Metaphysics. | Philosophical theology. | Theism—History. | Environmental ethics.

Classification: GE195 .T39 2020 (print) | GE195 .T39 (ebook)

Manufactured in the U.S.A.   DECEMBER 18, 2020

To my mother

The act of being is an act of giving, an act of knowing, an act of love.
—STRATFORD CALDECOTT (1953–2014)

Contents

Foreword by Larry Chapp xiii
Preface xix
Acknowledgments xxiii

Introduction: The Nature of Our Crisis 1

1. **The Enduring Questions:**
   The Development, Rejections, and Renewals of Metaphysics 9
   A Brief History of Being 10
   Rejections of Metaphysics 19
   Attempted Recoveries of Metaphysics 29
   The Metaphysics of Gift: A First Look 37

2. **Two Visions of Nature and Morality:**
   The Technological Paradigm vs. Eco-philosophies 46
   A Mechanical Cosmos: Technological Metaphysics 49
   Lost in the Flux: Emergent Science and Eco-philosophies 63
   Overcoming Mechanism 77

3. **The Person and the Leviathan:**
   The Technological Paradigm in Contemporary Liberal Bioethics 79
   Formal Rationality and Classical Liberal Bioethics 82
   Power over Life: A Sociopolitical Critique 89
   Reconceiving Bioethical Practice 101
   A Richer, Deeper Foundation 116

4. **Thinking through Gift: Contemplating Nature's Splendor** 118
   The Meaning of the Original Gift of Being 121
   Five Exponents of the Metaphysics of Gift 125
   Wonder, Beauty, and Gift 198
   An Ever-New Gaze 200

5. **Metaphysics of Gift in Action** 203
   Is Holism the Answer? 205
   To Do Good Work 213
   Solidarity through Dialogue 224
   To Live in the World 233

   Epilogue: Imagination and Our Ontological Covenant 236

   Bibliography 243

FOREWORD

Michael Dominic Taylor's new text on an integral ecological ethic in the light of a metaphysics of gift could not be more timely. As I type these words, I am in lockdown in my home due to the ongoing Coronavirus pandemic. And one cannot help but think that the ease with which the virus has spread has at least something to do with our ongoing technological exploitation of the natural world, the degradation of natural environments, and our out-of-sync relationship with the earth. And one does not have to be a radical environmentalist where humanity is viewed as a disease that needs to be purged to see that we have not been good stewards of the natural world. Therefore, there is a great need for works such as this one by Taylor where a vision is articulated that escapes the extremes of a reductionistic and technocratic materialism on the one hand and an escapist Gnosticism on the other. It also avoids the pitfalls of a form of environmentalism, mentioned above, that personifies nature itself and sees all human activity as an "assault" upon the integrity of a natural world that has been imbued with a quasi-mystical quality. In other words, Taylor gives us here a true metaphysics, deeply profound and embedded in a grand metaphysical tradition, that avoids both a mechanistic reduction of nature to a tool of human power, and the magical mystification of nature as something set against human agency.

Taylor also does a good job of showing that there are deep connections between our misuse of the environment and our politics and economics. What this current crisis has proved beyond any shadow of a doubt is that our globalist, technocratic, capitalist, and neoliberal order is both environmentally fragile and, because of that fragility, almost necessarily authoritarian. The last and only remaining "values" of the Liberal order (liberty and equality) have been summarily, and almost casually, set aside since the only possible remedy for the pandemic, given the current state of our culture, politics, and economics, is the blunt force of the state. What it shows is that after several hundred years now of mechanistic, naturalistic, reductionistic, and scientistic thinking, combined with Liberalism's acidic and corrosive destruction of traditional communitarian values and structures (the church and the family in particular), the modern *ordo* that dominates everything is nothing more than a thinly veiled proceduralism, where there are no values or goods that inhere in anything and that all such values and goods are simply "made such" by a stipulative agreement achieved through some equally facile process of political consensus. The whole thing is a kabuki theater masquerade—a fact proven by the rapidity with which those same stipulative goods are tossed out the window in the face of a crisis.

But all is not lost, and we should not succumb to cynicism or pessimism. Just as Tolkien rose from the horrors he witnessed firsthand in World War I, and penned his grand mythology in *The Hobbit* and *The Lord of the Rings*, so too can we learn from the current crisis how to approach things differently, which of course implies seeing things differently. And it is the project of "seeing things differently" that Taylor is pursuing here. The result is a stunning new way of looking at the natural world and our place within it. In many ways, as with Tolkien, the current work is as much a *cri de coeur* for a radical conversion of worldview as it is a profound academic work. It is thus written with both precision and passion—a rare combination in works of this type.

Thus, like Tolkien, Taylor shows that the environmental crises of our time and the political/economic crises of our time are deeply related. Taylor began his career trained in the sciences, doing biological field work in Alaska studying steelhead trout, and has now moved into more philosophical academic pursuits. Thus, he has a foot in both the scientific and philosophical worlds, giving him a unique perspective. It is not common to see a scholar equally adept in both of these worlds! Thus, Taylor is able to demonstrate that the Liberal proceduralism I noted above is itself rooted in an implied metaphysics, despite Liberalism's constant claim that it has no such metaphysics and that it is "neutral" in all such matters. And Taylor shows clearly that the putative neutrality of Liberalism is a mask that hides a metaphysics latent within all of its assertions, a metaphysics made all the more insidious by its stealth nature as a metanarrative that supposedly denies all metanarratives. In reality, what it denies is all metanarratives other than its own, corrosively absorbing all other communities of discourse into its "field of neutrality," and in so doing, destroying them. He then shows how this latent metaphysics has had such deleterious consequences for our approach to the environment, with all of the destruction and degradation that followed in the wake of the technocratic revolution.

Taylor demonstrates that this reductive metaphysics is the fruit of the scientific revolution and the Enlightenment, which conflated the realm of nature with the realm of artifice, separated "facts" from "values," championed a naïve empiricism as the source of an even more naïve belief in scientific "objectivity," relegated all questions of the spirit and of the moral sphere to the "private" and "merely subjective," and equated the "real" with the "quantifiable." Thus was spawned modern technocratic scientism, positivism, and the *de facto* atheism at the heart of modern economics, politics, and environmental policy. The Baconian reduction of what constitutes real knowledge to what can be manipulated and controlled sets the stage for a form of science oriented to technology and the subjugation of nature to human domination.

All of this has had, of course, deep consequences for our modern approach to ecological ethics wherein we see all of these sad tendencies at play. Unable to move beyond a purely procedural notion of what constitutes the good, modern ecological ethics plays in the sandbox of the politics of social consensus, a consensus which itself is always on the move as it fluidly conforms to whatever new mold society provides. The inability to consider the concept of teleology as a determinative principle is critical here. For if the idea that all things that exist are formally oriented to a spiritual end is excluded from all consideration, then a deep distortion and falsehood is interjected into the very heart of ethical deliberation. Furthermore, all that is left after such a rejection of nature's formal orientation to a higher fulfillment in Transcendence is its opposite—namely, that nature has no formal orientations at all. Nature is thus reduced to an absurd and random dance of particles, signifying nothing, and therefore open to whatever artificial teleology we might impose upon it.

Taylor thus argues that we are at an impasse in our metaphysical discussions. There is simply no way out of this thicket of naturalistic, voluntaristic, and mechanistic reductions so long as we refuse to open ourselves to the metaphysical question. This then constitutes the greatest achievement of Taylor's analysis: namely, his development of a metaphysics of gift as the most fruitful avenue for resolving our environmental crisis. At their root, all of the various ideological distortions and falsehoods that came to dominate Western culture have a common source: a false view of God's Transcendence and of the relationship between that Transcendence and the world. This question has been variously described, but at its root it is the age-old problem of the relationship between the One and the Many, between being-as-such and appearances, between unchanging substance and the flux and change of experienced existence. And owing to the degradation of the Christian view of God in the late medieval world, the true contours of the Trinitarian ontology at the root of the Christian answer to these philosophical problems was lost. Absent this deeper theological and metaphysical understanding of God, there arose views of the God–world dynamic that vacillated between a sharp dualism and a totalizing monism. The notion of analogical relation was eclipsed and in its place we got what Robert Barron calls a "competitive" notion of Transcendence that hobbled all that came after. The upshot of all of this in the sphere of ecological ethics was a rejection of any notion of the normativity of the teleology of natural things. Such teleological views were seen as overly "essentialist" and wedded to "discredited" theological underpinnings. Christian notions of Transcendence were mischaracterized as proposing precisely the kind of competitive Transcendence that Barron criticizes and were therefore set aside in favor of the dominant Liberal/technocratic/pragmatist paradigm that was incorrectly viewed as the best descriptor of reality.

What the metaphysics of gift puts forward, by contrast, is a view of the world precisely as a "creation" that is both radically contingent (and, therefore, not God) but also as possessing a true being all its own that is analogically related to God's non-contingent Being. Seen in this way, worldly being is now viewed as an open and receptive vessel, brought into existence by a relational and loving God who "gifts" the world with its own proper being—a being which is neither dualistically separate from God's being nor monistically reduced to it. It is a form of being shaped radically by its nature as "gift," i.e., a form of being that is, precisely as gift, truly its own in a worldly way, but also open to the fulfillment of its inner teleology in the Infinite.

The repercussions for ecological ethics are significant. I do not have the space to go into great detail about how Taylor applies the insights of a metaphysics of gift to the ecological questions of our time. Suffice it to say that the motif of nature as a receptive relationality open to the gift of a higher spiritual fulfillment implies that nature will lose even its worldly goodness if it cuts itself off from this gift. In other words, the closer the world gets to God the more "worldly" the world becomes, not less. The form of worldliness implied in a metaphysics of gift, then, is a worldliness characterized by an expectation that "something more" is needed and needed precisely as something gifted to it from outside of its own resources. In a sense then, such a metaphysics is marked by the sign of eschatology, wherein our worldly world recognizes its own insufficiency. For the "worldliness of the world" was never meant to be a self-enclosed and monadic reality and will lose even its most particular worldly integrity unless it opens itself up to this gift of a higher fulfillment.

In closing, I would like to add a personal note. I own and operate a Catholic Worker Farm, in the spirit of Dorothy Day and Peter Maurin. And one of the animating visions of this movement is that the beauty and the rhythms of the natural world contain a power to heal the human soul across all religious and ideological spectrums. Living on the farm and inviting others to join us in our work here is a broad ecumenical and humanistic endeavor that speaks to people of all kinds of differing persuasions. Thus, even though the metaphysics of gift articulated by Taylor has well-defined Christian theological underpinnings, the very principle of analogy embedded in that metaphysics allows us to encounter "the giftedness" of existence in and through the forms and structures of the world. Therefore, as with our farm, so too with our environment in general, people of differing views can make common cause so long as we all recognize that we are not the source of anything, but "receivers" of a gift. May the tribe of those who apprehend this truth multiply—and, I think, Taylor's excellent book will be of great help in achieving that goal.

—Larry Chapp, PhD
Professor of Theology (retired), DeSales University
Co-owner and manager of The Dorothy Day Catholic Worker Farm

PREFACE

As an undergraduate student of ecology in Maine, I came across a 2005 article in *Nature* magazine that offered a mathematical model of leadership and decision-making in the movements of large animal groups.[1] The model showed that the larger the group, the smaller the proportion of informed individuals that was necessary to assure that the group arrived at its proper destination; for example, only 5 percent of honeybees need know the location of their new nesting site for the entire swarm to reach it.[2] Among swarming, schooling, and herding animals, there is a fascinating dynamic between an individual's capacity for specific knowledge and trust in the group. I copied down the formula and kept it on my bulletin board for years. I'm not sure I knew why at the time. Perhaps it was the implication that animal life was anything but determined and mechanistic, requiring learning and trust. Perhaps it was wonder at the beauty and orderliness of nature as it adapts to the needs of reality. Perhaps it was confidence in the fact that we are capable of approaching a certain comprehension of the truth of such mysterious phenomena. But perhaps more than anything else it was the hope that just a few could make an essential difference in the trajectory of all, guiding many to their proper destination. In this book I wish to share the work of some of those whom I believe ought to be considered part of that few, worthy of our trust.

The philosophical presuppositions of ecology and empirical science were not capable of explaining my reasons for keeping that formula, unless I were to universalize their philosophical presuppositions to my entire life and reduce all the reasons to mere illusions of evolutionary utility. It ought to be clear to most people that just because we can't build an artificial tool to measure something or describe it mathematically doesn't mean it isn't real. The human person is the best "gauge" of the

---

1. See Couzin et al., "Effective Leadership and Decision-Making."
2. Seeley, *Honeybee Ecology*, 74.

truths of reality, beyond the empirical; we were made for this, in the same exact way that the bee was made to find the flower. But every person and every life is unique, and so individual "results" will vary necessarily and will also depend on each person's openness and receptivity to reality. This variance is not inaccuracy or imprecision or, much less, reason to despair that any truth exists at all beyond the empirical, as argue those who fail to see that the truths of reality stretch beyond the reaches of the human intellect. With the humility to accept that every person engages with reality truly, but from a unique perspective, this variance becomes an asset whereby *every* experience is enlightening and valuable in differing degrees. Thus the "few" I refer to is meant to denote those most open to reality and to solidarity, who would say with C. S. Lewis, "My own eyes are not enough for me; I will see through those of others. . . . Even the eyes of all humanity are not enough. . . . Very gladly would I learn what face things present to a mouse or a bee."[3]

Since my childhood I've done my best to pursue both wonder and knowledge, and I've found that each begets the other in an ever-upward dance. I am convinced that the natural world to which we belong is an endless source of direct and analogous wisdom. To observe the world around us is to open ourselves to this wisdom. This book is based on the observation that every living thing possesses the gift of being—of existence—each in a way unique to its individual dignity. This gift is intimately bound to truth, goodness, and beauty, both directly and analogously, in ways that are often overlooked. These three sisters are the mark of existence and go where it goes. It is no wonder that the development of life has favored forms that are most receptive to the truth of their surroundings, which has guided the evolution of increasingly more accurate sense organs and central nervous systems capable of interpreting the truth of reality. It has favored those creatures most capable of achieving the goodness appropriate to their particular nature, and so we admire the myriad ways living beings have adapted to reality. It has favored forms of life that manifest the beauty of their wholeness within the harmony of the order of nature, and so we marvel at the beauty of the mutual dependence of all things. And it has favored our ability to recognize and judge all these things. To deny that human beings are the greatest recipients of the gift of being would be to deny the reality of the gift *tout court* and to shirk the responsibility that it carries. To shirk

3. Lewis, *Experiment in Criticism*, 140.

the pursuit of truth, goodness, and beauty in our lives individually and collectively is to evade the gift of existence—the gift of being—and, as D. C. Schindler says, "to bring dis-order into the cosmos."[4]

Far from being a luxury into abstraction, philosophy (and especially metaphysics) is foundational to all our actions and our relationship to all of physical reality as we know it. One of the premises of this book is that the greatest crises of our times are, at heart, metaphysical. Ideas have consequences, and the less we are aware of this fact, the more helpless we are. Everything depends on the presuppositions about reality that we assume, and so the title of this book, *The Foundations of Nature*, refers to the analysis of the most common presuppositions and a presentation of a vision that has been forgotten by many. This method has directed me towards a long line of philosophers whom I refer to as metaphysicians of gift, philosophers, lovers of wisdom, who pursue the truth of reality. Gift, as we will see, is the best word we have to refer to the surprise and wonder at the fact that we exist at all. Finally, although the term "ecological" has been both overused and deeply politicized, in its original meaning it includes all the members of a family or household (*oikos*), all things that share in the gift of being, and so an "integral ecological ethic" refers to a vision of knowledge and practice that embraces all our actions—technological, economic, political, bioethical, and more.

I do not believe that the challenges that face the world are cause for fatalism but rather a call to step out of our self-absorbed worlds, out of the abstractions that bracket out the essential questions of life. To hide in abstractions is to evade reality and our calling inscribed therein. Abstracting ourselves from the rest of nature, inhabiting purely artificial and digital worlds, pursuing utility as our ultimate goal is one form. Positing that our actions are ultimately meaningless or shifting our own responsibility to some abstract force of nature that we must stay out of the way of or avoid angering is another. The hope derived from the humble realism of those whose work I have attempted to describe herein is a call to action, to the good work that can, I believe, do far more than doomsday predictions to change our behaviors and serve as the antidote to the paralyzing despair those predictions induce. This hope is far more than optimism because it is founded on love, not as a sentimental ideal but as the very meaning of being, which we participate in and can experience firsthand: to receive freely, and to give from what we have received.

---

4. D. C. Schindler, *Companion*, 87.

ACKNOWLEDGMENTS

I WANT TO THANK the many people who have played a part in bringing this work to fruition: first, Pablo Martínez de Anguita and María Ángeles Martín, for their endless hospitality and friendship. I would also like to express my gratitude to Don Francisco Javier Martínez Fernández, Archbishop of Granada, for his continuous friendship and support, and for his intellectual encouragement; to David L. Schindler, D. C. Schindler, Larry Chapp, and Adrian Walker, for their work and their constant effort to educate in truth, goodness and beauty; to Aaron and Melissa Riches, Ricardo Aldana, Ildefonso Fernández-Fígares Vicioso, David Alcalde Morales, Mátyás Szalay, Rut Castellano, Eduardo Segura, Sonsoles Navarro-Rubio, Sister Elizabeth Rose, Adam Ureneck, Kathy and Arthur Bom Conselho, and Elizabeth Moe, for their friendship, encouragement, and everything they have taught me. I especially want to thank my wife, Cassandra, who has continued to love, sustain, and inspire me through it all. To my sisters, Teresa and Jordan, for always supporting all of my endeavors. To my father, Michael, who has made everything possible, and to my mother, Mary, my first and best teacher, to whom this work is dedicated: thank you for giving me the greatest gift.

INTRODUCTION:
THE NATURE OF OUR CRISIS

Being is radiant because it is a gift.[1]

HUMANITY'S COLLECTIVE ENTHUSIASM AT the outset of the twentieth century, on display throughout *La Belle Époque*, was born from newfound technological prowess and material progress, but that high-minded optimism came crashing down with the start of the First World War. One of its largest battles, one of the bloodiest in history, was the Battle of the Somme, where new military technology clashed with tactics from a previous era.[2] Not long before, the world had been united in celebration of the same ingenuity and technical proficiency that had now killed or wounded more than one million men in just five months.

One of the survivors of that battle was John Ronald Reuel Tolkien, who would become the famed author of *The Hobbit* and *The Lord of the Rings*. In these works, he would take up the deepest questions of history with a new urgency: good and evil, suffering, fidelity, fellowship, loss, and hope. John Garth writes, "Middle-earth, I suspect, looks so engagingly familiar to us, and speaks to us so eloquently, because it was born with the modern world and marked by the same terrible birth pangs."[3] Tolkien's *Silmarillion*, which he began to write during the war,[4] is the "creation myth" set as the backdrop for his later works; it also contains a clear picture of his metaphysics.[5] "In creating his mythology," Garth says,

---

1. See Walker, "Foreword," 1–3.
2. July 1, 1916 – November 18, 1916. See *They Shall Not Grow Old*, directed by Peter Jackson; Frum, "The Lessons of the Somme."
3. Garth, *Tolkien and the Great War*, 309.
4. See Tolkien, *Letters*, 130.
5. See McIntosh, *The Flame Imperishable*.

"Tolkien salvaged from the wreck of history much that it is still good to have."[6]

In *The Silmarillion*, the original musical theme of Ilúvatar the Creator is sung in harmony by his first creatures, the Ainur (immortal spiritual beings). One of them, Melkor, attempts to mar it with discordant noise, to which Ilúvatar responds with themes greater still.

> It seemed at last that there were two musics progressing at one time before the seat of Ilúvatar, and they were utterly at variance. The one was deep and wide and beautiful, but slow and blended with an immeasurable sorrow, from which its beauty chiefly came. The other had now achieved a unity of its own; but it was loud, and vain, and endlessly repeated; and it had little harmony, but rather a clamorous unison as of many trumpets braying upon a few notes. And it essayed to drown the other music by the violence of its voice.[7]

When Melkor's clamor reaches its greatest disharmony, silence falls. Ilúvatar then shows the Ainur a vision. That which they had only heard becomes visible to the eye: the World in all its beauty and wonder. He speaks one word, Eä, "it is" or "let it be." The actuality of being, of all that is, unfolds from his word through the musical themes in which the Ainur participate.

Tolkien's literary style has been described as "an act of deliberate defiance of modern history."[8] Modern history and thought alike are scarred by dualisms that have led inevitably to conflict and continue to disfigure our world; meanwhile, postmodern thought, which began to take form after the Second World War, has only escalated those conflicts through an "ontology of violence" that precludes any amicable resolution.[9] While in modernism we can only understand reality as an array of oppositional antagonists locked in a zero-sum game, we discover in postmodernism a vision of reality

> determined by the boundless flow of diversity, setting entities over and against each another in a competition of becoming. The analogy that best describes postmodern ontology is music without a composer. When slamming a hand down on a piano

---

6. Garth, *Tolkien and the Great War*, ##.
7. Tolkien, *Silmarillion*, 4–5.
8. Brogan, "Tolkien's Great War," 356.
9. Milbank, *Theology and Social Theory*, xiv.

the diversity of notes clash with one another all at once, striving to be the loudest instead of working together to form a harmonious melody.[10]

By contrast, the gift of being to beings, like that envisioned by Tolkien, resounds in an originary alliance and an "ontology of peace."[11]

We live in a period dominated by conflict, opposition, and discordant ontologies that harm human and non-human life alike. Numerous scientists and cultural commentators have referred to the current era as the "Anthropocene," pointing to human domination of the earth as its principal characteristic.[12] Human population growth and over-consumption are blamed for decreasing animal and plant populations and increasing the extinction of species far above the natural rate.[13] One would think, then, that in the midst of such a period of unprecedented evolutionary success, human beings would be thriving; however, disturbing statistics are consistently reported about the human community. Hope for the future seems to be dismally low. The rate of suicide has increased by 60 percent over the last forty-five years, most notably among the young,[14] and across the developed world, abortion has become a common occurrence.[15] As Frederica Mathewes-Green notes, from a purely ecological perspective, human beings are displaying worrying behaviors:

> If you were in charge of a nature preserve and you noticed that the pregnant female mammals were trying to miscarry their pregnancies, eating poisonous plants or injuring themselves, what would you do? . . . You would immediately think, "Something must be really wrong in this environment." Something is creating intolerable stress, so much so that animals would rather destroy their own offspring than bring them into the world. You would strive to identify and correct whatever factors were causing this stress in the animals.[16]

10. Steele, "Postmodern Metaphysics."

11. Hart, *Beauty of the Infinite*, 36.

12. See Crutzen and Stoermer, "The 'Anthropocene'"; Edwards, "What Is the Anthropocene?"

13. See Ceballos et al., "Biological Annihilation"; de Vos et al., "Estimating the Normal Background Rate"; Pimm et al., "Biodiversity of Species."

14. World Health Organization, "Mental Health."

15. In 2017, 18 percent of all pregnancies in the United States were ended by abortion. Guttmacher Institute, "Abortion Incidence."

16. Mathewes-Green, "When Abortion Suddenly Stopped Making Sense."

There is no question that there is something wrong in the natural world of which we are a part, and the diversity of literature currently being produced on the subject of ecological and medical ethics is a testament to it. For example, in one such publication, the authors argue that "ultimately, our behavior is the result of a basic failure to recognize that human beings are an inseparable part of Nature" and offer numerous ecological reasons as to why "we cannot damage [nature] severely without severely damaging ourselves."[17] The truth of this claim goes well beyond its ecological implications. We should complete it by adding that, truly, we cannot become the kind of people that damage nature without damaging ourselves. Fundamentally, "the external deserts in the world are growing, because the internal deserts have become so vast."[18]

The problems confronting bioethics today may appear to be primarily moral matters of good and evil that give rise to good or bad policies, but they are first of all matters of ontology.[19] How we ought to confront the bioethical crises of our day must be answered on many levels: the technical, economic, political, social, and the ethical. The truth, however, goes deeper than our ecological interconnections and our ethical responsibilities, for moral questions about human action ultimately depend upon "what we take to be real"; they are first questions of order, which are metaphysical ones.[20]

As Pablo Martínez de Anguita has pointed out, each of these levels is significant in resolving problems, and each is dependent upon the levels that follow it.[21] Yet we confront considerable obstacles at the ethical level; antagonists will remain in conflict until another, deeper level is reached and addressed. Despite attempts to reduce complex discussions to supposedly easily agreed-upon common coin principles (autonomy, respect, etc.), consensus in ecological and bioethical debates is notoriously hard

---

17. Chivian and Bernstein, *Sustaining Life*, xii.

18. Benedict XVI, "Homily."

19. A way of acting always implies a way of understanding the world and vice versa. Ontology and ethics cannot be separated.

20. D. C. Schindler, "Why Socrates Didn't Charge," 398.

21. See Martínez de Anguita et al., "Environmental Economic."

to reach because the underlying philosophical presuppositions that shape one's ethical principles have no common ground.

Before we can adequately address how we ought to live in relation to nature and each other, we must identify what fundamental worldview we hold, which is determined by what we take to be real and how we understand what is good. The fundamental question, which considers the essential nature of reality, represents the deepest level, the metaphysical or ontological. This may seem esoteric, idealistic, or even impossible to apply to our day-to-day lives and debates, but its centrality becomes clearer when one considers two things. First, an ontological stance is inescapable, acknowledged or not. Second, the repercussions of what one takes to be real manifest themselves in ways that are ordinary rather than esoteric; if one believes that the universe is essentially chaotic, arbitrary, and violent, one's thoughts and actions will inevitably follow suit. Seeing the heart of reality as love leads to very different ends.

Metaphysical questions do not disappear if we ignore them, and so even a non-answer has ontological and ethical consequences. Our relationship with nature on the whole has become deeply confused and even toxic as a result. The technological paradigm, with its mechanistic ontology, makes silent yet powerful claims about human beings and nature, often to our detriment. While this paradigm continues to dominate, a broad spectrum of philosophical positions is growing in response to its deficiencies, ranging from various forms of holism to a kind of postmodern détente which holds truth in abeyance and goodness as conformity to predetermined ideological principles. These too carry significant metaphysical claims that are not adequately attuned to reality, and thus often only worsen the problems they seek to resolve. Thus, the question is not *whether* metaphysics should be considered, but rather *what* metaphysics we are considering: what metaphysics best reflects reality and therefore best addresses the bioethical dilemmas of our time?

The focus of this work is fundamentally metaphysical because, if we are going to heal our world's ecological crises, we must go even deeper than the roots of current proposals, to the very soil that is so often overlooked. The ontological assumptions of both mechanistic and postmodern worldviews contain elements of truth but lack others that are essential for the growth of healthy relationships, not only with the natural world but with each other. This study proposes "the metaphysics of gift" as the body of thought that most genuinely describes our human experience and most adequately incorporates the elements of truth found in other proposals, not only with regard to bioethical concerns, but for all areas of human activity. It is not a closed system of thought, but an open and active venture founded on being as that which is most universal, and it brings together what seems always to be at odds: the immanent finitude of reality and a familiar transcendence that runs through all existence.

"Gift" is used as the universal description of the primordial experience of being as such: a reality that precedes us, not merely as given, but as one being given, and not one we have constructed. Recognizing being as gift from the outset predisposes the person to those attitudes that are most suited for fruitful ontological reflection: wonder and gratitude. Gift as a point of reference serves as a counterbalance to the errors to which philosophical thought is most prone and which cause the most harm. As Martin Bieler cautions, "The fundamental temptation that faces philosophy, and indeed human thinking in general, consists in failing to recognize the gift-character of creation and thus to take note of its actuality. This violation of the truth has immediately destructive implications for one's interaction with creation."[22]

We will begin our reflection in chapter 1 with the first metaphysicians, the ancient Greeks, and briefly trace the progress of metaphysics up to the height of the Scholastic period, before examining how that work began to be undermined by some of the thinkers who were precursors to the modern era. Then we will address different attempts to recover metaphysics in the last century, which have taken shape on both sides of the Analytical–Continental divide, before offering an overview of metaphysics of gift.

Chapter 2 will address the dominant attitude towards nature currently at work in the world, the technological paradigm, followed by an examination of the critiques put forward by the eco-philosophies that reject it. The technological paradigm is founded on a mechanistic ontology born from modern philosophy, while the eco-philosophies have emerged from postmodern philosophies, primarily holism. Both contain elements of truth as well as metaphysical incongruences that must be considered together.

Contemporary bioethics as a fruit of the technological paradigm, specifically the principlism and proceduralism of Classical Liberal bioethics, will be examined in chapter 3. We address the postmodern

---

22. Bieler, "Introduction," xxii.

sociopolitical critiques levied against it and then examine both from an ontological perspective.

Metaphysics of gift will be presented most fully in chapter 4, chiefly through the thought of five of its most influential exponents. Thomas Aquinas, with his exposition of the real distinction and his use of analogy, has marked metaphysics forever. Erich Przywara, Ferdinand Ulrich, Hans Urs von Balthasar, and David L. Schindler have all been students and commentators of Aquinas who have added a great deal to his original intuitions, entering into dialogue with the major thinkers of the twentieth century and carrying forth that work into the twenty-first century. This chapter ends with a deeper look at philosophical wonder, which, as Plato first noted, is the beginning of and persistent mark of true philosophy.

Finally, chapter 5 will address some pending issues with the approach of postmodern holism as an introduction to a discussion of the more concrete applications of the metaphysics of gift to ecological ethics. Work, economics, encounter, and dialogue are all brought together in a fresh presentation of Martínez de Anguita's concentric-spheres model for addressing ecological problems, which may be extended to other bioethical concerns.

This study seeks to respond to "the urgent need to uncover (and treat) the deep roots of the environmental crisis, and to foster in our culture a less aggressive, more harmonious relationship with nature" through in-depth metaphysical analysis.[23] The task must be taken up at all levels, but first we must discover a more profound respect for the integrity of reality. In Tolkien's vision of Middle-earth, evil is always marked by a "twisting" of the world's natural order, but that abuse is only possible because of a deafness to the goodness and beauty of the world's harmony. We must become aware of the metaphysical music often unnoticed beneath our proposals and seek solidarity in a common recognition of its actuality. We must begin where every lover of wisdom begins: in childlike wonder, in the "amazement and gratitude, in praise for the sheer existence of so much beauty, so much actuality."[24] And room must be left for mystery, which "is not merely the unknown lying beyond, or 'underneath' what is known, but the excess of intelligibility implicit in every act of knowing."[25] Wonder, mystery, solidarity: these are the marks of a metaphysics of gift

---

23. Caldecott, *Radiance of Being*, 25.
24. Caldecott, *Radiance of Being*, 91.
25. D. L. Schindler, *Ordering Love*, 353.

that can aid us in the encounter of the truth, goodness, and beauty of the world and the harmony of its order in which we are called to participate.

1

The Enduring Questions

The Development, Rejections, and Renewals of Metaphysics

> *To find ourselves as existing, thinking beings, situated in interdependent relations with all manner of other beings within a cosmos that hangs together in a meaningful and orderly fashion; this is the primary marvel motivating any sort of sustained thoughtful reflection on the meaning of things.*[1]

From the beginning, the touchstone of philosophy has been wonder, the personal experience of openness before the gift of reality in all its mystery. This universal human experience before existence itself constitutes the essence of the contemplation of being, within which lie the foundations of nature. The mysterious nature of being is not due to its unintelligibility, but rather its superabundant intelligibility in relation to the scope of the human intellect, which it always surpasses. Reality will always exceed our comprehension of it, yet we can comprehend it truly and deepen into its truths in an endlessly fruitful way. This mystery of being, as Hans Urs von Balthasar has said, "resists any monism of concepts and definitions that would naively or even subtly paste over the polarity of true differences . . . [and] it satisfies again and again our every desire for understanding."[2]

1. Tyson, *De-fragmenting Modernity*, 12.
2. Balthasar, *Theo-Logic I*, 157–58.

Thomas Aquinas observed that being is "the first thing conceived by the intellect . . . because everything is knowable only inasmuch as it is in actuality. Hence, being is the proper object of the intellect, and is primarily intelligible; as sound is that which is primarily audible."[3] It was an editor of Aristotle's works who coined the word "metaphysics" when he organized the philosopher's works on the unchanging ultimate causes and the first principles of all things *after* (*meta*) those on the physical world, and the study of "being as such" or "being qua being" is the way most introductory texts on classical metaphysics define their subject matter.[4] The essential problems are what this means, how this study can be undertaken fruitfully, or even if it should be undertaken at all. The loss of the concept of being has been noted by many, often in a celebratory tone. Twentieth-century philosophers attacked earlier philosophy for what they saw as inflated ontologies, for furnishing the world with a phantasmagoria of extraneous and imaginary entities (the Absolute, Pure Being, Ideas, etc.), and for developing esoteric systems, abstruse and impractical for the modern world. In a study that claims that a different vision of metaphysics is the most promising perspective for our times, especially considering the critical challenges we face in relation to the natural world and in bioethics, it is essential to revisit the development, rejections, and renewals of the field.

A Brief History of Being

The twofold character of the intellectual intuition of being, to be given in any sensible experience, and yet to transcend all particular experience, is both the origin of metaphysics and the permanent occasion of its failures.[5]

The Dawn of the *Arche*

By all accounts, the history of philosophical thought, representing the first attempts at creating a unified account of reality, began with the ancient

---

3. Aquinas, *Summa Theologiae*, I, q. 5, a. 2.

4. The word "ontology" was coined in the seventeenth century to refer specifically to what would be called "general metaphysics" after metaphysics itself had become a very broad catchall for any question beyond epistemology, ethics, logic, politics, and other existing categories.

5. Gilson, *Unity of Philosophic Experience*, 253.

Greeks. Since that time, this desire for explanation has never waned and the proposal of new attempts has never ceased. Though these attempts have taken many forms, the common desire for a universal vision, for meaning and wholeness is, in itself, instructive. The range within which these attempts have fallen—the pendulum swings between seemingly opposing positions and the constant circling back to common themes—reveals that the intensity of the desire for an answer is matched only by the difficulty of obtaining one.

The first movement out of myth and into the realm of the rational goes back at least to the pre-Socratics of the seventh, sixth, and fifth centuries BC. They were known for their attempt to find the unifying feature of all things, the *arche* or "ultimate indemonstrable principle,"[6] hypothesizing that all nature was, in essence, one thing, such as water (Thales), or air (Anaximenes). Anaximander proposed the *apeiron*, referring to the boundless and indefinite infinite as the unchanging source (and destiny) of earth, air, water, and fire, which in turn gave rise to everything else. These attempts provide evidence that reason naturally intuits all things as originating from one source, and also point to their own inadequacy: the whole cannot be reduced to one of its parts, for no element would suffice as the *arche*.

The One and the Many, or Being and Becoming

Everything in the world appears to us as both unique in itself yet a member of a multiplicity of similar beings; hence we give many things both individual and universal names. At the same time, we experience the multiplicity of the world immediately through our senses, yet transcend that experience through reflection, memory, and deliberation. After the astonishment at being itself—the wonder that there is something rather than nothing—this twofold intuition of immanence and transcendence is the earliest insight of human reflection and the origin of metaphysical questions. Change and death reveal that no creature holds within itself the means to preserve itself in being, thus pointing to something transcendent that upholds the tenuous world. We know ourselves and the things around us as limited, yet are open to and aware of something we intuit as unlimited. Individuals are dependent, mutable, dying, yet we conceive of something beyond them, an underlying *something* that

---

6. Peters, *Greek Philosophical Terms*, 23.

transcends all contingency. The question of the One and the Many manifests itself as inquiries into the duality of the transcendent and immanent, the whole and the part, the infinite and the finite, eternity and history.

It seemed that the duality could be resolved by denying it: renounce either unchanging Being or continuous Becoming. The philosophers Heraclitus and Parmenides, the two most important pre-Socratic thinkers, have been taken as typifying the paradigmatic choices—Parmenides as the philosopher of Being, denying the changing reality of Becoming, and Heraclitus as the philosopher of Becoming, denying that there was any enduring Being. What we know about their thought is partial and filtered through other thinkers, but how it has been characterized goes to the core of the metaphysical debate. Together they seem to represent two mutually exclusive metaphysical positions and yet, as we will see, they are actually two sides of the same philosophical coin.

What fragments remain of Heraclitus's thought present a complex and ultimately ambiguous picture. Heraclitus proposed fire as the *arche*, the first principle of the universe, inasmuch as it represented transformation and change. "You cannot step into the same river twice" is his most famous adage, highlighting the awareness that everything is in constant flux, while the appearance of stability and constancy is an illusion, a momentary harmony in the tension between opposing forces. But his characterization as the philosopher of Becoming, of process and flux, is inaccurate, as "it ignores the fact the Heraclitus was a great, possibly the original, Greek thinker of *Logos* (the Greek word for divine, cosmos-ordering reason)."[7] The Logos for Heraclitus is the pattern that endures through strife and change, as the river endures, though at every instant, every drop of water changes.

Nonetheless, he has come to represent the notion of universal fluctuation (giving his name to the phrase "Heraclitean Flux," a fundamental idea that continues to hold sway over both science and philosophy, especially in postmodern thinking) which is the essential counter position to a philosophy in which what is illusory is *change*. In this converse position, opposed to the *Many* we have the *One*, for in man's intellectual quest for the *arche*, change alone, devoid of unity, seemed to contradict human intuition. To name change as the principle of the unity of the universe was rightly seen as philosophical defeatism and as self-subverting, essentially saying that there can be no principle of unity possible.

---

7. Tyson, *De-fragmenting Modernity*, 15.

Parmenides, as the apparent exemplar of this latter position, agreed with the Heracliteans that motion and change would destroy being, but since beings obviously do exist, motion and change must be the illusion. His only known work, *On Nature*, is divided into two parts.[8] The first, "The Way of Truth" (*Aletheia*), concerns "the Parmenidean One"; in it the philosopher is enraptured and taken out of the world of appearances, ascending to a realm of pure Being in which there can be no emanations or gradations of being, and that is eternal and unchanging. The second part, "The Way of Appearance" (*Doxa*), is generally interpreted to mean that the world of perception is taken by humanity to be reality, but they are mistaken; in the end, it is illusory. Once again, as with Heraclitus, Parmenides is mischaracterized, as his position is a bit more sophisticated, for he does not in fact deny the reality of the perceptible. While the intelligible is identified with One and Being, and the perceptible is located among the changeable, as John Palmer notes,

> Both Plato and Aristotle understood Parmenides as perhaps the first to have developed the idea that apprehension of what is unchanging is of a different order epistemologically than apprehension of things subject to change. . . . Most importantly, both Plato and Aristotle recognized that a distinction between the fundamental modalities or ways of being was central to Parmenides' system.[9]

Whatever the nuances of the teachings of Heraclitus and Parmenides, in their popular interpretations as opposites, the end result is similar. Focusing entirely on the One deprives the world and its inhabitants of their own reality, making them fleeting illusions, things to be escaped if one wants to reach the truth; focusing on the Many either absorbs Being into itself through pantheistic identification, or in modern forms reductively eliminates dimensions of reality from the realm of truth, whether meaning, value, goodness, or beauty, inevitably leading to skepticism. Both are incompatible with the world as we know it, with objective truth and value, and with individual dignity, betraying our most essential intuition that there must be something that belongs to all things and yet does not belong to any two things in the same way.

So far we have seen the failure of philosophers to explain the whole of reality using one of its parts as its first principle, whether it be one of the

---

8. See Parmenides, *Parmenides of Elea*.
9. Palmer, *Parmenides and Presocratic Philosophy*, 44.

elements or one of the two poles of our intellectual experience of reality. Within this tension found at the heart of being, we will find the history of metaphysics. Both perspectives are necessary. Just as we need both eyes to see in three dimensions, we must observe being in both its immanence and transcendence in order to train our minds to see the depth of reality and move within it without stumbling.[10] After the questions raised by the pre-Socratics, philosophy would turn to this dilemma.

Plato, Aristotle, and Aquinas

The three greatest metaphysicians who ever existed—Plato, Aristotle, and St. Thomas Aquinas—had no system in the idealistic sense of the word. Their ambition was not to achieve philosophy once and for all, but to maintain it and serve it in their own times.[11]

We owe the original solution of the seemingly intractable problem set up by Heraclitus and Parmenides to Plato, a proper renewal of whose thought will ultimately help us tackle our ecological crises. In *The Sophist* he confronts the question directly:

> The philosopher—the person who values these things the most—absolutely has to refuse to accept the claim that everything is at rest, either from defenders of the one or from friends of the many forms. In addition he has to refuse to listen to people who say that *that which is* changes in every way. He has to be like a child begging for "both," and say that *that which is*—everything—is both the unchanging and that which changes.[12]

Many students learned in introductory philosophy courses that Plato was a dualist who divided reality dogmatically between the world of perfect forms and their less-than-real images on earth. This misrepresentation made inevitable an opposition between matter and spirit, a negative interpretation of matter that is incompatible with a view of creation as generous and good. This error is what Étienne Gilson referred to as one of the permanent occasions of the failures of metaphysics

---

10. The developing brain requires two different perspectives on the same reality in order to develop three-dimensional vision; children born with only one working eye have trouble perceiving depth. Once our brains adapt to the depth of reality, however, we can see it even with one eye closed.

11. Gilson, *Unity of Philosophical Experience*, 254.

12. Plato, "The Sophist," 249d (271).

because the temptation to see the world as a mere shadow is constant and opens all of knowledge to the advances of skepticism. Additionally, philosophers from Nietzsche to Heidegger to Derrida blamed Plato for everything from the scientific disenchantment with being to ecological destruction to creating the "binary oppositions" postmodernity seeks to overcome, and more. Important recent scholarship has provided a corrective. John Milbank points out that Plato places appearance between being and nothingness: "The crucial mark of Plato's thought was his concern with the constitutive relation (*metaschesis*) between the one and the many contained even at the level of the forms themselves."[13] The key form is that of the Good: for D. C. Schindler, "Platonism" is the name for a dualistic "version of Plato that disregards the role of the good in his thought," when it is the Good that is the answer to the dilemma:[14]

> Parmenides made Being the highest principle, and thus saw otherness, differentiation, and multiplicity, as simply negative, i.e., nothing at all. By making goodness the highest principle, by contrast Plato offers a positive ground for difference. He thus affirms that the universal is beautiful and good, as the effect of a good cause.[15]

For Plato, Being is coextensive with Truth, which marks all that is intelligible, and with the Good—the ultimate cause of both. In this vision, "the world of forms is seen as immanent to the physical world . . . [which] possesses certain formal elements, and . . . may be said to be intelligible."[16] Plato stands firmly on the observation that human reason passes easily from the immanent and particular beings of this world, the realm of becoming, to the transcendent and universal forms, the realm of being. And so he is justified in binding the two realms together, despite their paradoxical aspect.

Why does this happen? The answer has to do with another question: what is the ultimate cause of being, or why is there something rather than nothing? The answer is found in what Plato calls the universal form of the Good, which is essentially different from any other of the universal forms. As Plato explains in *The Republic*, the Good is "both absolute (good in itself) *and* relative (good for us)."[17] This means that "self-sharing

---

13. Milbank, "Shares of Being," 2.
14. D. C. Schindler, *Plato's Critique*, 288.
15. D. C. Schindler, *Plato's Critique*, 303.
16. Sherrard, *Human Image*, 13.
17. D. C. Schindler, *Plato's Critique*, 37.

is therefore an essential part of the meaning of goodness."[18] The physical world exists because it was caused by the Good and participates in it; being is good because it was caused by the Good and, because of its goodness, it gives of itself to create the physical reality we can come to know truly. Human reason too is grounded in the transcendent form of the Good, which exceeds it. Reason is only capable of receiving the intelligibility of physical realities, Being, and the Good itself when it is properly ordered. It is this feature that allows reason to be itself: "Without being so ordered, reason finally loses its rationality. Reason cannot be reason proper outside the love of the good."[19]

Aristotle deviated from Plato's teachings, most notably regarding the doctrine of the forms. Plato had proposed the doctrine as a way of linking all the things of this world, through participation, to the ideal forms, which were the only true and unchanging realities, and what could be truly known. Without denying the reality of material things, he made them objects of "opinion" rather than of true knowledge. For Aristotle, however, being is only ever present in things that exist in this world. It was clear to him that "being is that which is 'common to all things,' yet at the same time particular and distinct in each single substance."[20] Hence his chief contribution to metaphysics would be known as his hylomorphism: the unity of eternal form and eternal matter as the act and potency of the physical things of this world, making them the only true beings. "Being is here made radically existentially temporal and material, whilst also retaining its intellective and eternal essence."[21] Consequently, true knowledge for Aristotle is only possible through the knowledge of the things of the world. He maintained the unity of knowledge and of all things through analogy: "things that are one by analogy are not all one in genus."[22] However, while Plato had the form of the Good as the cause of being, Adrian Pabst has pointed out that here Aristotle can show "how things exist under different categories . . . [but] cannot explain why anything exists in the first place."[23]

---

18. D. C. Schindler, *Plato's Critique*, 302.
19. Tyson, "Reasoning within the Good," 323.
20. Pabst, *Metaphysics*, 11.
21. Tyson, *De-fragmenting Modernity*, 20.
22. Aristotle, "Metaphysics," V, 6, 1017a2 (760).
23. Pabst, *Metaphysics*, 13.

These two visions of Plato and Aristotle would vie for influence in the ancient world, taking circuitous routes around the shores of the Mediterranean before reconvening in Europe in the thirteenth century, where Thomas Aquinas synthesized aspects of each into what would become known as his *philosophia perennis*. While we will delve more deeply into his metaphysics in chapter 4, it is useful to make mention of his main contributions here.

While Neoplatonist elements were well-established in Christian Europe by Augustine, the newly rediscovered Aristotelian act/potency relation and the concept of analogy would influence Aquinas's thought deeply, with a significant improvement: "the discovery of *esse*."[24] While for Aristotle, form or essence was the active aspect of every thing and the measure of its perfection, Aquinas saw that the "act of being" (*esse*) was primordial because the essence could not exist in the world without it, and consequently could not be known either. Thus Aquinas envisioned a new, more foundational understanding of things that saw being in the active role, while the essence was passive in relation to being: "In conceiving *esse* as actual in relation to the potency of essence (the formal element), Thomas in effect reverses the relation of form and act."[25] This would come to be known as "the real distinction" between *esse* and essence.

A remarkable transformation of Greek teachings, this would prove to be tremendously fruitful. The constant tension between immanence and transcendence, between the One and the Many, would find its resolution in the polar relationship, made possible through analogy, in which *esse* gives existence to things and things give *esse* a home within which to *be*. The acceptance of this paradoxical mutual dependence is the only way to properly integrate "the twofold character of the intellectual intuition of being," namely, "to be given in any sensible experience, and yet to transcend all particular experience."[26]

It is crucial to note here that Aquinas's achievement was not that of *completing* metaphysical reflection, as in extracting all of its conclusions, nor was it that of constructing a closed system by which all of reality is captured. What makes the metaphysics of gift unique is its openness and its recognition of human reason as being situated *within* reality, rather than being coextensive with it or being greater than it. In other words,

---

24. Healy, *Eschatology*, 43.
25. Healy, *Eschatology*, 43.
26. Gilson, *Unity of Philosophical Experience*, 253.

this metaphysics is "love of wisdom," rightfully recognizing the unknown not as an untamed wilderness to be conquered but as a mystery to be respected and explored with love and humility. The distinctly modern temptation against true metaphysics would be to conflate our ability to collect information with our ability to know reality, "for even though, as is impossible, all that which exists were known to us, existence itself would still remain a mystery."[27]

The Muddling of Metaphysics in the Late Medieval Period

While Descartes's idealism is often blamed for undermining Aquinas's metaphysics at the start of the modern age, the Late Middle Ages was critical. Many of Aquinas's works were condemned by the Bishop of Paris, Étienne Tempier, based on the fear that Aristotle's philosophy, which had recently been reintroduced to Europe through Muslim philosophers, led to heretical forms of theology; therefore, anyone associated with Aristotle was under suspicion. It was not until 1325, two years after Aquinas's canonization, that the condemnations would finally be suspended.[28] In the meantime, Duns Scotus and William of Ockham would develop a distinct line of philosophy in order to emphasize divine freedom and omnipotence, important elements of Franciscan theology.[29]

Aquinas distinguished different modes of being in order to account for the connection between the world and the ultimate source of all things while still preserving their differences: the beings of the sensible realm all participate *analogously* in divine being, the source of all things. Duns Scotus's notion of the *univocity* of being, flattening out being "in such a way that removes different ontological degrees of reality," contributed to the "intellectual malaise of late-scholastic ontology such that the ties between metaphysics, theology, and 'natural philosophy' (science) become astonishingly complex and abstruse."[30] In this intellectual environment William of Ockham asserted his nominalism, which made the claim that only individual things existed, and his attendant voluntarism regarding human freedom, which ended in the capriciousness of the will. He fundamentally challenged the way in which the cosmos had always been

27. Gilson, *Unity of Philosophical Experience*, 256.
28. Wippel, *Mediaeval Reactions*, 71.
29. See Lindberg, *Science in the Middle Ages*, 107–8.
30. Tyson, *De-fragmenting Modernity*, 17–18.

conceived, reducing it "to a juxtaposition of individual realities without depth, since every real universal, i.e., every principle of communion among beings, is denounced as linguistic illusion."[31] Stratford Caldecott described this theory and its consequences:

> [Nominalism] first became popular in Europe around the time of the Black Death and with even more devastating effect. . . . The nominalists and their successors (positivists, pragmatists, and members of other schools of thought hostile to traditional metaphysics) believe that the real world consists entirely of individual particles, elements or energies and their relationships, which can be described in a variety of ways. It is only the way in which we *choose to describe* certain things that determines whether they belong to one "species" or another. On this assumption there can be no reason to prevent one type of thing turning into another.[32]

The state of philosophy, metaphysics and theology in late medieval Europe was a morass of conflicting positions that would only worsen as further developments attempted to rectify this situation through philosophical innovations. In the closing centuries of the Middle Ages, a very different ontology began to assert itself: an early form of representationalism with its concomitant subject-object dichotomy that lies at the heart of modern epistemology. In chapter 2, we will discuss more fully the technocratic paradigm that was born from the nascent scientific revolution and modern philosophy. First, though, we will address other fundamental rejections of metaphysics in modern philosophy on both sides of the continental/analytic divide, as well as attempts at its recovery. An understanding of deviations from the metaphysics of gift enable us to delineate it more clearly.

Rejections of Metaphysics

Far from being a science long since exhausted, metaphysics is a science which has, as yet, been tried by but few. What passed by its name was almost always something else.[33]

---

31. International Theological Commission, "In Search," 71.
32. Caldecott, *Radiance of Being*, 52–53.
33. Gilson, *Unity of Philosophical Experience*, 256.

Rejections of Metaphysics by Contemporary Philosophy

Before exploring a recovery or renewal of an adequate metaphysics for ecological ethics, it is important to note that contemporary philosophers claim to have been undergoing such a renewal for quite some time. How can these other metaphysics be distinguished from the metaphysics of gift that is central to this study? The answer will turn on another query: what is the primary metaphysical question?

W. V. Quine summarized the ontological problem with the simple question: "What is there?"[34] The investigations range over things from everyday physical objects, to subatomic particles, to sets, to universals, to mind-independent moral truths, to theory-dependent terms, to non-existent entities (such as Russell's "present King of France"[35]). For Rudolph Carnap, this question quickly became, "What can we *say* about what is there, or what we think is there?"[36] However, neither can be the ultimate metaphysical question, but rather an evasion of it, for things and language are part of the history of nature, "which is to say the history of what already has existence. The question of existence, however, concerns *the very possibility of such a history*,"[37] the question of being itself. Martin Heidegger and Balthasar agreed that the "authentic metaphysical question"[38] is: "why is there something rather than nothing?"[39] Though the empirical sciences can tell us "what there is," they cannot ask, let alone answer, this ultimate question, for science always presupposes its subject matter as given. "What is lacking," says Nicholas Healy, "is precisely the element of a radical surprise over the fact that things exist at all. This is why only wonder corresponds to the basic metaphysical question, 'Why is there anything at all and not simply nothing?'"[40] If wonder comes into play as it does in eco-philosophies based on emergence, it is not true *metaphysical wonder*, but "at most only . . . admiration that everything

---

34. Quine, *From a Logical Point*, 1.

35. Russell, "On Denoting," 479.

36. Carnap replaced "What is?" with "How should we best articulate what we know?" Carnap, "Empiricism, Semantics, and Ontology," 73.

37. Hart, *Experience of God*, 98 (emphasis mine).

38. Balthasar, *Glory of the Lord V*, 613.

39. Leibniz, *Philosophical Essays*, 210.

40. Healy, *Eschatology*, 62.

appears so wonderfully and beautifully ordered within the necessity of Being."[41]

The two questions are analogous to the difference between questions of "creation out of something" and "creation *ex nihilo*," out of nothing. The former refers to *how* things came to be in the primordial past, a first act or first in a series of temporal events that begin with a "something," and the latter deals with the qualitatively different question of *why things exist at all*. Yet the human imagination tends to collapse the latter into the former: even as great a physicist as Steven Hawking confounded the differences—"spontaneous creation," his term for creation *ex nihilo*, is due to "something" already there, already latent: "negative gravitational energy."[42] Kenneth Schmitz pointed out that moves like this confuse *cosmology* with *ontology*. Similarly, to speak of "metaphysics of gift" as if it were an alternative to, or in the same class as, "semantic metaphysics" or "naturalized metaphysics" or "scientific metaphysics" is to make a category mistake.

We now turn to the rejections of metaphysics in recent philosophy, beginning with a brief overview of the major division today between analytic and continental philosophy.

The Analytic/Continental Split

A comprehensive history of the divergence between analytic and Continental philosophy, including as its last chapter the story of the overcoming of the very idea of such a "divergence," has yet to be written.[43]

When distinguishing between analytic and continental philosophy, two things should be noted: first, that the distinction is not always employed by continental philosophers, who see it as a way for analytic philosophers to dismiss something they do not understand; second, that despite the divergence, in recent years some convergence can be found. John Milbank notes that the twenty-first century's renewed interest in metaphysics no longer has much to do with the analytic/continental divide, but it has nonetheless left its mark.

---

41. Balthasar, *Glory of the Lord V*, 613–14.
42. Hawking and Mlodinow, *The Grand Design*, 180.
43. Sachs, "What Is to Be Overcome?," 303.

Analytic (sometimes "analytical") philosophy is predominant in the English-speaking world as well as in Scandinavia. It is a broad movement that dates back to work done in the early twentieth century by G. E. Moore and Bertrand Russell, following the predicate logic of Gottlob Frege, one of the founders of modern logic. Analytic philosophers aspired to the precision that characterized mathematical logic. To reach such rigor, they believed, metaphysics had to be jettisoned. Descartes's disjunction between nature and non-nature resulted in a disjunction "between the sort of knowledge proper to the study of nature (e.g., physics) and the sort of knowledge proper to what it would take to be non-nature (e.g., metaphysics and theology),"[44] and with Kant, epistemology replaced metaphysics as the "First Philosophy." Beginning in the late 1920s, the Logical Positivists decided that metaphysical questions were not simply concealed epistemological questions; they were really concealed questions about the meaning of words, and the Cartesian/Kantian turn to the subject was revised as a linguistic turn. Michael Dummett said that "what distinguished analytical philosophy . . . is the belief, first, that a philosophical account of thought can be attained through a philosophical account of language, and secondly, that a comprehensive account can only be so attained."[45] The idea was that vernacular language is merely an appearance that conceals the truth revealed in the logical structure.[46]

Of central importance to the Logical Positivists was A. J. Ayer's "verification principle," which stated that the only statements that are meaningful are those that can be verified empirically, or truths of logic. These relegated all other human questions in ethics, aesthetics, theology, etc. to the realm of the emotively expressive but factually meaningless, a dualism which still haunts us today and which in turn gave rise to still more dualisms.

Logical Positivism was dealt a death blow by Quine's 1951 "Two Dogmas of Empiricism": clearly there are many higher-order theoretical statements that are meaningful but not observable or testable; in addition, individual statements do not stand alone to be verified empirically, but are already deeply embedded in a theoretical position. What Quine called "interanimation of sentences" showed that language was more like a web than a series of building blocks; no propositions are true simply on

---

44. D. L. Schindler, "Introduction," 10.
45. Dummet, *Origins of Analytic Philosophy*, 4.
46. Sachs, "What Is to Be Overcome?," 315.

the basis of experience alone, but on the basis of the experience and the other propositions one holds.[47] The work of the linguistic positivists was shown to have many of the same problems they deplored in metaphysics, including an absolutist stance regarding its first principles: our perception of the world may not be determinate, they thought, but *language* is; perhaps we cannot say anything about the way the world really is, but surely we can say something about what we say there really is. Yet in the end, language turned out to be a far more elusive thing than previously supposed, and the attempt to develop a purely formal language was repudiated.

Nevertheless, analytic philosophy is still characterized by a preference for a rigorous methodology that uses science as its model, and, like physics, tends to divide into many specialties and sub-specialties, while abstracting problems from their cultural and historical milieu. This puts analytic philosophy in sharp contrast with continental philosophy, so named because it is primarily derived from the European continent. Its founding fathers were Husserl, Hegel, and Heidegger, and it was influenced by Nietzsche and Marx as well. It tends toward literary theory and hermeneutics as models rather than science and is wide-ranging rather than narrowly specialized. It brings in concerns from across many fields, situating problems in their social and political context rather than considering them in a formal abstraction. There is a great diversity among continental philosophers: there are phenomenologists, Hegelians, followers of Foucault and of Deleuze, and some who seem to fit in no category but their own.

Each criticizes the other: analytic philosophers tend to think continental philosophers lack precision, while continental philosophers reject the analytic philosophers' conception of precision. Many believe analytical science easily becomes "scientism" (the idea that "science itself does the work of metaphysics and offers a comprehensive vision of all of reality"[48]), which is itself a metaphysical system based on reduction. They also reject formal models in favor of the "hermeneutics of change":

> The aim here is not continuous progress, the gradual but steady accumulation of knowledge or accepted facts, as in modern

---

47. See Quine, *Word and Object*, 8. Ontology is relative because, he says, ontological statements, when taken absolutely, are circular. "What is an X" makes sense only in reference to background language; "inscrutability of reference" means there are no facts of the matter and in this it is like Nietzschean perspectivism.

48. Milbank, "Only Theology Saves," 8.

science, but continuous revolution: replacing received methods and styles with ones that are unforeseen or overlooked, so as to see the word anew. Hermeneutics, the interpretation or re-interpretation of the world, therefore takes precedence over formalisation or the mere advancement of knowledge. . . . the aim is not to render something more precise or better established, but to destabilize common patterns of thought.[49]

Despite their differences, until recently analytic and continental philosophers agreed in their rejection of metaphysics; both considered themselves post-metaphysical, whether turning toward formal logic or hermeneutics. Most agreed that we can only deal with the multiplicity and differences of appearances, not of "being itself" or "things in themselves."

Analytic and Continental Rejections

After modern philosophers solidified the growing idea that the immanent and transcendent, the empirical finite and the super-empirical infinite, were diametrically opposed, the problem of the relation between appearance and being and every other dualistically conceived pair became impossible to conceive of as held together *analogously* in a harmonious unity. Kant's solution was not so much to reject metaphysics outright, but to attempt to make it more "scientific." According to him, "good" metaphysics described what he saw as the *a priori* conditions of "possible experience," while "bad" metaphysics included claims that went beyond "possible experience."

Similarly, Carnap said that while there was a kind of metaphysics he was rejecting, namely "the field of alleged knowledge of things that transcend the realm of empirically founded inductive science," that rejection "does not include endeavors towards a synthesis and generalization of the results of the various sciences."[50] "Bad metaphysics" attempted to say something about ultimate reality; "good metaphysics" meant reflection on our conceptual apparatus. But he went further than Kant, who simply said that the knowledge of ultimate reality—the *noumenal*—was impossible for us. For Carnap, those claims are meaningless, since there is no way to verify them empirically. He had a long list of metaphysical terms

---

49. Trakakis, "Meta-Philosophy of Religion," 203–4.
50. Carnap, "Elimination of Metaphysics," 80.

that are without meaning: God, essence, manifestation, the Infinite, emanation, thing-in-itself, principle, the unconditioned, and more.[51]

If Kant is one of the fathers of the anti-metaphysical stance in analytic philosophy, Heidegger and Nietzsche might be seen as ground zero for contemporary continental philosophy's rejection of metaphysics. Nietzsche's rejection of metaphysical realism was a dismissal of objective truth; he famously claimed that the idea that "things possess a constitution in themselves quite apart from interpretation and subjectivity is quite an idle hypothesis; it presupposes that . . . a thing freed from all perspectives would still be a thing."[52] Heidegger, meanwhile, rejected the entire Western history of metaphysics from Plato on, accusing it of being "onto-theology": the hardening of Being into a conceptualization, the making of Being itself into just another being.[53] While this critique rightly applies to Hegel and others, it fails to hold up against Plato and Aquinas because true metaphysics does nothing of the sort.[54] In fact, they would agree that onto-theology is a failure of philosophy, hence the insistence on the openness of reason and the ever-greater mystery of reality.[55] As Merold Westphal explains, onto-theology has become "a one-word refutation of views too 'metaphysical' for postmodern preferences, and all too often it does so without careful analysis."[56]

Postmodern philosophy rightly rejects metanarratives meant to ground (thus offering the possibility of capturing) the whole of reality, whether economic, political, religious, etc. It sees the modern as encapsulating "a single metanarrative ambition: a desire to transcend the conditioned finitude and contingency . . . by way of representation of the

---

51. Carnap, "Elimination of Metaphysics," 67.

52. Nietzsche, *Will to Power*, 302–3.

53. Metaphysics is defined as, "the question about beings as such *and* as a whole. The wholeness of this whole is the unity of all beings that unifies as the generative ground. . . . This means: metaphysics is onto-theology" (Heidegger, *Identity and Difference*, 54).

54. "Contrary to the prejudice that Thomas engages in a reifying 'metaphysics of substance,' the Angelic Doctor himself already interprets substance itself in light of its radical origin. His interpretation of substance, in other words, places it in the context of what he calls the *esse habens* (the 'that-which-has-being'), which has received the gift of being, hence, is itself a gift given to itself—and, as such, has its own ground in itself ('subsists')" (Oster, "Thinking Love," 668–69).

55. Heidegger "shows no signs of ever having truly understood the radical break with Greek ontology in Aquinas's notion of being" (McGrath, *Early Heidegger*, 212).

56. Westphal, *Overcoming Onto-Theology*, xvi.

absolute, universal, or rational."[57] Onto-theology, and metanarratives in general, render "the whole of reality intelligible to human understanding . . . . [a] pride that refuses to accept the limits of human knowledge."[58] However, Heidegger's accusation that metaphysics is onto-theology is, in reality, the "totalizing metanarrative" *par excellence* that throws the baby out with the proverbial bathwater.

John Caputo exemplifies those who want to reject "totalizing" metaphysics in order to privilege finitude and contingency to "avoid false totalities/absolutes (closure) and . . . to be honest to the way things are and to affirm concrete actuality/reality/existence and genuine otherness (openness)."[59] Taking his cue from Heraclitus and Derrida, the philosophers "of the flux par excellence,"[60] he seeks immersion into immanence, becoming, and "the Many."

Caputo sees metaphysics as making light of "the difficulty in existence"[61] by suppressing movement in an attempt to impose an order that "arrests" (a word he uses repeatedly, always negatively, as an endeavor rooted in folly) its turbulent flux.[62] A philosopher needs the courage to "stay with the flux" rather than denying or subverting or "reconciling" it as metaphysics does.[63] The central problem with metaphysics, according to this line of thought, is that it is a turn toward abstraction, fixated on the One as refracted in essences, or in universals, or in necessities (necessary beings, necessary laws). In contrast, he says, "Think of radical hermeneutics as a kind intellectual fire department that arrives on the scene to douse the flames of essentialism wherever they threaten to flare up and consume us."[64] Universals are rejected in favor of the difference of the particular; drawing on Kierkegaard, the philosopher of "the individual," he says that "the universal . . . cannot embrace, circumscribe, encompass, the singular."[65]

For contemporary philosophy, a belief in natural essences as an underlying basis for identity is like a belief in the ether. Nominalism and

57. Hart, *Experience of God*, 6.
58. Westphal, *Overcoming Onto-Theology*, 4, 7.
59. Simpson, *Religion, Metaphysics, and the Postmodern*, 4.
60. Caputo, *Radical Hermeneutics*, 116, 202.
61. Caputo, *Radical Hermeneutics*, 1.
62. Caputo, *Radical Hermeneutics*, 34.
63. Caputo, *More Radical Hermeneutics*, 12.
64. Caputo, *More Radical Hermeneutics*, 3.
65. Caputo, *Demythologizing Heidegger*, 203–4.

anti-essentialism go hand in hand; talk of essences is seen as talk about the constructed character of the world. As for necessity, Kant thought that Hume was right when he argued that there is no necessity in nature and everything derives from experience. His solution was to argue that if there are necessary laws, their source is the transcendental subject that constitutes them. If postmodern philosophers speak of necessity at all, it tends to be something on the order of: "the only necessity is that the laws of nature are contingent."[66]

In the end, the rejection of essences, necessity, and universality is a rejection of any claim to be in on a "metaphysical secret," to have "privileged access" to absolute knowledge about the way things are, or to reality, or to whatever else one might claim that surpasses "the limits of offering a mere mortal interpretation."[67]

Pragmatism

In short, my strategy . . . is to move everything over from epistemology and metaphysics into cultural politics, from claims to knowledge and appeals to self-evidence to suggestions about what we should try.[68]

Pragmatism, to be discussed in more detail later, also rejects metaphysics while cutting across the analytic/continental divide. Richard Rorty defies "the American Church of Analytic Philosophers of the Strict Observance" and sends "shock waves through the American 'continentalist' establishment [by stealing] the best lines from their high priests," Nietzsche, Heidegger, and Derrida, and is championed by nominalists and non-essentialists.[69] In *Philosophy and the Mirror of Nature*, the rejection of "representationalism"—the position that holds that the mind reflects realities in nature—is equated with the rejection of traditional metaphysics.[70] Rorty believes that we can *pragmatically evaluate linguistic*

---

66. Badiou, "Preface."
67. Caputo, *More Radical Hermeneutics*, 1–3.
68. Rorty, *Truth and Progress*, 57.
69. Caputo, *More Radical Hermeneutics*, 84–85.
70. See Rorty, *Philosophy and the Mirror*. Following the Enlightenment, consciousness is seen as an enclosed box in which impressions and concepts occur, and it is to these that our awareness is directed. "We can try to get outside by making inferences: we may reason that our ideas must have been caused by something outside us, and we may construct models or hypotheses of what those things must be like, but we are not

practices without making ontological claims. What is useful depends on our purposes, as tools depend on the job we need them for. Our vocabularies, Rorty suggests, "have no more of a *representational* relation to an intrinsic nature of things than does the anteater's snout or the bowerbird's skill at weaving."[71]

Preliminary Criticisms

While a metaphysics of gift also rejects representationalism and essentialism (without rejecting essence), some preliminary criticisms of other postmodern positions might be briefly stated here. First, Paul Ricouer saw the Heideggerian project of including all of Western thought since Plato under the unity of one grand metanarrative as

> an after-the-fact construction of Heideggerian thought, intended to vindicate his own labour of thinking and to justify the renunciation of any kind of thinking that is not a genuine overcoming of metaphysics. But why should this philosophy claim for itself alone, to the exclusion of all its predecessors, that it breaks through and innovates? It seems to me time to deny oneself the convenience, *which has become a laziness in thinking, of lumping the whole of Western thought together under a single word, metaphysics*.[72]

Jean-Francois Lyotard's famous definition of postmodern thought is "incredulity toward metanarratives."[73] In the eyes of some philosophers, this incredulity is itself another metanarrative that "completes not only the critical but the metanarrative projects of modernity (which prove to be indistinguishable)."[74] For this reason, D. B. Hart and David L. Schindler, among many others, see postmodernity as simply *a logical extension of modernity* and not a truly radical alternative to it.

---

in any direct contact with them. . . . We do not know how to show that our contact with the 'real world' is not an illusion, not mere subjective impression" (Sokolowski, *Introduction to Phenomenology*, 9–10). Representationalism is discussed in chapter 4.

71. Rorty, *Truth and Progress*, 48.

72. Ricoeur, *The Rule of Metaphor*, 368.

73. Lyotard, *The Postmodern Condition*, xxiv.

74. Hart, *Experience of God*, 7. Some postmodern philosophers agree: "The announcement of the 'End of Grand Narratives' is as immodest as the Grand Narrative itself" (Badiou, *Manifesto for Philosophy*, 30).

Next, critics of postmodernism take issue with anyone who claims that others are seeking to go "beyond the limits" and imagining a "secret," while at the same time claiming the right to determine the limits of human knowledge. That claim is not neutral, since to set a limit is to predetermine something of what is on the other side.[75]

Finally, a criticism of Pragmatism's "whatever works" will follow, but here we can note the repercussions: "If the only measure of the truth of a practice is its success, then anything that works is regarded as just as good as anything else, so long as it works also, without regard for any judgment as to the inherent desirability of what has been constructed.... Truth becomes detached from the good."[76] The dissolution of metaphysics ends in basing ethical views on a working consensus, which neither avoids arbitrariness nor resolves any philosophical problem—it merely displaces it from the individual to the group and leads to ethical skepticism. Edward Feser notes the result in chilling terms: "It could at least in principle be morally innocuous to strangle an infant or a homeless schizophrenic just because you felt like it, as long as there was no one else to whom these people mattered. These human beings can have no value or standing unless others decide to give them value or standing."[77] Thus, Pragmatism equally fails to provide a satisfactory solution to the consequences of rejecting metaphysics.

Attempted Recoveries of Metaphysics

The twenty-first century has seen a renewed interest in metaphysics. Milbank speaks of three families of thought: *speculative materialists* (some of whom, like Daniel Dennett and Richard Dawkins, reduce philosophy

---

75. "This idea of limit, even if intended to be only disciplinary in nature, will inevitably carry some tacit conception of what lies beyond the entity's limit" (D. L. Schindler, *Ordering Love*, 386).

76. Milbank and Pickstock, *Truth in Aquinas*, xi. However, John Rothfork, in defense of postmodernity in general and Rorty in particular, pits "a lived way of life, embodied knowledge" against *principles*, which primarily lead to totalitarianism ("deadly serious talk about religious and philosophic principles has created havoc in Europe this century"). This conflates principles with ideology, and sets up the false dilemma of *either* abstract, absolutist principles, *or* Rorty's pragmatism, embedded in real life. The philosophers of the metaphysics of gift have always sought lived experience, practices, knowledge embedded in the traditions of the community, while not eschewing principles, and avoiding blind ideologies (Rothfork, "Postmodern Ethics," 21).

77. Feser, "Contract Schmontract."

to physics and are "prepared to pay the price of the loss of the reality of mind and reason"), which we see in the thought of Quine, Davidson, and Rorty; *speculative idealists* ("even if . . . nominally materialist in character"), represented by Badiou and Meillassoux; and *speculative realists* (who, in "seeking to do justice to the reality of both mind and matter. . . . do not seek to sustain both worlds, so much as to situate the human spirit entirely within the first world of the real external cosmos" and thus remain immanentists), represented by Graham Harman and Bruno Latour.[78] Milbank is right that these groups are more explanatory for the twenty-first century than the analytic/continental divide, but we will use the terms for the sake of historical context. Of necessity this section will be brief; practitioners will find it incomplete, even unfair. However, the point is not to present a complete picture of these philosophies, but rather enough to provide a contrast to the metaphysics of gift.

In Analytic Philosophy

Quine, one of the most authoritative and influential analytic philosophers of the century, represented a turning point, both as the culmination of the anti-metaphysical attitude as well as a harbinger of the possibility of a renewal, albeit in a different guise, of metaphysical thinking. In the midst of the twentieth century's widespread hostility toward metaphysics, he wrote an essay entitled "On What There Is" that "single-handedly made ontology a respectable subject."[79] However, in Quine's view, ontology does not reveal anything about "being *qua* being" or disclose anything about the ultimate nature of reality, or speak of our transcendental, Kantian constructions, or expose something that is supposedly "hidden" in our semantics, as the positivists would have it, but rather *clarifies the "ontological commitments" we make within our theories.*

Quine is noted for having argued that to be is to be the value of a bound variable. So, for example, to say "some dogs are white" (in formal logic, $(\exists x)\, D(x) \wedge W(x)$ or "there exists some X such that X is a dog and X is white") means that the bound variable X ranges over white dogs, but does not need to include or make any reference to essences or universals, to "dogness" or "whiteness." A class of dogs consists of the members of the class only, and there need not be any idea "behind" the class. "The

---

78. Milbank, "Stanton Lecture 8," 4–5.
79. Putnam, *Ethics without Ontology*, 78–79.

point is *not* that to exist amounts to nothing more than being the value of a bound variable, but that to *commit* oneself to the existence of something is nothing more than *to say* that there is such a thing."[80] A philosopher translates our theories from regular language to formal language and becomes convinced of a particular ontological presupposition *if and only if* we need that supposed entity among the entities our variables range over in order that the affirmations *in the theory* be true.[81]

We now turn to some examples of recovery.

Relative Essentialism

Analytic philosophy had distinguished statements that were *necessary and a priori* from those that were *contingent and a posteriori*.[82] American philosopher Saul Kripke, whose work was "as influential in the latter Twentieth Century as ... Logical Positivism and Logical Atomism were in the early part of that century,"[83] against the Positivists and a whole tradition stemming from Kant, said that truth claims could be *necessary and a posteriori*. Consider a "natural kind" term like gold: its atomic number, 79, was discovered *a posteriori*. If gold has the property of having an atomic weight of 79, it does so necessarily even though it is not known *a priori*. "Gold" then becomes, as a name, a "rigid designator" true over all "possible worlds."[84] Kripke's 1970 lectures recorded in *Naming*

---

80. Soames, "Ontology, Analyticity and Meaning," 3. This appears to be pure nominalism, denying universals, but Quine states that it is "nominalistic neither in doctrine nor in motivation. I was concerned rather with ascribing ontologies rather than evaluating them" (Quine, *Logical Point*, viii).

81. Quine, *Logical Point*, 13.

82. Essentially, a necessary truth, as opposed to a contingent one, is one whose denial would be a contradiction. *A priori* and *a posteriori* are epistemological terms that refer to conclusions that can be known independent of experience and those that cannot. Of course this theory is more sophisticated, and complicated by differences in the meaning of "experience."

83. Green, "Kripke, Saul Aaron," 1361.

84. "Possible worlds," in the spirit of Leibniz, is a way to envision logical possibility. The person baptized "Shakespeare" would be Shakespeare in all possible worlds, even those in which he did not write *Hamlet*; opposed to this is the idea that names are concealed descriptions, so that "Shakespeare = the author of *Hamlet*," and the description would pick out *whoever* did that, even if it turned out not to be William Shakespeare. "A formula is necessarily true just in case it is true in all worlds in the model; possibly true just in case it is true at some. The semantics of the modalities *necessary* and *possible* is then cashed out in terms of the familiar quantifiers *all* and *some*" (Green, "Kripke, Saul Aaron," 1362).

and Necessity inaugurated a resurgence of metaphysics in analytic philosophy; rather than being dismissed, "metaphysics of the essentialist kind is regarded as a core field of philosophy."[85]

What *kind* of essentialism is another story. Philosopher Samuel Wheeler became convinced that Kripke's intuitions were right: that "there had to be natures of things and the *de re* necessities that would be the consequences of such natures" and that some sort of realistic metaphysics was required.[86] But it seemed more plausible that these new "*a posteriori* necessities" were not about the "stuff" of the world, like gold, at all, as Kripke thought, but rather about the *conditions* for something to be gold. Rather than essences "*de re*"—in the things themselves—and rather than nature itself being divided into objects at "natural joints,"[87] Wheeler speaks of "*relative essentialism.*" There *is* essentialism, for the universe is not an amorphous flux which can be divided any way we please, but that essentialism is *relative and tied to predicates*, treating entities as "posits required for thinking rather than articulations of reality." He continues, "Thus, in a somewhat Kantian way, positing beings and properties is a precondition for thought. I argue that the happy fact that reality seems to come in beings which have properties is not our conformity to a given articulated world, but rather our doing."[88] In the end, the ghost of Kant cannot be escaped: metaphysical claims are considered merely claims about the structure of thought.[89]

Naturalized Metaphysics

James Ladyman et al. in their book *Every Thing Must Go: Metaphysics Naturalized* propose "naturalized metaphysics," grounded in empirical science.[90] Their Primacy of Physics Constraint states that fundamental physics is primary and other sciences should not violate it.[91] Their

---

85. Wheeler, "*Saul Kripke,*" 284–85.

86. Wheeler, *Neo-Davidsonian Metaphysics*, 2.

87. This is a reference to Plato's *Phaedrus*, in which Socrates compares the comprehension of the forms of nature to the work of a butcher who cuts "along its natural joints" (Plato, "Phaedrus," 265e [542]).

88. Wheeler, *Neo-Davidsonian Metaphysics*, 7.

89. See Lowe, *Survey of Metaphysics*, 7–11.

90. Ladyman et al., *Every Thing Must Go*, 38.

91. Not all physics is fundamental, only "that part of physics about which measurements taken anywhere in the universe carry information" (Ladyman et al., *Every Thing Must Go*, 55).

scientific "metaphysics" is concerned with unifying the sciences, systematically relating them to each other: a new metaphysical claim can be taken seriously only if it can show how two or more scientific hypotheses "jointly explain more than the sum of what is explained by the two hypotheses taken separately."[92] This is a far cry from anything that hitherto has been considered metaphysics and usurps the original meaning of the word in order to convey their universal ambitions for scientific consilience, a materialistic ambition popularized by E. O. Wilson that we will address later.[93]

Neo-Aristotelian Metaphysics

The philosophers of another recovery program, "Neo-Aristotelianism," object to metaphysics as empiricist or naturalized, as simply clearing up linguistic confusion, and as what they see as the Kantian error: "supposing that metaphysics concerns the structure of our thought about being rather than being itself."[94] They instead ask questions about "metaphysical explanation," mind-independent relations within the world such as why something is true, or why something exists.[95] Neo-Aristotelians attempt a defense of essentialism, but in a non-transcendental form that does not hold up to scrutiny. Their only argument against the Heraclitean flux is an appeal to "the constancy of scientific law—but the whole idea of a law prior to 'the way things happen to go' is an anthropomorphic projection alien to the most radical spirit of modern physics."[96]

Continental Recovery

There has been in recent years a renaissance in continental philosophy as well, as evidenced by book titles like Graham Harman's *Guerrilla Metaphysics: Phenomenology and the Carpentry of Things*.[97] The "metaphysical turn" that continental philosophy has taken extends over a large and

---

92. Ladyman et al., *Every Thing Must Go*, 37.
93. See Wilson, *Consilience*.
94. Lowe, *Survey of Metaphysics*, 14.
95. See Tahko, "In Defence of Aristotelian Metaphysics."
96. Milbank, "Stanton Lecture 3," 7–8.
97. See Harman, *Guerrilla Metaphysics*.

diverse field, from Alain Badiou's set theory in mathematics as ontology[98] to Adrian Johnston's work on "transcendental materialism."[99] Johnston is candid: an aversion to the empirical-only route of knowledge acquisition leads to "an unruly, proliferating swarm of confabulations, delusions, imagining, fantasies, and ravings passing themselves off as rigorous, responsible philosophizing."[100]

The continental turn towards metaphysics has been more concerned with realism and the relation between appearance and reality than with formalizing language about ontological commitment, but it is *not* the realism of the past. The various forms this realism takes are very different from each other. Consider the following examples:

1) Metaphysics that makes human consciousness central and turns to phenomenology.

Dwayne Tunstall says that phenomenological metaphysicians do not attempt to examine the structures of a mind-independent world, "as though we could ever describe the world as it is in itself." Rather, they, "disclose the essential, invariant structures of our acts of meaning bestowal (for example, constituting objects of human cognition and scientific inquiry) as well as our acts of appreciating certain interpersonal phenomena (for example, love and faith)."[101]

2) Metaphysics that *rejects* phenomenology, proposing not only that objects exist independently of human perception, but that object–object relations are on the same ontological footing as human–object relations.

Speculative Realists[102] are opposed to "correlationism," Meillassoux's term for any philosophy based on the mutual interplay of the

---

98. See Badiou, *Being and Event*. It is because of, not in spite of, the many paradoxes in mathematics, as shown by such figures as Kurt Gödel, that ontology as set theory is so interesting. According to Milbank, it is the paradoxes "which allow a mathematical ontology to be non-reductive: by exposing the holes, gaps or cracks in ontological reality they suggest the obscure spaces in which both phenomenal and the subjective realities can emerge into being: singular, self-founded realities 'beyond being' in the sense of the ontological repertoire, and so themselves not subject to any mathematical accounting" (Milbank, "Stanton Lecture 3," 15).

99. See Johnston, *Adventures in Transcendental Materialism*.

100. Johnston, "Points of Forced Freedom," 91.

101. Tunstall, *Doing Philosophy Personally*, 10.

102. "Speculative realism," as the name indicates, means that contra Kant, we

mind and the world—the idea that knowledge is a matching up of mental states, observations, or propositions with a "really existing" thing or state of affairs in the world. Correlation leads to skeptical, epistemological questions like, "How do we know the correspondence is right?" For Speculative Realists, ontology, not epistemology, is the primary concern. Meillassoux's own hardline objectivist realism stands against all constructivism, linguistic anti-realism, pragmatism, hermeneutics, and any philosophy that restricts us to speaking only about how the world is for us, and that believes that "truth is co-extensive with the scope and limits of attainable human knowledge."[103]

3) Metaphysics that occupies the "middle ground" between mind-independent and mind-dependent ontologies.

Markus Gabriel sees mind-independent realism as unable to account for the modern insight that humans make decisions as to "what is what"; meanwhile anti-realists go too far in the other direction, imagining that "we somehow *create* a volcano by individuating it."[104] In a position midway between the two, he says,

> One could simplify further and say that metaphysical (old) realism is exclusively interested in the world without spectators, whereas constructivism is exclusively interested in the world of the spectators (oscillating between phenomenologically bracketing the world without spectators and its outright denial). New ontological realism accordingly occupies middle ground by recognizing the existence of perspectives and constructions as world-involving relations.[105]

These pendulum swings over whether to privilege the world, or the mind as spectator of the world, or to somehow hold on to the tension of a middle position, reflect the perpetual problem of every sort of dualism that sees the partners as standing in opposition rather than analogical relation to each other. Edward Oakes, writing about Erich Przywara on the topic of analogy, said that he saw "the pathos of individual thinkers

---

can speculate philosophically, going beyond the phenomenal, and we *can* be realists, speculating about mind-independent reality.

103. Norris, "Speculative Realism," 38.
104. Gabriel, *Fields of Sense*, 9.
105. Gabriel, *Fields of Sense*, 11.

who were unable to hold the two poles together" and that "the whole of philosophy was the story of this unfulfilled passion for wholeness."[106]

Though both analytic and continental philosophy opposed speculation and sought to bring about the end of metaphysics as First Philosophy, it has been argued, most notably by Milbank, that both stem from the same source. From Scotus came the notion of univocity of being, and also the related *priority of possibility over actuality*:

> Scotus, unlike Aquinas, no longer thought of "contingency" as simply the dependency of creatures upon God, but thought that in order for something to be contingent, something else must always be equally possible, tracking the real like an uneasy shadow. Furthermore, by a curious inversion Scotus made this lurking shadow of the possible more primary than the actuality whose light one might have supposed to have cast this shadow in the first place.[107]

The current of "possibilism" (which differs from Aristotelian potency[108]) flowed to Kant, in whom metaphysics becomes epistemology, through Suarez and Wolff, with the fateful elaboration that the conditions of possibility of knowledge were *only such for the knowing subject*.[109] In twentieth-century philosophy, logical possibility, either as modal theory, or as the "new logical instrument" of phenomenology, which separated appearance from "what might really be the case," became the preferred way to solve philosophical problems.[110] Finally, there is the thesis that "possibility really precedes actuality in the ontological realm."[111]

In the end, says Milbank, we lose sight of the notion that natural necessities, essences, etc. are *actualized* as "gift." "Instead one has a doubly arid mere *givenness* without taint of generosity or gratitude. Possibilities are just 'there' without real receiving, while actuality is an existential instantiation of essence, equally sheerly 'there' without the 'why'

---

106. Oakes, *Pattern of Redemption*, 37.

107. Milbank, "Stanton Lecture 1," 6.

108. "For Aristotle, a potential is a potential for something, for some state or other, which is always primarily defined in terms of its actuality. But to say that the possible comes first is to say either that defining essence precedes existence or that a defining force precedes relatively static states of existence" (Milbank, "Stanton Lecture 2," 8).

109. Milbank, "Stanton Lecture 1," 8.

110. Milbank, "Stanton Lecture 1," 11.

111. Milbank, "Stanton Lecture 2," 1.

of donation."¹¹² We will return to the consideration of contingency and necessity, potency and actuality, later on. The "why" of donation brings us to a first look at what we could call a true recovery of metaphysics: the metaphysics of gift.

The Metaphysics of Gift: A First Look

*Being is given to us; we are given to be, and to be as mindful; we do not first produce being, or make it be as for us; originally it is given as an excess of otherness which arouses our astonishment that it is at all. . . . The metaphysician keeps alive this elemental astonishment.*¹¹³

Markus Gabriel describes metaphysics as "a combination of an account of reality versus appearance, and a theory of totality."¹¹⁴ The two are intrinsically related, for the "attempt to say what reality is in opposition to appearance . . . typically turns reality into the totality of what is the case anyway."¹¹⁵ Caputo agrees both on the reality-versus-appearance opposition, rejecting any metaphysics that imagines itself "as a kind of super-science that cuts through the soft surface of appearances and hits the hard rock of Reality,"¹¹⁶ and on the rejection of a metaphysics that tries to survey the flux in one "totalizing sweep."¹¹⁷ The trend continues with Rorty and other anti-representationalists rejecting any philosophy that demarcates appearance from being. Another hallmark of postmodernism is the rejection of essentialism, whether by outright denial (by claiming that the world does not divide at Plato's "natural joints"; rather, *process* takes precedence) or by a Kantian "relative essentialism."

The questions of appearance and being, of reason as a totalizing metanarrative, and of essences versus process are all permutations of the problem of the One and the Many: in rejecting Enlightenment dualism and absolutist monism, the only alternative for postmoderns seems to be to construct a variety of immanent ontologies in a form of indiscriminate pluralism. Indifferent pluralism, monism, and dualism all suffer from the

112. Milbank, "Only Theology Saves," 47.
113. Desmond, *The Intimate Strangeness*, 5.
114. Gabriel, *Fields of Sense*, 6.
115. Gabriel, *Fields of Sense*, 6.
116. Caputo, *More Radical Hermeneutics*, 7.
117. Caputo, *Radical Hermeneutics*, 166.

same problem: as Pabst says, "All three refuse any mediation between the infinite one and the finite many."[118] To oppose them (and with them other permutations such as the collective and the individual), he continues, "is simply to assert that they represent contrary principles and that as such they are incompatible, producing conflict and violence."[119]

However, there is another group of philosophers who, though they do not pertain to one particular school, also reject a totalizing reason that purports to capture all of reality, who also reject the representational epistemology and dualisms of the Enlightenment, and who also reject an abstract metaphysics divorced from lived human experience. They do not cling to essentialism, though they do not reject essence either, and they call for a recovery of metaphysics, but not one that is a simple nostalgia for the ancient or classical tradition, nor for one of the current ontologies of immanence, whether construed as positivism or as transcendentalism. In the oscillation between privileging being or appearance, unity or diversity, these philosophers do not opt for an *opposition* of one against the other but rather for a genuinely mutual *polarity*, a unity-in-distinction, in which "difference is always interpreted in the context of a prior unity, and that unity, properly understood, is always fruitful, which means that it is always generative of further difference."[120] Throughout this study we will refer to these thinkers as metaphysicians of gift, for, it could be said, they all share a distinct "sense of all of reality as gift" and an openness to being that represents a "sense of the '*pre*modern,' in a word, that precisely enables [their] genuine *post*modernity."[121] What follows will be a brief presentation of the major themes we have covered in this chapter, from the perspective of a metaphysics of gift.

Appearance as a Revelation of Reality

A being appears, it has an epiphany: in that it is beautiful and makes us marvel. In appearing it gives itself, it delivers itself to us: it is good. And in giving itself up, it speaks itself, it unveils itself: it is true (in itself, but in the other to which it reveals itself).[122]

118. Pabst, *Metaphysics*, xxviii–xxix.

119. Pabst, *Metaphysics*, xxx.

120. D. C. Schindler, "Beauty," 21–22.

121. D. L. Schindler, "The Significance," 33. While David L. Schindler wrote these lines about Balthasar, they could be applied to any of the metaphysicians of gift.

122. Balthasar, *My Work*, 116.

Metaphysics of gift offers a unique perspective on the classic quandary of appearance versus reality. The information gathered by our senses can sometimes seem to contradict itself, which was the foundational observation for Descartes's doubts; metaphysics of gift goes beyond this initial impression. It does not *oppose* appearance and being, or appearance and reality, or appearance and "things-in-themselves." On the one hand, appearance is not the only truth we have, since "being" or "things-in-themselves" are supposedly inaccessible, as in Kant's *equivocal* view of reality as noumenal and phenomenal. On the other hand, appearance and being are not collapsed into each other in a *univocal* logic of identity; they are not the same thing. Rather, in the *analogical* sense, there is both a clear distinction as well as a mutual relation between the two. Appearance is an *epiphany* of being. At the epistemological level, this means we are not necessarily deceived by appearances; they are not illusions concealing reality—they simply cannot reveal the fullness of truth. What we know, we may know *truthfully*, though not *exhaustively*. As we will see, analogy is truly the sword that cuts the Gordian knot of appearance and being.

This is not just a theoretical issue; it also has political and social effects. If "being" represents the reality of a thing as distinct from its being perceived, and the criteria for knowledge lies with the perceiver alone, how do persons connect with each other in a truly intrinsic manner? How do we come to a common truth? "The question is no longer 'what is true?' but 'what is capable of bringing about the most desirable outcome?' There is a total collapse into effective power."[123] We will examine this more fully in the next chapter on the inadequate metaphysics of the technological paradigm.

The Openness of Reason

To say that reason is grounded in the good means that reason has its proper place within a context that exceeds it. The implications of this are endless. One of them is that we cannot limit reason to its formal aspect.[124]

---

123. D. C. Schindler, *Plato's Critique*, 64. He says: "The problem with relativism is that it is essentially dogmatic: by equalizing all perspectives in a wholly undifferentiated manner, relativism makes each perspective in itself a kind of self-contained totality, which is therefore on its own terms incontrovertible and thus definitive" (*Plato's Critique*, 14–15).

124. D. C. Schindler in Tyson, "Reasoning within the Good," 326.

What characterizes the metaphysics of gift is its *openness* to the totality of reality, not a claim to have *captured* that totality or to be capable of doing so eventually, as proponents of consilience do. In fact, it makes no claims about grasping a "totality" at all and thus has no stake in modernity's "metanarratives." D. C. Schindler describes reason as essentially *catholic* (in the philosophical sense, from the Greek *cat-holon*, "according to the whole") in both its principles (it is defined by its relation to being as a whole, and it involves the whole person) and in its exercise (it grasps the whole as universal *and* as a concrete individual thing in each particular act).[125] "Only the affirmation of the catholicity of reason preserves genuine humility, so that the typical strategies for avoiding the 'excesses' of reason that one finds in modern and postmodern thought, to the extent that they impoverish reason or attempt to impose artificial limits on its use, inevitably undermine their own aims."[126]

Metaphysics of gift sees the wholeness of reason not as a circle that can enclose everything, but a parabola, open to a context that exceeds it, an ever-deeper mystery. One could argue that the concession of mystery is even a logical necessity: in order to posit a "limit" to reason, one is already presupposing something unknown beyond that limit. And so the wholeness regarding reason in metaphysics of gift is not only *not* totalizing, "but is rather the only adequate resistance to it."[127]

While at first we might be tempted to think that this philosophical attitude goes against the tendencies of a scientific mindset, we must recognize that in reality it is the dominant technocratic culture that betrays its own roots. This humility and recognition of the ever-greater is as necessary for the "hard sciences" as it is for a solid metaphysics. A scientist seeks empirical evidence and limits himself to what is measurable, yet within the realm of the empirical, he can never close his mind to any possible explanation. Through research, his questions and hypotheses are not converted into facts but rather into ever-deeper questioning such that, as knowledge grows, so does the awareness of how much we do not yet know. The problem arises when the scientific methodology of only considering empirical evidence valid takes the place of the humility of an open reason.

---

125. See D. C. Schindler, *Catholicity of Reason*, 3–32.
126. D. C. Schindler, *Catholicity of Reason*, 3.
127. D. C. Schindler, *Catholicity of Reason*, 3.

The Nature of Essence

Metaphysicians of gift do not reject essence but are not "essentialists" in the way that postmoderns imagine. Some sort of concept of substance deriving from Aristotle "is indispensable for defending any adequate notion of being as gift," for there must be a "stable 'what,' or substantive subject of gift" for the idea to make sense.[128] But Aristotle's matter/essence hylomorphism of substance was not the last word; as we noted above, there is in a sense a "second hylomorphism," the crucial Thomistic distinction of essence and existence. Thomas said: "*Principia essentialia rerum sunt nobis ignota*" ("the essential principles of things are hidden from us")[129] in the sense that there is always the ever-greater mystery—an excess of intelligibility that cannot be simplified or captured—of *existence* on the other side, so to speak, of the essence–existence distinction within each entity. There can be no "totalizing" essentialism, only an openness such that to learn anything or discover anything is an invitation to seek further, and that manifests itself also as openness to other beings in relationships of giving and receiving.

In addition, for the metaphysics of gift, substance is not a "static, unknown substratum to which relations are added extrinsically, from outside,"[130] nor does it dissolve into a flux. Rather, relationality is *constitutive*. Tracey Rowland says an anthropology of persons must be

> sufficiently multidimensional to include within it both substantiality (the notion of a universal human nature), and relationality (an appreciation of the uniqueness of each and every human life, its individuality determined by its relations with similarly unique others) . . . the two dimensions [must be] held together rather than eclipsing either the historical or the ontological edge of the pole.[131]

In fact, *all* beings must be seen both in their essential substantiality as well as their relationality: two poles that are mutually interdependent.

---

128. D. L. Schindler, "Being, Gift (Part One)," 228.

129. Aquinas, *Commentary on Aristotle's* De Anima, lib. 1, l. 1, n. 15.

130. D. L. Schindler, "Being, Gift (Part One)," 228.

131. Rowland, *Benedict XVI*, 93. Neo-Aristotelians make a distinction between constituent and relational ontologies, and as we will refer to the metaphysics of gift as "relational," we must note that the meanings are different. "Constituent ontology versus relationality ontology" for Neo-Aristotelians refers to whether or not *properties* such as "whiteness" can be considered ontological "parts" of an object, and does not take into account relation with other entities.

To Aristotle, relationality was one of the "accidents" or "chance circumstances of being"; substance, on the other hand, was "the sole sustaining form of the real."[132] But for the metaphysicians of gift, "the *relatio* stands beside substance as an equally primordial form of being."[133]

Metaphysics as Pilgrimage

At the foundation of a dramatic notion of reason is [the] insight that consciousness is "born," i.e. it is constituted in the simultaneously interpersonal and ontological event of the mother's smile. . . . The conditions of possibility that structure reason do not belong to it prior to its encounter with the real, but are "dramatically" constituted in the gift of its participation in and with the reality the child's mother lovingly offers.[134]

Hans Urs von Balthasar was one of the most prolific thinkers of the twentieth century and one of the most creative and insightful readers of Aquinas. Aquinas's *essence* and *existence* are counterparts to Balthasar's *limited* and *limitless* being; the communication and reception of being by creatures is counterpart to the giving and receiving within the metaphysics of gift. At the interpersonal level, the Thomistic "real distinction" is manifest in an encounter in which both the "essential" and "existential," being and appearance, are understood as dimensions of the same reality. They are not torn apart by the dualistic fissures of Descartes and Kant (between what can and cannot be known) or the linguistic philosophers (between what can and cannot be said).[135] The objection of philosophers since Heidegger is that metaphysics is onto-theology, where "one specific kind of being [is] elevated to the level of being itself, set down as the foundation of all others,"[136] but it has been said of Balthasar's unfolding of the real distinction that it effectively "prevents us from conceiving the transcendent ground as another being among beings—thus collapsing metaphysics into onto-theology."[137]

132. Ratzinger, *Introduction to Christianity*, 183.

133. Ratzinger, *Introduction to Christianity*, 183.

134. D. C. Schindler, "Hans Urs von Balthasar, Metaphysics," 110–11.

135. "The 'fourfold difference', which many regard as the copingstone of Balthasar's philosophy, represents Balthasar's version of Thomas's 'real distinction'" (Healy, *Eschatology*, 61).

136. Harman, *Bells and Whistles*, 9.

137. López, "Eternal Happening," 217–18.

Balthasar characterized the structure of reason as that of a dramatic encounter. His four-part distinction is elucidated in the famous "Smile of the Mother," which we will address more fully in chapter 4. The best way to grasp the seemingly ineradicable problems of consciousness/mind/language and world/things/being is *not* in conceptual or formal abstraction. The origin of metaphysics lies neither there, nor in theoretical posits, nor in ontological commitments, but in the "simultaneously interpersonal and ontological event,"[138] which Balthasar describes in what he calls four "unfoldings."

Briefly, the child's first experience, the smile of the mother, is the experience of *giftedness* and *unity-in-diversity*: that the child both has been granted existence, for he is not the source of his own existence, and at the same time "is one in love with the mother, even in being other than his mother."[139] This experience is the proper context for the fundamental question of metaphysics: why is there something rather than nothing? "The reception of a gift provokes a natural desire to know the source of the gift. To whom do I owe my gratitude?"[140]

In the second and third movements of the "fourfold distinction," we see that the mother too is in the same position of having been gifted with existence, as are all other limited beings; hence being appears as a limitless source upon which each existent depends. Yet if each existing thing participates in being and thus needs being, said Balthasar, the reverse is also true—being stands in need of the existent.[141] To preserve the distinction between the two, to preserve the reciprocal relationship, and to account for the multiplicity of existent things, one cannot privilege one over the other, whether through mechanistic materialism or through idealism. The question of why there is something rather than nothing "cannot be answered at the level of a distinction between being and the existent. As non-subsistent, being cannot be the ultimate source of the existent."[142]

And so both the interpersonal communion and the mutual dependence of the existent upon being and vice versa point to the fourth and final distinction: a mysterious "more" flowing from subsistent Being behind non-subsistent being. The inseparability of wonder and gift arises

---

138. D. C. Schindler, "'Wie kommt der Mensch?,'" 665.
139. Balthasar, *My Work*, 114.
140. Healy, *Eschatology*, 65.
141. Balthasar, *Glory of the Lord V*, 619.
142. Healy, *Eschatology*, 68.

because this "more," that which is "ever greater," is richer than even the ontological difference itself, and so our wonder is "directed beyond the reality of the world"; that which "lies at the heart of being reaches all the way to God, who is present in creation as a gift that has been truly given away."[143]

Of course, it would appear to many that we have here left philosophy behind and entered the realms of theology or poetry. But the ontology of which we speak implies that "the features of gift such as those noted above are really present in things, and that it is thus possible in principle for all reasonable beings . . . to recognize these features."[144] Kenneth Schmitz has pointed out that the dynamic of giving and receiving is present at every level of existence, from physical and chemical transference of energy, to physiology's stimulus and response, to the mutual exchange of commerce, and up to the highest social interactions.[145]

For many of those practicing philosophy today, the various permutations of metaphysical questions are compelling: the analytic view of metaphysical entities as logical and linguistic confusions, the phenomenological choice of a science of appearances over classical metaphysics, questions about ontological commitments within scientific theories, etc. These things should not be set aside or rejected, but rather caught up in and transformed by the deeper understanding of a metaphysics of gift. "As a 'logic' of 'being' (onto-logy), it is understood . . . to include in its most basic terms the logic of the whole person in his encounter with the totality of things."[146]

The point is that the "recovery of metaphysics" in analytic and continental philosophy is not the recovery this study seeks. We may still ask "What is there?" and "What can we say about what is there?" but the foundational metaphysical question is qualitatively different, and that question is primary. The metaphysics of gift cannot be construed as one subject among many, for it aims at an open and unifying vision of being within which all fields of study contribute. Since the real life questions about how to care for creation, how to live, and what to do politically, economically, socially, ethically, and in charity toward others *follow* from metaphysics, the authentic metaphysical question does not issue forth

---

143. Healy, *Eschatology*, 68–70.
144. D. L. Schindler, "The Given as Gift," 85.
145. See Schmitz, *The Gift*, 77.
146. D. L. Schindler, "The Given as Gift," 56.

into a subject matter or field, but into a *way*, a *camino*. In Peter Casarella's felicitous phrase, it is "metaphysics as pilgrimage."[147]

---

147. Casarella, "Trinity and Creation," 30.

2

Two Visions of Nature and Morality

The Technological Paradigm vs. Eco-philosophies

As often as not, it is the questions we fail to ask—and so the presuppositions we leave intact—that determine the courses our arguments take.[1]

WHEN CONFRONTING ECOLOGICAL PROBLEMS, the belief that science-based solutions are sufficient is ubiquitous today. What combination of technical, economic, political, and social forces should be used is just a question of analysis, while ethical or religious arguments are often seen merely as motivational factors that can strengthen the social adherence to a particular solution. By default, we gravitate towards pragmatic resolutions that look something like this: apply whatever technological solution that will solve the material problem in the most economical way and that is socially acceptable and politically achievable. More often than not, these solutions have proven to be shortsighted because the method used to reach them carries with it a reductionist view of reality that can partially or completely—immediately or eventually—undermine the positive elements the solution could have, or worse, exacerbate the problem it was supposed to fix.

Though we may not be conscious of it, we navigate the world according to deeply rooted metaphysical assumptions, which "exert a powerful influence on our lives. Indeed, the less aware we are of our metaphysical

---

1. Hart, "The Illusionist," 109.

assumptions, the more we are subject to them."² This does not mean that a full-blown metaphysics must be developed before we can come to an ethical position. What we intuit as ethically good can illuminate our understanding of what is metaphysically real and vice versa; one's metaphysics and one's ethics grow up together. Yet, if we do not explicitly confront a problem on its deepest level, we may be blindly accepting assumptions that could frustrate all of our efforts. Recognizing the fundamental role of metaphysics for the comprehension of reality implies adherence to the principle that "reality as a whole is unitary and necessarily self-consistent" and, therefore, "truth is single and indivisible."³ Because all truths are rooted together in the heart of reality, if we are conscious of our presuppositions, we can be confident about the kind of foundation upon which we build.

Contrary to modern dogma, there is no neutral foundation from which to begin because every assertion of truth or goodness depends intrinsically on a metaphysical underpinning, which is itself an affirmation of what we take to be real. This chapter will seek to expose the metaphysical assumptions that determine the dominant modern worldview.⁴ This worldview has been referred to as the "Technological Paradigm"⁵ because, at its heart, it represents a theoretical framework resulting from a way of understanding the world *according to what we can do to it.*

In this paradigm, knowing is qualitatively reduced not simply to what is empirical but to what "works." Meanwhile, no ethical, economic, or even rational boundary is put on our actions; what can be done, should be done and what cannot be done should be tried until it is achieved.⁶ This method has become nothing less than the intellectual "trajectory of modern times"⁷ precisely because the metaphysical assumptions inherent within it have been universalized beyond their natural scope to eclipse the way we see the world; they are now part of the air we breathe. The technological paradigm is synonymous with a mechanistic view of

2. Vieira, "Which Is More Fundamental?"

3. Lowe, *Survey of Metaphysics*, 3.

4. See Heidegger, *The Question Concerning Technology*; Guardini, *Letters from Lake Como*.

5. See Hanby, "Creation as Aesthetic Analogy"; Francis, *Praise Be to You*, §101–36.

6. This is most strikingly observed in the biotech industry, where any conceivable advancement in knowledge is enough to justify any type of experimentation.

7. Benedict XVI, *Saved in Hope*, §17.

nature in which natural elements have no deeper reality than that which can be explained by physics: *what can be done to and with them.*

Most environmental thinkers today reject this paradigm and the intellectual tradition that gave rise to it, giving voice to a new perspective built on the concept of emergence that describes a vision of the material universe that goes beyond mechanism, which they rightly see as reductionist. Many adopt Heidegger's critique of technology, which blames Plato and his metaphysics—mistakenly—for technology's dominance of Western culture. Though a series of modern and ancient figures have been put before the tribunal—Francis Bacon, Descartes, Galileo, Plato, and even Abraham[8]—what is certain is that the modern environmental crisis has brought about widespread rejection of modernity: "In the late twentieth century, the environmental crisis and developments in postmodern science and philosophy have called into question the efficacy of the mechanistic worldview, the idea of Enlightenment progress, and the ethics of unrestrained development as a means of dominating nature."[9] These authors also reject the philosophical positivism that stipulates that true knowledge can only be derived *a posteriori* from empirical data.

What the technological paradigm and emergentist theories have in common is that both can be called forgetful, or perhaps willfully ignorant, of the true nature of the metaphysical dimension, though the latter at least attempts to address it, seeking to account for a richer understanding of reality. For example, emergent philosophers insist on the importance of relationality to the point of proposing a monistic holism as the proper metaphysical lens through which to view our world and as a foundation upon which to develop our ethics. This relational holism is opposed to "the anthropological machine" that has been constructed upon "metaphysical distinctions to separate and elevate the properly human from the less-than-fully-human and the natural world."[10]

While the technological paradigm is essentially based on a Cartesian-Newtonian worldview, the emergent authors point out that the findings of quantum physics have rendered the universal application of Newtonian physics obsolete. This observation has led to the rejection of the material reductionism inherent in the technological paradigm by more and more scientists, but we must recognize that it is so embedded

---

8. See White, "Historical Roots."
9. Merchant, *Reinventing Eden*, 225.
10. Smith, *Against Ecological Sovereignty*, xii.

in our lives that it is almost impossible to avoid. It is based on metaphysical presuppositions derived from modern science, often unnoticed and un-critiqued, that have been assumed by the broader culture, and it has widespread effects on our lives and on the natural world.

In this chapter we will discuss the technological paradigm and the alternative to it offered by mainstream eco-philosophy, namely holistic theories based on emergence, along with critiques of these proposals.

A Mechanical Cosmos: Technological Metaphysics

The present global technological situation of man has itself a metaphysical side to it besides the more obvious practical one. The meaning of the technological revolution is thus part of, indeed the completion of, the metaphysical meaning of the scientific revolution.[11]

It does not take a keen observer to see how technology has invaded our lives and caused the deterioration of our natural world.[12] Technology can be a powerful tool for ecological care and restoration, if used properly; however, the technological *paradigm* is a different story, as much a cultural and political reality as it is a scientific and practical one. The philosopher Michael Hanby uses "technocratic totalitarianism" to describe this era, which is "uniquely 'post-political,'" whose power lies not in coercion by the force of law but in the fact that people are rarely aware that they are being coerced and there is no one truly in control. Though there are elements of both, our situation is looking more like Aldous Huxley's *Brave New World* than George Orwell's *1984*: "In a perfectly absolute society, whose rule was indeed *total*, . . . there would simply be truths that could no longer be perceived, ideas that could not be thought, experiences that could no longer be had, and no one would ever know what he was missing."[13]

Here, however, we choose to speak directly to a *techno-logical* paradigm in order to focus on the underlying metaphysics at its foundation. We are not being subjugated by an outside force but by what is still, in essence, a product of our chosen vision of reality. This is not

---

11. Jonas, *Philosophical Essays*, 48.

12. Though the technological paradigm tends to concentrate environmental costs in some areas while leaving others untouched, social media and journalism makes us aware of many of the ecological impacts of technology.

13. Hanby, "A More Perfect Absolutism."

about condemning technology, for there is not one among us who is not grateful for some part of its innovations, but about understanding more deeply *what it is*. Its etymology is on point; the technological paradigm is, first and foremost, "a model" (*paradeigma*) of the world in which our "understanding" (*logos*) is determined by our "method of making or doing" (*technê*). This goes beyond epistemology alone as what *we can* think about things necessarily determines what we think they *are*, which, in turn, dictates our ethical responsibilities towards them. For this reason we will discuss the technological paradigm as provoking a metaphysical and ethical crisis.

Defining Metaphysics in Science

The technological paradigm is undoubtedly the fruit of modern science, but it was also paradoxically the seed from which modern science came into being. Galileo is credited with first developing the scientific method in general terms: the explicit omission of all "subjective appearances" in favor of empirical measurements, thus removing the scientist—along with anything unempirical—from the scientist's understanding of reality. In order to develop and apply this method, however, Galileo and the pioneers of modern science already had to think *within* these parameters. Hans Jonas explains the intellectual revolution that the scientific revolution required:

> The scientific revolution changed man's ways of thinking, *by* thinking, before it materially changed, even affected, his ways of living. It was a change in theory, in world-view, in metaphysical outlook, in conception and method of knowledge. It did not at first—and for a long time—concern itself with the realm of practice, even though some of its most eloquent philosophical prophets assigned to it this role early enough: that assignment itself was in the realm of thought.[14]

At the root of this new metaphysical outlook was the mechanistic view of creation: in simplest terms, that means conceiving all natural things, and indeed the entire universe, as a complex set of machinery. This idea was so packed with consequences that it is difficult to imagine that early scientists could have foreseen its impact. Of course, it first came about as a mere methodological tool, but it became an entirely new

14. Jonas, *Philosophical Essays*, 47.

worldview that would remake not only the world but even the conception of God, from the immanent and active source of all being to a cold and distant clockmaker.

According to this perspective, the surest, most reliable form of knowledge is empirical, representing those results that are repeatable and verifiable, and thus the most "real" reality is physical. As has often been pointed out, empirical science quickly became the archetype of true knowledge and all other fields of study, now considered "less exact," sought to conform themselves to this model.[15] Thus, all subjects had to conform to empirical standards to escape being deemed "subjective," a derogatory term for non-scientific forms of knowledge. This was indeed a radical turn. All the collected wisdom in art and literature suddenly became irrelevant, inconsequential, and dualistically separated off from the progress that science and technology offered humankind.

Philosophy, and metaphysics along with it, would no longer be considered useful or reliable as an application of human reason. In fact, Descartes's entire philosophical enterprise can be considered an attempt to justify certain "unscientific" beliefs—in the soul and in God—not *in the face* of the new intellectual paradigm, but *from within it*. As Hart points out,

> Descartes was remarkable not because . . . his vision was especially "vivid and compelling"—in comparison to the subtleties of earlier theories, it was crude, bizarre, and banal—but simply because no one before him had attempted systematically to situate mental phenomena within a universe otherwise understood as a mindless machine.[16]

Thus, built into his thought from the outset was the propagation of the mechanistic worldview, a radical dualism between a material, objective world and an immaterial, subjective world.[17] He had no qualms about philosophically justifying his infamous *res cogitans—res extensa* dualism, as it was already inherent to the technological paradigm. The same procedure is still employed by popular writers when facing the enigma of consciousness.[18]

---

15. See Benedict XVI, "Faith, Reason and the University."

16. Hart, "The Illusionist," 109.

17. Descartes notoriously posited that these two worlds were connected through the pineal gland.

18. "I am not philosopher enough to discuss what ['consciousness'] means, but

The conception of human rationality would now be concentrated solely in its instrumental capacity to apply and reapply the scientific method to the material world, resolving every practical problem put in its path. This would overturn medieval conceptions of human reason, which was understood to have a unified, yet twofold nature: first, the receptive contemplation of the *intellectus*, which would "passively" welcome in the whole of the experience of reality, and, secondly, the instrumental discursive function of the *ratio*, which worked "actively" on those experiences.[19] Thus man's intellectual capacity was no longer primarily a receptive function open to the fullness of reality. It was now destined for the primary purpose of teasing out all of reality's empirical elements and learning how to control and manipulate nature. According to Bacon, human reason had to become a tool capable of "a form of induction that takes experience apart and analyzes it."[20]

Understanding natural things in this way implies the possibility of the exhaustive intelligibility of *all* things. There is nothing that human rationality cannot capture within its understanding, and, eventually, all mysteries will be revealed. This is another radical departure from the previous worldview that understood the material reality of an object as a manifestation of its immaterial reality, considered in four different causal dimensions. Suddenly that has been wiped away and we are left with the mere materiality of objects, each of which is understood as a conglomeration of parts.

Another major consequence of the mechanistic conception of things is that of their relationality. The only possible relations between things are those described by physics: deterministic forces that are measurable and calculable. This means that there are no intrinsic, immaterial relationships in nature but only extrinsic relationships of essentially unrelated objects. Living things are only quantitatively more complex than nonliving things and can be considered, in the words of Descartes,

---

fortunately *it does not matter for our present purposes because it is easy to talk about machines that behave as if motivated by a purpose*, and to leave open the question whether they actually are conscious. These machines are basically very simple, and the principles of unconscious purposive behaviour are among the commonplaces of engineering science" (Dawkins, *Selfish Gene*, 64–65; emphasis mine).

19. "The Greeks—Aristotle no less than Plato—as well as the great medieval thinkers, held that not only physical, sensuous perception, but equally man's spiritual and intellectual knowledge, included an element of pure, receptive contemplation, or as Heraclitus says, 'listening to the essence of things'" (Pieper, *Leisure*, 28).

20. Bacon, *New Organon*, 17.

"*bête-machine*" (beast-machines) and "natural automata."[21] In fact, the thesis that "animals are machines"

> forms part of Descartes' general scientific "mechanism," and, roughly translated, means that all animal behavior is subsumable under physiological laws, which, for Descartes, are ultimately derivable from mathematical principles. Essentially, when Descartes says that "all motions of animals originate from the corporeal and mechanical principle," he is concerned to promulgate a scientific animal physiology which seeks explanations in terms of efficient rather than final causes.[22]

For Descartes, there is no qualitative difference between machines made by man and the machines "made by God," like our bodies and those of animals. All of the layers of the depth of reality present in the Aristotelian conception of nature have vanished. With only cosmetic differences, this same conception of biological organisms is fully present among today's popular authors such as Richard Dawkins, who refers to living organisms as "gene machines," "selfish machines," "survival machines," and "purpose machines" throughout his work.[23] For Descartes, Dawkins, and the entire mainstream scientific tradition between them,[24] which fully embraced the placement of mechanism at the heart of science, the whole universe can be considered a conglomeration of machinery controlled by deterministic physical principles that we may manipulate to suit our needs.

Mechanistic Rationality

The mechanistic conception at the heart of the technological paradigm involved two subtle yet fundamental philosophical shifts: the conflation of making and knowing and the conversion of nature into artifact. These represent the epistemological and ontological counterparts of what is portrayed as a merely practical method.

---

21. Cottingham, "'A Brute to the Brutes?,'" 552–53.
22. Cottingham, "'A Brute to the Brutes?,'" 552.
23. Dawkins, *Selfish Gene*, 59, 86, 65.
24. Here we would have to leave out scientists like Johann Wolfgang von Goethe, Michael Polanyi, and many quantum physicists.

Conflation of Making and Knowing

As its name indicates, technology binds understanding to making. However, the question is: what is the exact nature of their relationship? As Hanby rightly points out, there is a great deal of unity between knowing and making, but they ought to be conceived of in a hierarchical relationship such that one knows far more than one is capable of making.[25] The problem arises when this relationship is inverted and knowing is subsumed within the bounds of making, disfiguring both. As Bacon maintained,

> Although the road to human knowledge and the road to human power are very close and almost the same, yet because of the destructive and inveterate habit of losing oneself in abstraction, it is altogether safer to raise the sciences from the beginning on foundations which have an active tendency, and *let the active tendency itself mark and set bounds to the contemplative part.*[26]

However, what Bacon was describing was already built into the scientific project. Control and power were never merely the goal of scientific examination but also the means:

> It's not simply that we now know nature for the sake of control; it is rather that we know by means of the various kinds of control we are able to exercise over the phenomena of nature, and the truth of our knowledge is measured by the success of our experiments in predicting, retro-dicting, or manipulating these phenomena. . . . The imperative to control is not principally a matter of subjective will or intention; rather it is inherent in the structure of scientific cognition and experimental rationality.[27]

It was not the fact of its undeniable technological successes that caused the river of science to swell so completely that it flooded into other disciplines; the new vision of nature according to modern science "contained manipulability at its theoretical core and, in the form of experiment, involved actual manipulation in the investigative process."[28] We cannot underestimate the extent to which the conflation of making and knowing was driven by the desire for control. Indeed, Bacon would

---

25. See Hanby, "Gospel of Creation," 727–28.
26. Bacon, *New Organon*, 103 (emphasis mine).
27. Hanby, "Gospel of Creation," 728–29.
28. Jonas, *Philosophical Essays*, 48.

have looked fondly on "the subjugation of the whole natural realm to the service of man."[29] It was also Bacon who would equate this new scientific-mechanical knowledge of things with power: "Therefore those two goals of man, *knowledge* and *power*, a pair of twins, are really come to the same thing."[30] If you define "knowledge" as the exhaustive understanding of the physical causes of a thing and "power" as the ability to control those causes, then yes, knowledge in that sense is power, and the scientific method was set up with exactly this ambition in mind. Jonas, commenting on this fateful aphorism, described precisely the change it signified for common wisdom: "To put it in the form of a slogan, the modern knowledge of nature, very unlike the classical one, is a 'know-how' and not a 'know-what,' and on this basis it makes good Bacon's contention that knowledge is power."[31] This "imperative to control"[32] is built into the scientific method and its rationality, on the ontological level, and for this reason it is a method for the domination and manipulation of nature.

Transpositioning of Nature into Artifact

It would appear that the principle change provoked by the technological paradigm is an epistemological one that does not truly impact things themselves, but as Hanby points out, "this *subjective* conflation of knowing and making has as its ontological counterpart the *objective* conflation of nature and artifice, whose fusion now characterizes our culture from top to bottom, in thought, word, and deed."[33] In order to understand what he means by this, we must first understand what "nature" is and why artifacts are not nature.

Common sense points to the fact that there is a significant difference between a natural object and an artifact fashioned by man,[34] but for the technological paradigm, these two things are qualitatively equivalent. At the heart of Aristotle's understanding of the world was a distinction between things that "exist by nature" and things that exist "from other

---

29. Caldecott, *Radiance of Being*, 30.
30. Bacon, *New Organon*, 24.
31. Jonas, "Practical Uses of Theory," 82.
32. Hanby, "Gospel of Creation," 729.
33. Hanby, "Gospel of Creation," 729.
34. Or even one fashioned by an animal for that matter. It is well documented that animals such as chimpanzees and ravens can make simple tools to get food, birds build nests, bees build hives, and so on.

causes"[35] which are "products of art"[36] or "artificial products."[37] Things, or better yet, substances that exist by nature include "the animals and their parts, ... and the plants and the simple bodies (earth, fire, air, water)."[38]

The essential difference seems obvious: products of art are made by an active agent and natural things are not, but for Aristotle the explanation of the differences is more subtle, and he uses an analogy with the former to explain the latter. Aristotle defines nature as "a source or cause of being moved and of being at rest in that to which it belongs primarily, in virtue of itself and not in virtue of a concomitant attribute."[39] Thus, natural elements contain within themselves "a principle of motion and stationariness,"[40] where, by motion (*kinesis*), he does not mean physical movement but "the fulfillment of what exists potentially, in so far as it exists potentially."[41] In Aristotle's words, all products of art, "a bed and a coat and anything else of that sort . . . have no innate impulse to change" except to the extent that they are composed of natural elements and thus possess the innate principles of those natural objects.[42] For example, a wooden chair will fall to the ground or rot or burn not because it is a chair but because of the innate principles of the wood of which it is made. In other words, what an active agent is to an artificial product, nature is to natural objects. Thus, a natural object is never just a static body at rest that is not *doing* anything until it is acted upon by some other body or agent, and it is not something that can be understood by simple empirical weighing and measuring. The same could be said about artifacts to the extent to which they never lose the natural principles of their materials.

Aristotle called metaphysics "first" philosophy, and physics is the "second" philosophy that depends on the metaphysical investigation into forms and causes by the "first philosophy." An entity is composed of passive and active components—matter and form—while the four causes (material, formal, efficient, and final) describe four dimensions of one indivisible reality, none of which are purely physical in the empirical sense.

35. Aristotle, "Physics," II, 192b7 (236).
36. Aristotle, "Physics," II, 192b18–19 (236).
37. Aristotle, "Physics," II, 192b28 (236).
38. Aristotle, "Physics," II, 192b9–10 (236).
39. Aristotle, "Physics," II, 192b21–23 (236).
40. Aristotle, "Physics," II, 192b14–15 (236).
41. Aristotle, "Physics," III, 201a10–11 (254).
42. Aristotle, "Physics," II, 192b16–19 (236).

The material cause is not merely what it is made of, but should be conceived as the passive principle and source of an object's potentialities. The formal cause, the form of an object, is the active principle that actualizes a certain set of potentialities possessed by the material. Neither of these causes exists in the real world independently of the other, existing only as a hylomorphic unity. This is the first reason why the causes cannot be separated; they are united in comprehending a singular reality in different ways. The efficient cause is related to Aristotle's concept of movement (*kinesis*) and acts by bringing about an effect or a change. This could be outside of the object or it could be internal, corresponding to the nature of the entity itself. Meanwhile, the final cause is conceived teleologically as the purpose or reason a potential change occurs or is brought about. Sometimes these causes can coincide, as is often the case in natural beings, and *nature* can feature in any of these inseparable causal functions.

To Aristotle, the physical world we experience is the result of constant movements from potentiality to actuality brought about by causes that act on but transcend the physical, the greatest of these being *telos*. All things are connected, sharing in Being itself, but humans hold the special capacity of and responsibility for being active agents in the world. "First" and "second" philosophy are intimately entwined because "first" philosophy's metaphysical investigation can only take place through the observation of physical things. For Aristotle it would have been unthinkable to try to disentangle metaphysics from physics.

Only with this understanding in mind can we fully appreciate the difference between an artifact and a natural substance that, by nature, contains its own ontological autonomy, uniqueness, and destiny. However, even for Aristotle an artifact will maintain the natural form of its material elements and, in a sense, never be completely artificial. We can now better appreciate the following deconstruction of Aristotle's *Physics* by Bacon in *The Advancement of Learning* (1605). He says he intends to use "metaphysics" in a different sense than in the past, and that by it he means completely separating physics from metaphysics: "Physic should contemplate that which is inherent in matter, and therefore transitory; and metaphysic that which is abstracted and fixed.... *The one part, which is physic, inquires and handles the material and efficient causes; and the other which is metaphysic, handles the formal and the final causes.*"[43]

---

43. Bacon, *Major Works*, 193–95 (emphasis mine).

It is this division of causes, and thus the division of physics from metaphysics, that essentially erases not only the formal and final causes but also the Aristotelian understanding of the material and efficient causes from the gaze of the scientist. A natural object no longer possesses any inner *nature* as a source of change from potentiality to actuality and therefore neither does an artifact by virtue of its material. All objects are qualitatively the same, according to Bacon's conception of material and efficient causes, and have no immaterial reality; they are only discoverable empirically, through measurement. Fifteen years after publishing *The Advancement of Learning*, Bacon would publish the following in his *New Organon* in 1620, which would come to mark the universal position of modern science:

> Thus, let the investigation of forms, which are (in the eye of reason at least, and in their essential law) eternal and immutable, constitute Metaphysics; *and let the investigation of the efficient cause, and of matter, and of the latent process, and the latent configuration (all of which have reference to the common and ordinary course of nature, not to her eternal and fundamental laws) constitute Physics.* And to these let there be subordinate two practical divisions: to Physics, Mechanics; to Metaphysics, what (in a purer sense of the word) I call Magic, on account of the broadness of the ways it moves in, and its greater command over nature.[44]

Metaphysics had not been forgotten but had been banished from the realm of practical importance for the burgeoning bourgeois European societies. One might argue that this division had to take place in order for science and technology to progress, so that it might bring us all of the advancements and benefits we know today. However, science and metaphysics ought to grow up together through mutual reinforcement and correction in a unified model of knowledge. The key is in the intimate, inseparable connection between Aristotle's Physics and Metaphysics. Metaphysics can only be studied through the careful observation and investigation into that which manifests itself through what is physical, not exclusively by seeking to manipulate it but by contemplating it in order to seek first to understand *what it is*.

Many other figures played important roles in this transformation of nature into artifact as we have described it. Ockham's fourteenth-century nominalism and voluntarism cannot be ignored, as they served

---

44. Bacon, *New Organon*, 109 (emphasis mine).

as theological and philosophical encouragement for Bacon as well as Galileo, Descartes, Newton, and others with regards to accepting the incipient technological paradigm into their theoretical conception of the world.[45] Perhaps Descartes's qualification of corporeal entities is the most striking in its minimalism: "Each substance has only one principle property which constitutes its nature and essence, and to which all other properties are related. Thus, extension, in length, breadth, and depth, constitutes the nature of corporeal substance."[46] This shows the power of the technological paradigm as a scientific ideal that loses sight of *nature* and thus preordains it for neglect and exploitation:

> I know of no distinction between these things [things made by human skill] and natural bodies, except that the operations of things made by skill are, for the most part, performed by apparatus large enough to be easily perceived by the senses. . . . It is as natural for a clock, composed of wheels of a certain kind, to indicate the hours, as for a tree, grown from a certain kind of seed, to produce the corresponding fruit.[47]

By conflating nature and artifact, modern science essentially forgot what nature was and reassigned it the task of providing the universal mathematical laws that would allow the scientific endeavor to march on as it had been preconceived.

Abstraction and Limits

In order to correct these errors we must, in the words of D. C. Schindler, "recover within science a more self-conscious sense that *one is not studying only a part, but rather the whole, even if it is in a particular respect.*"[48] There is an essential distinction between studying *only a part of reality* and studying *the whole of reality in a particular respect*. The former implies autonomy and independence within its realm of expertise and a certain disinterest towards "the whole" with which it has little in common, especially when the goals of a society are principally material. The latter emphasizes a sense of collaboration and mutual enlightenment between different perspectives, different branches of knowledge, and a common

---

45. Hanby, "Creation as Aesthetic Analogy," 352–53.
46. Descartes, *Principles of Philosophy*, 23.
47. Descartes, *Principles of Philosophy*, 285–86.
48. D. C. Schindler, *Catholicity of Reason*, 28 (emphasis mine).

goal of working towards a shared understanding of reality, of which wonder and beauty are a part.[49] It is not difficult to see that the former is a way of doing science that is more susceptible to scientism and more likely to conceive of *its part* as the only part that matters, or even *the only part that is real*, especially considering the deeply-rooted tendency for human reason to seek a unified comprehension of the world.

Modern science came about under that guise of studying *its own part* of reality—the empirical part, hypothetically separated from everything else. The method led to any number of puzzling problems when the subjective world we experience and the empirical scientific world diverged.[50] As Hart notes, science seeks universal explanations, "so it was inevitable that what began as an imperfect method for studying concrete particulars would soon metastasize into a metaphysics of the whole of reality." With the subjective world reduced to illusion, the mind became nothing more than "an emergent product of the *real* (which is to say, mindless) causal order,"[51] leaving two alternatives: maintain the Cartesian separation of mind and body, or subsume mind in a materialistic monism. In the end, the result is fundamentally the same: science remains the only arbiter of knowledge in a world that is entirely physical.

This is the course Dawkins took in *The Selfish Gene*, referenced earlier; here we wish to focus on his method of *abstraction* and how it predetermines the results of any reflection or investigation. Scientific abstractions necessarily suggest the notion of *limit*, a boundary that sets the object off from its context, such that one's understanding of the object is essentially indifferent to what lies beyond the limit; it is inessential. In Dawkins's case, by setting aside the question of consciousness as *not a scientific question* he presumes to already know that it has no bearing on the question of brain activity, a presumption made without argument. It simply excludes the possibility "that consciousness *might be an integral whole that includes the brain and its mechanical dimension even as it transcends it*,"[52] an exclusion which is itself a positive claim.

---

49. It must be acknowledged that many scientists already do science in this way to varying degrees.

50. For just one notable work of reflection on the body-mind problem, see Nagel, *Mind and Cosmos*. He explains in no uncertain terms that "a true appreciation of the difficulty of the problem must eventually change our conception of the place of the physical sciences in describing the natural order" (Nagel, *Mind and Cosmos*, 3).

51. Hart, "The Illusionist," 110.

52. D. C. Schindler, *Catholicity of Reason*, 27 (emphasis mine).

The most common corollary to scientific abstraction is the notion that science is, in itself, a neutral tool that can be used for good or evil; supposedly, problems only arise when scientists stray from asking "how" questions and try to answer "why" questions (this is Stephen Jay Gould's famous proposal of "non-overlapping magisterium": religious values and scientific facts do not overlap and thus should work independently of each other).[53] While the method appears to have proven its worth in many areas, it has also been blamed for the creation of, most famously, nuclear weapons. In response, it has been suggested that the moral and aesthetic dimensions of life be included in scientific endeavors via the *intentions of scientists*.[54] Perhaps the abstractions of science can be corrected by adding ethical or aesthetic values after the fact.

This suggestion, however, does not escape the root problem, but has implicitly given it a pass. David L. Schindler points out that every appeal of this type already embeds an implicit ontology in its proposal. The suggestion that morality and other values can simply be added to science after the fact is, in itself, "fraught with a mechanistic ontology that reinforces the very logic of the reductive science" we are trying to correct.[55] Simply put, it is mechanistic because the moral/aesthetic dimensions are understood to be *external* to the scientific-empirical dimension. It also assumes that all things are only connected *extrinsically*, that any relations between them are *unessential* to them, like parts of a machine that can be easily replaced. This procedure will evidently be epistemologically mechanistic as well, assuming that our knowledge of things can simply consist of the listing of facts learned by the study of each individual part separately.

While it is true that a scientist with a deeper appreciation of the unity of all being and a clear sense of the fact that science cannot exhaust the intelligibility of the object of study can make a certain correction in the interpretation of his or her work to include these elements, they remain conceptually exterior to it. Modern science in itself remains flawed, awaiting a paradigm shift that reconciles relationality and returns the observer and his values to the realm of the real.

In the end it is not enough to assert that wonder and beauty ought to be important to scientists, for this does not go far enough to escape

---

53. See Gould, *Rocks of Ages*.
54. See Lancellotti, "Science, Contemplation, and Ideology."
55. D. L. Schindler, "Given as Gift," 63.

the technological paradigm. Rather, Schindler proposes that wonder and beauty "are integral to the logic of scientific abstraction and the order of the world properly understood"[56] while pointing out that

> it is just this view of wonder and beauty as pertinent to, indeed, primary within, the *objective* order—both the given causal order of things and the method of scientific knowledge—that the mechanistic ontology dominant in today's culture denies. We must take account of all that is implied in this denial if we are to enable a fuller and more adequate science *precisely as science*.[57]

As to what this science could look like, it is enough for now to point out the essential role the observer plays in quantum physics, for example, to show that this paradigm shift has, on some level, already begun.[58] The other areas of science continue to operate primarily within a mechanistic paradigm and seemingly without looking back, because they still *work*.

Pragmatism

The achievements of modern science are undeniable; this is not in question. However, many new problems have come about and our argument from the beginning has been that the environmental crises we see around the world represent the collateral damage of the technological paradigm. While these crises could appear to be minor setbacks in the ceaseless advance of progress, we argue that they are symptoms of a fundamental failure rooted in an inadequate ontology.

The first and most common objection to any concern raised against the technological paradigm is one of pragmatism. The claim is that "science with its dominant modern mechanistic idea of method and order has *worked*."[59] Much could be said about the philosophical principles of the American school of pragmatism founded at the turn of the twentieth century, whose philosophers saw their work as offering a "method for settling metaphysical disputes that might otherwise be interminable."[60] In our context, however, there are only two points we must address: what it means to "work" and the purpose of metaphysical analysis.

56. D. L. Schindler, "Given as Gift," 64.
57. D. L. Schindler, "Given as Gift," 64.
58. See Caldecott, "A Science of the Real," in Caldecott, *Radiance of Being*, 25–41.
59. D. L. Schindler, "Given as Gift," 94.
60. William James, *Pragmatism*, 18.

The claim "it works" represents only a partial success: "'it works' can only signify what is at best an approximation, a matter of statistically frequent occurrence—that is, what is at best a fragmented part of the whole of what it means to 'work.'"[61] In other words, the conception of what it means "to work" is based on a concept of practical effectiveness resulting in material well-being, which itself is both a vague and ambiguous goal. For example, scientists celebrated the creation of DDT for its ability to reduce mosquito populations and, by doing so, protect millions of people from malaria, which were their chosen goals and their conception of what "worked." Responses also "worked" in only one direction: the *banning* of DDT to save birds caused malaria deaths to rise. And lest we forget, the atomic bomb also "worked."

The purpose of turning to metaphysics and critiquing our current practices is fundamentally to assure that our actions "work" in the best way possible, and this is only achievable if our decisions are made according to reality. The technological paradigm, for all that has been achieved, only provides us with a fragmented and partial understanding of reality. Our chosen goals and our conception of what it means to achieve them have aligned themselves to the technological paradigm, losing sight of other values, such as beauty and the inherent dignity of human life. For this reason, the appeal to practical effectiveness simply misses the point. In the end, the real question is: after close examination, are we truly satisfied with the current definition of what "works"? Or better, does it *really* "work"?

Lost in the Flux: Emergent Science and Eco-philosophies

For the reductionist, only particles in motion are ontologically real entities. Everything else is to be explained by different complexities of particles in motion, hence are not real in their own ontological right. But organisms . . . cannot be deduced from physics, have causal powers of their own, and therefore are emergent real entities in the universe.[62]

The technological paradigm brings about a great deal of a particular kind of knowledge and progress, but it also carries with it a great deal

---

61. D. L. Schindler, *Ordering Love*, 423n55.
62. Kauffman, *Reinventing the Sacred*, 3.

of blindness. Mechanism arose in modern science as the view that the world could be reduced to a set of basic elements externally related to each other, thus remaining substantially independent of each other. This view was extrapolated from physics to apply to everything, including living organisms, which had previously provided the counterexample to mechanism. Johann Wolfgang von Goethe resisted this paradigm, seeking to expand scientific methodology through his theory of universal archetypes and his call for scientists to include themselves in their studies, against Galileo's original construction of a scientist-less science.[63] Quantum physicist Werner Heisenberg would call for the same thing more than one hundred years later.[64] The twentieth century's advances in relativity and quantum mechanics meant that mechanism in physics came to be seen as wholly inadequate. Among some thinkers, the comparison of the natural world to a machine would increasingly give way to the model of an organism, that is,

> a pattern of relationships, preserving itself in a meaningful homeostasis or equilibrium in the midst of change, while the matter of which it is composed is in constant flux. The development of the sciences of organization—cybernetics and General Systems Theory—established a conceptual framework for the study of systems as such: that is, of wholes whose properties depend not just on the sum of their parts but on their interrelationships. But this in turn made theoreticians increasingly aware of the need for some kind of metaphysics; hence the various attempts to find illumination from Eastern religious philosophy, Western Hermeticism, and German Romanticism.[65]

Emergence has become central in almost every alternative to the traditional mechanistic and technological vision of nature. First and most notably, James Lovelock, writing in 1979, compared the earth to an emergent cybernetic system, which he called Gaia.[66] While a description of the activity of the earth can be made to conform to a cybernetic description of feedback loops and synergistic self-regulation, many believe he went too far in ascribing this system with a personified identity.[67]

63. See Amrine et al., *Goethe and the Sciences*, ix–xv.
64. See Lehrs, *Man or Matter*, 27–28.
65. Caldecott, *Radiance of Being*, 37–38.
66. See Lovelock, *Gaia*.
67. "Life and its environment are so closely coupled that evolution concerns Gaia, not the organisms or the environment taken separately" (Lovelock, *Ages of Gaia*, 19–20).

Regardless, postmodern thinkers from all fields reject (or claim to reject) reductionism, dualism, and mechanism, specifically as they imply "a primacy of controlling power and determinism and exact measurability and calculation, all of which are necessary for the exhaustive intelligibility of an object."[68] To take one representative example, Stuart Kauffman, a medical doctor and theoretical biologist, is one of many who denounce the reductionist view that holds "that, in the end, when the science is done, the explanations for higher-order entities are to be found in lower-order entities" and that reality is merely and ultimately "particles (or strings) in motion in space."[69] For Kauffman it is clear that "science is not, as Galileo claimed, the only pathway to truth,"[70] as we have also argued, but his path to that conclusion, and its significance, is very different. The postmodern scientific critique, which consists in both an evolutionary theory and an eco-philosophy, invariably rests on the notion of *emergence*.

What Is Emergence?

Intuitively there is something very different about life that goes beyond even the "local reversal of entropy," since anything living "is an entity whose nature sustains itself (temporarily) against the universal rise of entropy, by means of energy drawn from outside itself."[71] Darwin notably left the question of *the origin of life* out of his explanations, a question whose answer would be essential to establish a materialist explanation of life.[72] Postmodern scientists fill this gap by calling life "emergent."

It is the radical difference between the behavior of living things and the particles they are made of that leads to the conclusion that the latter ought not be reduced to physics. In the simplest terms, emergence expresses the fact that the whole is greater than the sum of its parts. Though Aristotle was the first to describe a phenomenon in this way, G. H. Lewis is often credited as coining the word "emergent" in the late nineteenth century in essentially the same terms. There is an extensive volume of twentieth-century literature on emergence, especially from

68. D. L. Schindler, "Given as Gift," 71.
69. Kauffman, *Reinventing the Sacred*, 3–4.
70. Kauffman, *Reinventing the Sacred*, xii.
71. Caldecott, *Radiance of Being*, 25.
72. See Harold, *The Way of the Cell*, 235.

Great Britain, attempting to analyze and categorize the surprising interactions of nature. In 1999, in the first issue of the journal *Emergence*, Jeffery Goldstein described emergence as "the arising of novel and coherent structures, patterns, and properties during the process of self-organization in complex systems."[73] Returning to Kauffman: "Emergence is therefore a major part of the new scientific worldview. Emergence says that, while no laws of physics are violated, life in the biosphere, the evolution of the biosphere, the fullness of our human historicity, and our practical everyday world are also real, not reducible to physics nor explicable from it, and are central to our life."[74] He goes on to elaborate the difference between "epistemological emergence" and "ontological emergence":

> Epistemological emergence means an inability to deduce or infer the emergent higher-level phenomenon from underlying physics. Ontological emergence has to do with what constitutes a "real" entity in the universe: is a tiger a real entity, or nothing but particles in motion, as the reductionists would claim? If the tiger is a real entity in its own right, it is ontologically emergent with respect to the particles comprising it.[75]

Despite claims of being a radical and "new" science, emergence is simply a reformulation of Darwinian evolutionary theory, freed from the strictures of mechanism, strictures to which Darwin himself did not seem to pay credence.[76] It does not reject physical laws of nature, but simply claims that

> they are incomplete: corresponding to *some* kinds of organized complexity there are additional laws, interfacing with the fundamental laws, that are no less basic, though they have application only in limited contexts. These laws identify holistic properties of specified system kinds and describe both the preconditions and causal impact of their occurrence. This is nothing objectionably strange or "magical" in such a layered picture of physical reality as against the "flat" picture of the reductionist: both are pictures of the world as law-governed and causally unified,

---

73. Goldstein, "Emergence as a Construct," 49.
74. Kauffman, *Reinventing the Sacred*, x.
75. Kauffman, *Reinventing the Sacred*, 34.
76. Darwin's theory included a second evolutionary force beyond brute natural selection: the irreducible impact of mate-selection. See Prum, *Evolution of Beauty*, 17–53.

open to scientific exploration and description. Hence, deciding whether our world manifests emergence should be a matter of empirical *evidence*, not a priori presumption or bias in favor of the tidiness of reductionism.[77]

The observation that physical laws do not explain all of reality is certainly accurate and the hypothesis of other empirically testable laws that are embedded in the fabric of the universe is intriguing, but little progress seems to have been made in ascertaining how those might work. As Thomas Nagel rightly implies, it seems that emergence is simply synonymous with inscrutability: "the brute fact of emergence [is] not explainable in terms of anything more basic, and therefore essentially mysterious."[78] Despite making many claims that we deem true and well supported, the bigger problem with emergence is that it simply exchanges one type of reductionism for another, while claiming to be anti-reductionist.

Critiques of Emergence as a Scientific Principle

The sociologist Christian Smith observes that water "is irreducible to that of which it is composed," and remarks with genuine marvel that "literally and truly something new has come into existence that is more than the sum of its parts."[79] Indeed, many emergent theorists describe how water is different than the hydrogen and oxygen atoms it is made of and therefore is an "emergent reality" that essentially changes what we know about physics.[80] While water is worthy of marvel and is truly different than both hydrogen and oxygen, the designation of these features as "emergent" does not explain anything or further the discussion past the rejection of emergentists' own definition of reductionism, which, to many, is self-evident. Hart summarizes this form of explanation in this way:

> Natural "emergence" . . . [is] the seemingly simple idea that in nature there are composite realities whose peculiar properties and capacities emerge from the interaction of their elements, even though those properties and capacities do not reside as such in those elements themselves. An emergent whole, in other

---

77. O'Connor, "Do We Have Souls?"
78. Nagel, *Mind and Cosmos*, 60–61.
79. Smith, *What Is a Person?*, 27.
80. See Goodenough and Deacon, "Sacred Emergence of Nature," x.

words, is more than—or at any rate different from—the sum of its parts; it is not simply the consequence of an accumulation of discrete powers added together extrinsically, but the effect of a specific ordering of relations among those powers that produces something entirely new within nature.[81]

What comes to the surface here is the importance of interrelationship and the novel results that can come from it. However, there are a number of critiques that must be made of this position that will, in turn, reveal why these observations are true yet still insufficient, necessitating the consideration of a truly metaphysical dimension.

Reductionism and Irreducibility

Up until this point we have referred to the inherent reductionism of the technological paradigm as the removal or ignoring of the metaphysical dimension of things. Empiricism, logical positivism, and scientism conceive of reality as mere material, as postmodern proponents of emergence essentially do. However, the emergentist vision of an unreduced reality is only *quantitatively* richer; while it does not rely on physical laws alone for the explanation of the world, it still proposes that these other laws are empirically testable. In other words, the very scientific method that birthed the paradigm they oppose will prove them right.

The principle goal of these thinkers is to give credence to the (true) claim that physical laws do not determine all of reality, but, because they are still struggling within an empirical framework, their arguments are less than convincing. They ignore the fact that, "at the purely material level, whatever is emergent is also reducible to that from which it emerges; otherwise, 'emergence' is merely the name of some kind of magical transition between intrinsic disparate realities."[82] In a typical passage, Smith states that water "is irreducible to that of which it is composed."[83] If, by "irreducible," Smith means different, then perhaps we could agree; water can put out a fire, while hydrogen or oxygen cannot. But this, says Hart, is to confuse identity with irreducibility: "Water's resistance to combustion is not *identical* with any property resident in either hydrogen

---

81. Hart, *Splendid Wickedness*, 236.
82. Hart, *Splendid Wickedness*, 237.
83. Smith, *What Is a Person?*, 27.

or oxygen molecules, but it is most definitely *reducible* to those special molecular properties that, in a particular combination, cause hydrogen and oxygen to negate one another's combustion propensities."[84] Emergent theorists are right to reject reductionism, but their deeper problem is their view of causality.

Causality

Aristotle's formal and final causes have been abandoned, as we saw in Bacon's work, and his efficient and material causes have been repurposed into the mechanistic paradigm by stripping them of their immaterial potentialities. Because proponents of emergence seek empirically testable theories, they, like the modernist materialists they oppose, confuse causality or reduce it to laws for which they cannot account.

Smith gives another example to clarify the claims of emergence: a computer. He notes that the activity of a computer is qualitatively different than the conglomeration of the silicon, plastic, metal, and electric current that compose it. The emergent properties depend not on composition; they exist because the component parts are "related to one another by careful design." He continues,

> The visual, informational, and computational abilities of my computer are new realities, yet not present in the sum total of the inputs of which my computer is constituted. It is only through their systematic relationships that those amazing abilities have being.... Reality is thus significantly constituted through relationality, not merely composition.[85]

However, what gives a computer its novel capabilities, beyond those of its component parts, "is not any *emergent* property at all, but rather the causal influence of a creative intellect acting upon those elements from without."[86] The components of a computer behave according to the laws of physics at the material level, exactly as one might predict, and in this sense the computer is certainly "reducible" to physical laws. What makes the computer special is the person who created it. Emergence can be ascribed to the formal causality of a creative intellect that has purposefully arranged these components with a final end in mind.

84. Hart, *Splendid Wickedness*, 237.
85. Smith, *What Is a Person?*, 27.
86. Hart, *Splendid Wickedness*, 237.

Advocates of emergence are not "against" reductionism in the same sense that we are arguing. In reality, "what reductionism fails to account for, and in fact fails even to see, is not the principle of emergence, but the reality of formal causality."[87] Ultimately we agree that there truly are emergent realities that render mechanism and materialism false. One of the principle aims of this study is to point out the fact that being itself, existence, is categorically irreducible to physical causes; it is the *non subsistens* par excellence.[88] Emergentists are correct that physical reductionism is wrong about the world, but emergence as an alternative fails to explain why because of its own unexamined presuppositions.

Information Reductionism

Scientific theories of emergence are wide ranging but basically seek to explain all things through an evolutionary process different than the traditional, mechanistic approach, based on complexity. As Caldecott summarizes, these thinkers argue that "greater complexity develops less through environmental pressure or selection from outside than through self-organization from within."[89] They consider living things as dynamic systems that maintain their stability through positive and negative feedback loops. Up to this point, we would argue that these theories certainly take a step in the right direction.

The difficulty comes when they try to explain mental phenomena. Caldecott points out that their explanation of consciousness relies on another reduction: reducing all mental processes to the flow of information. He dubs this an information reductionism: "By reducing mental processes to the flow of information, [they] are also ignoring the spiritual or interior dimension of consciousness."[90] In this sense, emergentists get little further than mechanists in the discovery of the actual cause of consciousness. While mechanists attempt to reduce the mind to the measurable activity of the brain, emergentists reduce it to the information it contains. The irreducibility of consciousness is well established, but not for lack of effort on the part of scientists and theorists. As early as 1946, Erwin Schrödinger argued that "consciousness can never be the external object of scientific investigation because it is always interior to

87. Hart, *Splendid Wickedness*, 237.
88. See Aquinas, *De Potentia Dei*, q. 1, a. 1, co.
89. Caldecott, *Radiance of Being*, 48.
90. Caldecott, *Radiance of Being*, 48.

the observer."[91] Nagel discusses consciousness at length, along with all the most prominent (yet unsuccessful) attempts to explain it physically, as the principle obstacle for a physical explanation of reality in his aptly titled *Mind and Cosmos: Why the Materialist Neo-Darwinian Conception of Nature Is Almost Certainly False*. The problem of consciousness cannot be solved through an empirical methodology because consciousness is, by most common sense accounts, irreducibly immaterial. Though some scientists still reject that claim, it is fundamentally impossible to resolve through empirical methods.

Eco-philosophies of Identity

While emergence has been applied as an alternative within scientific explanations of the physical world, it has also provided ample material for philosophical reflection by eco-philosophers. Emergent theorists' stated goal is to seek ways to capture beauty, meaning, relationality, and value, and to a large degree, they have provided compelling arguments for the reality of those things that are systematically excluded or ignored by the technological paradigm. They seek to express, in a unified theory, more of the depth of the human experience. Kauffman lists "four injuries," four ruptures that "split our humanity down the center," that this perspective seeks to heal: "the artificial division between science and the humanities," the idea that "we live in a world of fact without values," the claim that "spirituality is foolish,"[92] and our lack of "a shared worldwide framework of values."[93] He argues that all of these things can be resolved by the "new" scientific worldview based on emergence, which can explain all of reality, including human agency, as a catenation of natural emergent events:

---

91. Caldecott, *Radiance of Being*, 48.

92. Kauffman, *Reinventing the Sacred*, 8. By spirituality, Kauffman is referring to a natural sense of wonder and gratitude based on a concept of "God" that is entirely immanent and naturalized as contrasted with the Great Architect "God" of Deism without ever considering the fully transcendent and fully immanent God of Christianity: "Is it, then, more amazing to think that an Abrahamic transcendent, omnipotent, omniscient God created everything around us, all that we participate in, in six days, or that it all arose with no transcendent Creator God, all on its own? I believe the latter is so stunning, so overwhelming, so worthy of awe, gratitude, and respect, that it is God enough for many of us. God, a fully natural God, is the very creativity in the universe" (Kauffman, *Reinventing the Sacred*, 6). This method mirrors that of his, and all emergentists', metaphysics, and thus, the same mistake.

93. Kauffman, *Reinventing the Sacred*, 8.

> Biology and its evolution cannot be reduced to physics alone but stand in their own right. Life, and with it agency, came naturally to exist in the universe. With agency came values, meaning, and doing, all of which are as real in the universe as particles in motion. . . . While life, agency, value and doing presumably have physical explanations in any specific organism, the evolutionary emergence of these cannot be derived from or reduced to physics alone.[94]

While escaping the reductionism of mechanism, emergence-based philosophies fall into some of the same errors because of their anti-metaphysical presuppositions. The irony of these philosophies, and the reason they have been dubbed philosophies "of identity," is that despite their aim to counter the destructive tendencies of mechanism, without recourse to formal or final causality they theoretically dissolve all organisms into a singular material identity, a monism in which the individual is lost to the material and temporal flux of the universe. As Hanby explains, "Since form is subsequently identified with a generative *process*, the organism remains identical to its system function and is treated as the accidental end product of the generative process rather than its source and subject."[95] For example, it is common in ecology to consider an individual organism important insofar as it is a member of its species and to consider a species important insofar as it functions in an ecosystem. Yet, if we consider the appearance of the species on a longer time scale, we realize that it can be considered only as an instantiation of a constantly evolving universe with no motive or end other than self-perpetuation. This perspective leads to many consequences, intended or not, in ethical positions and values.[96] Certainly one of the most troubling distinctions lost in this vision is that of the dignity of the human person.

Biological Reductionism

The emergentist worldview, it is supposed, can address all the philosophical and religious concerns of human life, from existential questions like "Why is there anything rather than nothing?" to spiritual

---

94. Kauffman, *Reinventing the Sacred*, ix–x.
95. Hanby, *No God, No Science?*, 359.
96. The Voluntary Human Extinction Movement is perhaps the most radical. Antinatalism is another.

questions like "Why is there evil and suffering?" to moral questions about responsibility, trust, and compassion.

Acknowledging that these are deeply human experiences with real value is an improvement over mechanism's typical dismissal of these questions, but, when pressed, the emergentist can give no explanation to these except that they have simply evolved this way: "Those who are courageous, reverent, fair-minded, and compassionate . . . . will be more likely to be chosen as mates and to nurture their children with care and wisdom."[97] Although our ethical lives are not completely independent of our biological lives (as Alasdair MacIntyre and others have pointed out[98]), a materialist account of all human values represents just another form of reductionism, of simplifying the qualitatively different experiences of metaphysical, moral, and religious values to mere evolutionary fact. Most importantly, this position does not resolve the value-fact dualism that emergent theorists accuse mechanists of creating; it merely reduces these values into facts, thereby creating the illusion of having resolved the dilemma.

Dismissal by emergentists of the experience of immateriality and transcendence, which escape evolutionary theory, is particularly telling. For example:

> Reductionist understandings of how minds work are fascinating, but they are also irrelevant to what it's like to be minded. While we don't know what it's like to be a bat, we know what it's like to be a human, and it entails a whole virtual realm that doesn't *feel* material at all. The beauty of the emergentist approach to mind is that it suggests that to experience our experience without awareness of this underlying mechanism *is exactly what we should expect from an emergent property.* The outcome has been given reverent names, like spirit or soul, names that conjure up the *perceived* absence of materiality. But we need not interpret this as evidence of some parallel transcendental immaterial world. *We can now say that the experience of soul or spirit as immaterial is simply a reflection of the way the process of*

---

97. See Goodenough and Deacon, "Sacred Emergence of Nature," 869.

98. "I now judge that I was in error in supposing an ethics independent of biology to be possible. . . . No account of the goods, rules and virtues that are definitive of our moral life can be adequate that does not explain—or at least point us to an explanation—how that form of life is possible for beings who are biologically constituted as we are, by providing us with an account of our development towards and into that form of life" (MacIntyre, *Dependent Rational Animals*, x).

emergence progressively distances each new level from the details below. We can now turn the page.[99]

In the same breath, these authors criticize "reductionist understanding" while revealing that they have total confidence in the success of the mechanistic proposal to achieve a material description of the mind. They accept that the experience of consciousness and spirituality "doesn't *feel* material at all" but claim that this illusion is "exactly what we should expect" from an evolutionary fact that is purely material without offering any evidence. In addition, they present a caricature of the transcendental realm, which is not "parallel" to this world but indivisible from it, yet always remains partially out of reach. By misrepresenting philosophical and religious traditions, they are arguing against a straw man.

Given the fact that emergentist thinkers seek to reinterpret the collective experience of most of humanity, which throughout history has conceived itself as a material and immaterial unity, as an illusion perpetuated by the "expected" deceptiveness of the process of emergence, as described above, it seems that they ought to do more to justify their materialistic presuppositions. The difficulty of this, however, is the same difficulty that faces all materialists: it is a *premise* and not a conclusion. And so, while emergentists are certainly free to choose their philosophical premises, they ought to acknowledge that this is a philosophical *choice* rather than something they have proven.

The late German philosopher Robert Spaemann described how the emergent proposal based on systems theory bears little difference from the mechanistic accounts that it so opposes in this regard, referring to them collectively as "naturalism":

> Naturalism functionally reduces all experience of meaning, which overcomes contingency, to the preservation of contingent forms of life whose being is better than their not-being only for themselves. Since this interest is only a function of the existence of a living system, it cannot ground this existence for reflective being. When every value is only a function of preservation, then the value character of appreciating disappears along with the

---

99. Goodenough and Deacon, "Sacred Emergence of Nature," 864 (emphasis mine). Emergentism cannot offer anything resembling true transcendence: "Formal theories or sequences like that of Fibonacci may 'emerge' from numbers, and the sequence may have properties not found in the constituent numbers, but the sequence does not 'transcend' the numbers, for it is on the same quantitative level; the mathematician transcends both the numbers and the sequence" (Mary G. Taylor, "Healing the Rift?," 23).

subject of value appreciation. It is an arbitrary affair whether the continued existence of humanity and of the other living things on earth play a role or not in the motivation of action. To this extent naturalism and existential nihilism imply each other.[100]

There are many other ways of understanding the tendency towards self-preservation; for example, for Aristotle, each finite being possesses an intentionality that tends towards permanence because of the nature of being in which it participates.[101] From this perspective, the universe is a web of inseparable purposes and, rather than the most basic form of interaction—physical force—it was the richest manifestation of natural evolution—the intellect—that served as a model to understand the rest: "Hence the mind, rather than an anomalous tenant of an alien universe, was instead the most concentrated and luminous expression of nature's deepest essence."[102]

This type of explanation is not mutually exclusive with the recognition that, biologically, creatures that survive and reproduce possess inheritable traits; it is a deeper layer of explanation that embraces material causes within it. From a materialistic perspective, however, such explanations are predetermined as incomprehensible and left unexamined. If human values require a scientific explanation, any sensation of transcendence is illusory and we remain slaves to our genes despite all evidence to the contrary. No form of biological reductionism can help but lose the human being—our values, dignity, and freedom—in the flux of the immanently natural. Despite their efforts to escape the negative consequences of dualism and mechanism, because they restrict transcendence[103] and mystery to the immanent realm, they predetermine this outcome.

Contingency

At the heart of the metaphysics of gift lies the radical contingency of all things, the radical dependency of all things on the free gift of being.

100. Spaemann, *Happiness and Benevolence*, 47.
101. See Aristotle, "De Anima," II, 4 (560–64).
102. Hart, "The Illusionist," 110.
103. Note that "traditional" transcendence is misrepresented before it is flattened out. "Transcendence is explored from two perspectives: the traditional concept wherein the origination of the sacred is 'out there,' and the alternate concept wherein the sacred originates 'here'" (Goodenough, "Vertical and Horizontal Transcendence," 21).

According to emergent theorists, "Emergentism offers fresh ways to think about contingency."[104] However, by "fresh" they mean to contrast their view not with that of classical philosophy or the metaphysics of gift, but with a dualistic caricature of it. Michael Kalton expresses the emergentist perspective of contingency in evolutionary terms: "On the tree of life, we as a species are more a probing twig than an established branch, and civilization, let alone industrialization, is a radical experiment that depends on conditions civilization itself may systemically undermine."[105] He contrasts this with what he sees as "traditional western forms of transcendence [that] negate contingency not only by creating an absolute dimension, but also by writing humans into the very fabric of existence by framing mind or consciousness as the origin of the cosmos."[106] In this way he sets up a false dilemma between "the Absolute" and the apparent contingency of our finitude.

We agree that humanity, and indeed all physical realities, are radically contingent, but not only in the sense of being conditional, tenuous, mutable, temporal, dependent, or mortal. As Aquinas noted,[107] even an infinitely large and eternally lasting universe would still be radically contingent in a more fundamental sense, for "contingency is a *logical* designation: it is the condition of any essence logically distinct from its own existence—which is to say, the failure of a thing's proper description to provide any intrinsic rationale for that thing's existence."[108]

In other words, all finite beings are dependent on another cause for their very being; this is a true radical contingency, far more radical than being materially dependent on one's parents or even the entire trajectory of evolution. This is the logically necessary, radical contingency that the metaphysics of gift seeks to appreciate and which leads to true metaphysical wonder. Even if the world did not have a beginning, even if we appear to be discussing a closed, material, naturalistic, physical system, such a system is "closed" only at a mechanical level, not the ontological. Once again, it is the failure to see the gift quality of existence, which no thing gives to itself but must receive, that blinds us to the truly contingent nature of reality.

104. Goodenough and Deacon, "Sacred Emergence of Nature," 866.
105. Kalton, "Green Spirituality," 191.
106. Kalton, "Green Spirituality," 199.
107. See Aquinas, *Summa Theologiae*, I, q. 2, a. 3; Spitzer, *New Proofs*, 110–43.
108. Hart, *Experience of God*, 100 (emphasis mine).

> The ultimate source of *existence* cannot be some item or event that has long since passed away or concluded, like a venerable ancestor or even the Big Bang itself—either of which is just another contingent physical entity or occurrence—but must be a constant wellspring of being, *at work even now*.[109]

Kalton claims that "the problem is . . . the people who cannot recognize and live by the implications of contingency" and that "until we grasp our radical contingency, we have small chance of really understanding the nature of what is at stake."[110] These comments seem directed at those trapped in a Cartesian mind–body dualism and do not accurately represent the basic, classical understanding of reality. Until those enchanted by the illusion of emergence as an escape from that dualism grasp the meaning of metaphysical contingency, to which physical and evolutionary contingency are analogous but not identical, they will never be free from reductionism or its consequences.

Overcoming Mechanism

The mechanistic gaze, fruit of the technological paradigm, is a form of "sick blindness," as Balthasar put it, that "arises from regarding reality as raising no questions, being 'just there,'" and it "signifies the death of philosophy."[111] The new methods of modern science were primarily pragmatic at first; they helped achieve empirical results that proved particularly useful in certain areas of life. These new methods would give rise to a materialistic vision of the world. The modern sense of nature is "the source and product of the technocratic paradigm. It presupposes the conflations of knowing and making, nature and art, truth and possibility that characterize this paradigm."[112] The unintended consequence would be the technology that surrounds us today, along with the ecological degradation and plunder that accompanies it.

The dualisms established by this paradigm between fact and value, and all their concomitant dichotomies, create a profoundly unsatisfying view of human life. In response, many theorists sought for richer modes of explanation. But the recognition of emergent properties in nature

---

109. Hart, *Experience of God*, 109.
110. Kalton, "Green Spirituality," 190–91.
111. Balthasar, *Theo-Drama II*, 286.
112. Hanby, "Gospel of Creation," 745.

could not elude the mechanism they sought to escape. In the final analysis, as Hanby points out:

> Emergentism remains a form of mechanism—albeit one transformed by a more sophisticated conception of systems dynamics—trapped within the conflation of nature and artifice and unable to account adequately either for the unity and interiority of living things or for our experience of them and of being alive. ... The *metaphysical* history of modern biology ... has left biology without the metaphysical equipment to say what it wants to say, indeed to say what, to some degree, it cannot help but say. And it has left biology with a theoretical apparatus that remains inadequate to the phenomenon of life.[113]

It is only through a metaphysics capable of acknowledging the fullness of human experience, including the experience of those dimensions of reality that mechanism dismisses as absurd and emergentism explains away as illusory, that we can recognize the individual organism in its rightful place in nature. The living organism, as the recipient of the gift of being, is an indivisible unity and "ontological identity that transcends, and hence *ontologically* precedes, the temporal and material flux,"[114] not reducible to its genes, the atoms that make up its material body, or the particles that make up those atoms. A proper metaphysics, one that comprehends that the necessary gift of being to all things constitutes their radical contingency, permits a deeper appreciation of the intuitions that emergence theories recognize but fail to explain.

Next we must turn to ethics, specifically how the technological paradigm, through political liberalism, has shaped the field of bioethics and how metaphysics can defend bioethical proceduralism from itself. Neither the technological paradigm nor the eco-philosophies that oppose it are capable of properly conceiving the value of a single organism, whether it be a wildflower or a human child. Bioethics is the field of study whose stated goal is to defend against the abuses of science, but it can only do so if it is built upon a metaphysics capable of appreciating each one's unique dignity.

---

113. Hanby, *No God, No Science?*, 283.
114. Hanby, *No God, No Science?*, 359.

3

The Person and the Leviathan

The Technological Paradigm in Contemporary Liberal Bioethics

In a certain sense, ethics has become part and parcel of the technological order. It has been professionalized as an autonomous discipline external to medical practice. It is dominated by an engineering model of moral reasoning and impregnated with the idea of a technical rationality, applying principles to practices.[1]

THE FRAGMENTATION AND DISINTEGRATION that characterize postmodernity have affected all aspects of our life, but they have hit bioethics particularly hard because it is a relatively new field with a great deal of power over human lives. While bioethics first sought to protect the vulnerable through reasoned debate and a consensus that would bridge the moral pluralism of societies, mainstream bioethics works diligently to relativize all moral claims, paradoxically becoming "amoral."[2] Despite acknowledging many postmodern positions, much bioethical debate is still wedded to political liberalism's embrace of the Enlightenment-inspired dualism between fact and value, such that what had been seen as common morality based on the reality of nature is now viewed as subjective, private,

---

1. ten Have, "Medical Technology Assessment," 13.
2. In the sense that ethical positions are seen as options with no reference to objective truth.

and even irrational. This restricts the field to the procedural functions of the regulation of debates coupled with the relativization of any notion of the true or the good.

The two-tier morality that follows from public-versus-private, fact-versus-value dualism and a two-tier practical rationality between an internally coherent privatism and an empty proceduralism in the public sphere is still the most mainstream position. While this appears to be a solution—people can believe whatever they want privately but when they enter the public sphere they adopt "public reason"—in truth, "for anyone interested in ethical dialogue . . . the solution virtually reduces the whole task of ethics to a strategy of political co-existence"[3] that increasingly deforms the ideals it seeks to uphold. Bioethics as a field has only mirrored society as a whole as it has canonized the formal rationality at the heart of the technological paradigm that dominates nearly every aspect of our public lives.

There is no denying the enormous successes and material gains formal rationality has brought about, but there is also no denying the repercussions of it replacing ontology, that is, when it is taken as the best way to approach reality. When the abstraction of a strict procedural formalism is forced upon the realms of politics and bioethics as a solution to conflicts, the unintended consequences are inevitably a lack of relation and of meaning, extrinsicism, commodification, and monetization of every aspect of life, and, according to a sociopolitical critique, even violence in various forms of coercion. The concomitant uncoupling of ends and means reflects a detachment from a prior commitment to the good. The "freedom" ostensibly built into the principle of autonomy tends to become preapproved compulsion, the solidarity that ought to be expressed through mutual respect tends to become coercion labeled as "consensus," and "reason" is truncated into a formalism devoid of content while vital principles are reduced to a hollow proceduralism.

These failings are deeply rooted in presuppositions at the ontological level expressed in the formal rationality used to construct modern bioethics, indeed, modernity as a whole. All of these errors stem from an ontological conception of man as an "isolated individual," which, nevertheless, "is a pure fiction: one's personal identity always develops through dialogue and intersubjectivity."[4]

---

3. Dell'Oro, "Theological Discourse," 133.
4. Allodi, "Persona e Società Post-Secolare," 24 (English translation mine).

It might appear that metaphysics would be extraneous to contemporary society, and especially to any pragmatic field of study. However, metaphysics has seen a widespread revival, albeit with differing meanings, as more and more thinkers become disenchanted with the deficiencies of positivistic or proceduralist calculation. Though it seems that bioethical debates concern the spheres of technical efficiency, economic feasibility, political acceptability, and finally, some sort of moral consensus, and that there is no need to move to an ontological level, as D. C. Schindler explains, moral questions "always turn out to be epistemological questions, which in turn are determined by ontological and metaphysical realities. The way one acts (virtue) is inevitably a function of what one takes to be real (knowledge), which depends on the various ways reality can present itself."[5] And so our aim is to outline the scope, and especially the depth, of the bioethical project, which is a microcosm of and parallel to ecological ethics on the whole, through an ontological critique that appreciates but goes beyond sociopolitical criticism, providing an aperture through which a more adequate understanding and dialogue might arise.

It is not the purpose of this study to offer possible policy solutions, nor to disparage the difficult work being done by bioethicists, nor to deny the immense complexity of the decision-making process; any examples provided are simply meant to illustrate the scope of the problems we face and point towards a more solid foundation for bioethical discussion. The first part reviews the rise of formal rationality in general and in bioethics in particular, and the "Classical Liberal" view, which claims that the unique conjunction of pragmatism, proceduralism, and American Enlightenment philosophy "will drive any *adequate account* of ethics consultation in a liberal society."[6] The second part looks at the alleged neutrality, pragmatism, pluralism, principles, proceduralism, and consensus that are at the center of the above from the perspective of a sociopolitical critique, which claims that procedural liberalism in bioethics subverts the very things it seeks to defend. The third part comprises a second critique from the metaphysics of gift starting with the importance of constitutive relationality, which shows that the sociopolitical critique

---

5. D. C. Schindler, "Why Socrates Didn't Charge," 398. The distinction does not imply a strict division into areas of specialization. Instead it reflects different aspects of one acting person and the deep interconnection between how we think, believe, and act.

6. Moreno, "Can Ethics Consultation Be Saved?," 23 (emphasis mine).

does not get to the root of the problem. Only from these critiques will we be able to point to some constructive elements that can improve the current situation within bioethical proceduralism.

Formal Rationality and Classical Liberal Bioethics

Despite the fact that ethics was one of the very things that scientific rationalism consciously excluded from its purview, or perhaps because of it, the ethical practice of making medical and environmental decisions has been pushed to become ever more scientific over the last several decades. One of the results of this push has been the rise of formal rationality in ethics. Bioethical debates have been "thinning" out, that is, what is considered acceptable in the debates has become more formalized, juridical, and, it is argued, "neutral" at the cost of leaving out elements deemed imperative by many who have been left to watch from the sidelines.[7]

There have been several attempts to explain this development. The "Macro-Historical Process" explanation claims that this "thinning" was an inevitable, natural progression away from religion and toward neutral, scientific rationality. Some bioethicists believed that there was a natural evolution, "free of actors and interests, from less calculating and particularistic to more calculating and universal,"[8] that is, from substantive to formal rationality. In the "Expanding Democracy" explanation, the ostensible reason for the thinning of the debates is that in a pluralistic society where each individual has his own interests, discourse that arises out of theological or cultural backgrounds is at best parochial and at worst irrational, superstitious, and authoritarian; therefore the only way to resolve disagreements is through maintaining a strictly "neutral" stance about any particular conception of the good.

According to John Evans, the resolution of disagreements could come through two forms of consensus—*political* (or "procedural") or *overlapping*.[9] The first refers to the activity by which a pluralistic consensus survives a competitive debate. The second is conceived after the notion of the Venn diagram. Ends to be forwarded are legitimate if all parties in the debate share them, not after political give-and-take, but

---

7. See Evans, *Playing God?*, 11–44.

8. Evans, *Playing God?*, 24. See also: Fletcher, "Evolution of Ethical Debate"; Juengst, "Germ-Line Gene Therapy."

9. The term originated with John Rawls. See Rawls, *Political Liberalism*, xix.

after reflection, usually by "experts." In neither case is any truth about the human good nor the morality of an action accepted *a priori*; there is no "right" or "wrong" from the outset because the goal is simply to agree. In the first case, any claim is legitimate if it is voted for. In the second, anything is legitimate if everyone agrees on the necessity of predetermined principles. With conscience protections under attack in the few countries that still have them, and with the rise of unelected decision-making bureaucracies, ordinary citizens have very little say in the ethical decisions that control their lives.

Formal Rationality in Bioethics and Ecological Ethics

In his analysis of human action, Max Weber describes the distinction between substantive and formal rationality. *Substantive rationality* provides people with goods "shaped by economically oriented social action under some criterion . . . of ultimate values."[10] For Weber there can be an "infinite number of possible value scales"[11] and these ultimate values, or ends, are neither universal nor commensurable. Substantive rationality would argue that ends and means are intertwined, asking "are the means being considered consistent with their related ends or values?"[12] By contrast, *formal rationality* concerns the quantitative calculation of procedures necessary to attain a desired end most efficiently. It is "formal" because it creates a formula to which any particular content is added; the process is the same no matter what end is sought. The commensurable unit that made this possible was money, but the formalization of rationality is not limited to economics; Weber believed that the calculable logic of formal rationality, that is, the instrumentalization of reason, would inevitably spread into every modern institution.

However, it is not unique to modern times. D. C. Schindler discusses Socrates's debates with the Sophists on the art of rhetoric. For Plato's Socrates, speaking well meant *making the truth evident*; for the Sophists, however, speaking well meant speaking *persuasively*, no matter what one was arguing for, which required a radical separation of means and ends and the abandonment of truth:

---

10. Weber, *Economy and Society*, 85.
11. Weber, *Economy and Society*, 86.
12. Weber, *Economy and Society*, 86.

> The novelty of sophistry lay in the fact that it made *efficiency* a principal goal, and it was attractive because of its discovery of the power of *purifying* means, both in the sense of rationalizing them, excising inefficiencies so that they can be harnessed and controlled, and also in the sense of cleansing them of content and so rendering them neutral. In a word, sophistry represented in a decisive and symbolic way the absolutizing of instrumentality.[13]

The Sophists imagined they were neutralizing reason by purging it of inefficiencies and particular content. Similarly, science in the modern era prided itself on bracketing out all but the experimentally quantifiable, regarding this as a *proper self-limitation of reason*. "There is clearly only a small step—if there is any step at all—between Galileo's mechanism and Descartes' mind-body dualism."[14] The dualism is simultaneous with the formalization: whatever is stripped out as non-quantifiable is relegated to the realm of the private and subjective and is deprived of truth value. Only what can be deemed public and objective is accepted as legitimate. The choice to do this is a *metaphysical decision*, as the idea that "only that which is empirically verifiable is true" is not empirically verifiable itself, but a presupposed principle.[15]

Ethics was one of the areas exiled to the realm of the subjective. However, Max Weber's prophecy played out in bioethics as debates came to be governed by instrumentalized rationality over which means would maximize the predetermined ends of the process, ends that were not up for debate.[16]

How did formal rationality become so prevalent? John Evans suggests that this dominance is best illustrated by the development of double-entry bookkeeping in 1494, more than a century before Galileo's major work.[17] The new accounting method had two closely related benefits. First, proceeds and costs were combined into one metric: profit. Second, it discarded material extraneous to the decision-making process

---

13. D. C. Schindler, "Redeeming Work," 268.
14. D. C. Schindler, *Catholicity of Reason*, 134–35.
15. See Oakes, "Achievement of Alasdair MacIntyre."
16. Habermas says the "system" (institutions governed by formal rationality) is colonizing the "lifeworld" where people have free debates about ends, thus limiting public debates to talking about cost-effectiveness, efficiency, and expedience. See Habermas, *Theory of Communicative Action*, 303–31.
17. See Evans, "A Sociological Account." John Milbank traces formal rationality still further back. See Milbank, "Franciscan Conundrum," 468.

that characterized the former "narrative" form of account keeping.[18] This made calculations far more streamlined and precise. In the narrative form, where proceeds and costs were listed separately, it was not immediately clear whether a particular exchange maximized the potential "take." Commensurability, the ability to measure different properties by a common standard, became the desired goal not only in finance but in every other area previously requiring prudential judgments. Money and utility are prime examples. As with modern science's rejection of secondary qualities, commensurability eliminated any aspects of a problem that could not be measured by the common unit.

According to some of its proponents, before bioethics debates yielded to formal rationality, they were "a mixture of religion, whimsy, exhortation, legal precedents, various traditions, philosophies of life, miscellaneous moral rules, and epithets."[19] In the interest of making these debates acceptable, they would need to find a set of universally accessible, commensurable units. The solution was the institution of the "principles": three in the case of the 1979 Belmont Report and four in the definitive *Principles of Biomedical Ethics* by Tom Beauchamp and James Childress.[20] The list of principles (respect/autonomy, beneficence, non-maleficence, and justice) became the dominant paradigm for bioethical decision-making and was quickly institutionalized. The ambiguity of the terms and the inevitable collapse into a utilitarian calculus of harms and benefits has accompanied this "principlism" since its inception. The logic of accounting and the logic of principlism are one and the same. Therese Lysaught draws an apt comparison: "We cannot have real moral discourse between particular communities, it is claimed, absent a more overarching transactional system which can determine the moral 'exchange rate.' In other words, we will get nowhere as long as we bring francs and lire to the table; what we need is a moral Euro."[21]

But while so many traditions affirm that there is no exchange rate for a human life, though so many technocrats insist on calculating one, the "moral Euro" of proceduralism is not a neutral coinage. The cost of a seat at the table is the abandonment of Plato's interest in making the true

---

18. The narrative form would include such things as the circumstances of the persons involved, the context of the issue, disagreement, or special exceptions sought, and the end values of the community.
19. Clouser, "Bioethics and Philosophy," 10.
20. Beauchamp and Childress, *Principles of Biomedical Ethics*.
21. Lysaught, "And Power Corrupts," 114.

and the good evident through dialogue, and the adoption of the Sophist's instrumentalization of language in which, at best, one can hope for a utilitarian calculus of harms and benefits, and at worst, sheer coercion.

While much of this discussion revolves around medical ethics, modern environmental ethics (or "the instrumental rationalism of resource managerialism"[22]) is based on the same formal rationality. The environment is seen as a "system of systems" that can be rationalized and exploited for human benefit. Wilderness areas preserved for natural beauty and recreation are considered human benefits. Conflict resolution and policy-making include a three-part strategic framework, with efficiency as the key goal:

> First, define a problem (e.g., global warming) as "environmental." Second, craft a technical remedy (e.g., cap-and-trade). Third, sell the technical proposal to legislators through a variety of tactics, such as lobbying. . . . Conservational environmentalities, such as green consumerism or sustainable development, tout the importance of more efficiently disposing of things used by people and policing global production with strategic environmental initiatives to root out inefficiencies in society's industrial metabolism.[23]

Any environmental action that seeks to "conserve, restore, recycle, or otherwise manage natural resources when those resources are seen only in terms of their utility, and where sustainability is understood as nothing more than utility extended into the future"[24] is a form of rationalized environmental ethics that seeks to maximize a quantifiable end. Sustainability indicators may be useful tools but too often their defining feature is "a reductive mode of thinking based on an antecedent calculative utilitarianism in which all factors are stripped down to the measurable for a single goal."[25] That goal is construed almost solely in terms of material well-being rather than in ethical/philosophical/spiritual terms of *the good life*, with emphasis on the good. In the end, the technological paradigm within bioethics operates in the lowest spheres of decision-making.

---

22. Luke, *Ecocritique*, 78.
23. Nordhaus and Shellenberger, *Break Through*, 9.
24. Mary G. Taylor, "Deeper Ecology," 592.
25. Mary G. Taylor, "Deeper Ecology," 591.

The Classical Liberal View of Proceduralism

The prevailing form of this reduction of ethics and philosophy to utility and the power of politics is Classical or Procedural Liberalism. Debate has been designed to proceed in the manner of the Sophists regarding "neutrality" toward the good and instrumentalization of language. Lysaught paints a troubling picture of the limitations placed on bioethical debate by proceduralism today. She argues that bioethics

> privileges a particular conception of what counts as legitimate in moral discourse (the impersonal/public/universal/intellectual/rational/objective/secular . . .); of moral anthropology (autonomous individualism); of moral agency and authority (freedom to define, choose, and pursue one's own goods); of society (a composite or collection of discrete individuals who exist in competition and do not *a priori* hold goods in common); of rationality and knowledge (disembodied, mentalist, positivistic); and so on. These and related commitments are part of the extralocal apparatus that work via the practices of bioethics to produce particular sorts of persons, thereby reproducing the truth of these commitments in the world.[26]

The "particular conception" of what bioethicists consider legitimate discourse grows out of an unarticulated ontology that parallels the Western tradition of Liberalism stemming from the Enlightenment in both its "liberal" and "conservative" forms. It too is based on the centrality of the atomistic individual—abstracted from intrinsic relations to others and from mediating communities like family, church, or other local groups—who operates under the freedom of "choice," that is, one negatively conceived as freedom from the imposition of others. In this view, humans are essentially self-interested, and as such enter into contractual relations with others in order to maximize their interests, not unlike the way businesses behave in pursuit of profits.

American bioethicist Jonathan Moreno claims that the heart of bioethics today reflects the "wildly successful merger of Continental liberalism [John Locke, etc.] with early twentieth-century American pragmatism. . . . America's civic narrative is the most vivid political realization of the Enlightenment linkage between progress and science."[27] Like the Sophists, American philosopher Ronald Dworkin believed that politics,

---

26. Lysaught, "And Power Corrupts," 118.
27. Moreno, *Body Politic*, 185.

laws, institutions, and actions in the public order must be "independent of any particular conception of the good,"[28] that is to say, of ontological and moral positions concerning the highest or ultimate goods. Moreno agrees: "Classical liberalism aims to construct a public space that is neutral in its conception of the good life, so individuals can pursue their preferences."[29] Bioethics committees, then, are "instruments for the construction of moral consensus . . . . guided by certain *procedural values* that are widely embraced, at least in Western culture."[30] Therefore less attention is paid to principles than to purely formally rational procedures; this is the "ethics facilitation approach," which is thought to be most consistent with individual rights and pluralism and is conducive to the "inclusive consensus-building process" championed by proceduralists the world over.[31] "The ethics consultation process is not a value-neutral one, but its values are mainly *procedural*, a view that emerges directly from classical liberalism" and which foregrounds conflict resolution, a method for managing differences "without recourse to violence."[32]

Robert Dell'Oro has described this position as the "loophole solution" to the problems of postmodernity, in that it attempts to steer a neutral course between the public, procedural functions of regulation and the private, closed hermeneutics of multiple traditions in an attempt to keep everyone happy.[33] But this supposed neutrality, with its hope of peaceful agreements rather than forcible impositions, is in reality a non-negotiable claim about the nature of truth and goodness in themselves; specifically, this claim holds that for all essential purposes they are beyond reason, and hence must be excluded from debate as "meaningless." Thus, Moreno's method for managing differences must be taken with a grain of salt, as the way deep differences are acknowledged and managed is suspect. There are a number of differences that are simply off limits, ruled out *a priori*. Any criticism of the technological paradigm, whether from "traditionalists" or "postmoderns," from the right or the left, or from a crossover of the two which would fall under Moreno's category of "bioconservative" (which can include left-wing environmentalists), can

28. Dworkin, "Liberalism," 127.
29. Moreno, "Can Ethics Consultation Be Saved?," 24.
30. Moreno, "Can Ethics Consultation Be Saved?," 23–24.
31. Moreno, "Can Ethics Consultation Be Saved?," 30.
32. Moreno, "Can Ethics Consultation Be Saved?," 29 (emphasis mine).
33. See Dell'Oro, "Theological Discourse," 127–36.

only be the result of a Luddite reactionary blindness borne of ignorance, fear, and having to deal with "tension between their antitechnological stance and an implicit acknowledgement of the undeniable benefits of technology."[34]

However, the presuppositions that shape any debate under procedural liberalism are, according to both the sociopolitical critique and that of the metaphysics of gift, subversive of any claim for a "nonviolent" respect that leads to true consensus. The former critique occurs at the political level, the level of power, and the latter traces the problem back to the ontological level. We will examine both in turn.

Power over Life: A Sociopolitical Critique

Far from being an open, public deliberative practice . . . bioethics ought properly be understood as a disciplinary matrix that serves the modern Leviathan of state and market.[35]

A number of bioethicists have criticized the entire program of procedural bioethics from the outside, so to speak. As an example of what we might call a "pre-ontological critique," Lysaught has used the categories of Foucault and his mechanisms of governmentality—discourses, practices, institutions, and the "disciplinary matrices"—to critique what many see as deliberately disingenuous about the function of ostensibly neutral debates in the current situation, arguing that bioethics serves to perpetuate the power structures of the market/state binary.

"Discourses" are the concepts and statements that enable truth claims within specific fields of knowledge.[36] They define what can be spoken about meaningfully through rules and practices. The whole complex is then institutionalized and guaranteed by the power of the state "to effect social and political ends, even while rhetorically claiming to be apolitical, neutral, and objective."[37] One can trace the fall of one set of discourses (theological, philosophical, moral) and the rise of another

---

34. Moreno, *Body Politic*, 136.

35. Lysaught, "And Power Corrupts," 96.

36. "Indeed, the inherent power and domination of the situation are disguised insofar as the monopoly created by specialist knowledge has been legitimated by the sanction of law and professionalism" (Finkelstein, "Biomedicine and Technocratic Power," 14).

37. Lysaught, "And Power Corrupts," 100.

(state-approved). This first required creating "a body of esoteric, technical, formal knowledge that would be portrayed as inaccessible to the common person, while simultaneously constituting objects of knowledge and defining the acceptable parameters for discussion."[38] The discourse was then embodied into practices, including controlling what was allowed in professional journals; here the state entered as the major provider of funding and legitimacy. This sociohistorical account considers the *agents involved* rather than positing the "rational formalization" of bioethics as either inevitable or as rising up from the will of the citizens.

A Historical Review of American Bioethics

Bioethics can be traced back at least to Hippocrates and his famous, though now often unobserved, oath; however, it only arose as a discipline in the twentieth century. In the United States, early concerns centered around human experimentation and the genetic control of the human race. The history of eugenics in the United States, when theories about the genetic inferiority of people from Africa and Southern Europe were the norm, resulting in draconian immigration laws as well as involuntary sterilization of those deemed "feeble-minded," is truly sordid. So sordid, in fact, that after the ideas spread from the United States to the genocidal policies of Nazi Germany, made public by the Nuremburg Trials, they were all but abandoned.[39] However, a new movement of "reform eugenics" coalesced in the 1950s around the ideas of "improving" humanity; among the reformers were men like Julian Huxley and Theodosius Dobzhansky, who dreamt of the scientific control of humanity. While some people mistakenly see any criticism of work involving genes as anti-technological, few reject humanitarian work. Instead, it was the hubris of the language that provoked debate, as various ends were put forth with almost religious fervor. In 1970, the president of the US National Academy of Sciences suggested that genetics was the key to everything: "Who can help but find deep satisfaction in contemplating the ingenious elegance

---

38. Lysaught, "And Power Corrupts," 102.

39. There is a voluminous literature on the relationship between the United States and the Nazi eugenics movement. See Kühl, *The Nazi Connection*; Black, *War against the Weak*; Kevles, *In the Name of Eugenics*; Whitman, *Hitler's American Model*.

of the manner in which the complementary double-stranded structure of DNA solves *the most profound questions concerning the nature of life?*"[40]

Theologians were the first to challenge this claim. Some liberal theologians of the time such as Paul Ramsey saw scientists as "playing God" by supposedly challenging theology's jurisdiction, while others outside of theology also saw the claim as problematic.[41] Leon Kass illustrated his view with a well-known example: "Good afternoon, ladies and gentlemen. This is your pilot speaking. We are flying at an altitude of 35,000 feet and a speed of 700 miles per hour. I have two pieces of news to report, one good and one bad. The bad news is that we are lost. The good news is that we are making very good time."[42]

Scientists were making "very good time" in developing new technologies without having any goal in mind other than to control nature and human life. At the time, theologians were still considered important to the debates. In fact, Catholics founded the first bioethics institutes: Daniel Callahan started the present-day Hastings Center in 1969, and in 1971 what is now the Kennedy Center of Ethics was founded at Georgetown, a Jesuit university. But very soon after these debates emerged, theological and even many moral concerns were relegated to the periphery, except insofar as they could be instrumentalized for efficiency. Many have argued that before this happened, the debates on ethical questions, especially on genetically engineering the human race, did not favor special interest groups by limiting what topics could be discussed.[43]

Evans views both of the explanations with which we began this chapter—"Macro-historical" and "Expanding Democracy"—as radically deficient because they do not look at the agents who changed the debates or the power relations among them. Rather than adopting either, Evans claimed that the debate changed because the change *forwarded the interests of certain groups*.

In a detailed and well-researched account of the history, players, documents, and events involved, Evans debunks these myths. Regarding the "expanding democracy" explanation, he recounts how the theologians called upon the public to be involved, but this backfired when the scientists *pushed against* public involvement through legislative activity

---

40. Handler, "Science's Continuing Role," 1103 (emphasis mine).
41. Ramsey, *Fabricated Man*, 138.
42. Kass, "New Beginnings in Life," 15.
43. John Evans, Jürgen Habermas, Michael Walzer, and James Gustafson are just a few of the thinkers expressing this view.

and instead *pushed for* "bureaucratic control through government advisory commissions . . . [as the] ultimate arbiters."[44] The reason was that they feared the public might shut down any research it did not understand. Their motivation was actually to *circumvent* pluralism in order to avoid funding cuts. "In place of elected representatives, *unelected representatives* of the public on advisory commissions—who are much more distantly accountable to the public than elected officials are—would make ethical decisions for the public. *They* would discern the overlapping ends of the public a priori, and apply them to controversial issues."[45]

Rather than an inevitable evolution, the rise of formal rationality in bioethics was the result of "a complex interaction of professions competing in an environment for jurisdiction. . . . [A] debating community dominated by eugenicist scientists had begun a quest to expand its jurisdiction beyond the lab benches toward explaining, through genetics, the meaning and purpose of human life to the public."[46]

The distrust of unelected officials—bureaucrats unaccountable to the public—is high in the United States. Evans points to this as a reason for the initial reliance by government institutions on what was ostensibly quantifiable data alone; it was hoped that "neutral rules" would be trusted even if unelected officials were not.[47] The first government commission (the National Commission for the Protection of Human Subjects of Biomedical and Behavioral Research) was tasked by Congress to compile a list of ends, ends that "had to be portrayed as universally held by the citizens, but had to be applied *without a method of determining empirically what the ends of the citizens were.*"[48] The subsequent task "was to establish these ends as truth, to diffuse them throughout the institutional infrastructure of research and patient care, and through the practices of bioethics to persuade the citizenry to adopt these as their own ends."[49] The ends had to be applicable in all areas and there had to be one commensurable, universal scale for ends: utility.

The institutionalization of the formal rationality of principlism is most relevant to the rise of the technological paradigm in bioethics:

44. Evans, *Playing God?*, 7.
45. Evans, *Playing God?*, 36–37 (emphasis mine).
46. Evans, *Playing God?*, 35.
47. Evans, *Playing God?*, 85.
48. Evans, *Playing God?*, 83 (emphasis mine).
49. Lysaught, "And Power Corrupts," 107–8.

The principles became public law for federally funded research facilities, meaning that all Institutional Review Boards that were federally funded had to apply the principles. Professional journals only published research reviewed by these boards, hence the principles inevitably became the standard for privately funded research as well.[50]

In other words, there was an incestuous relationship between the scientists, commissions, and journals, such that the only way to join the debates was to speak the accepted language and follow the accepted rules, with the power of the state as guarantor. In this consists the disciplinary matrix.

Two Essential Aspects of the Bioethical Matrix

The Coherence and Content of the Principles

Since they were first proposed, there has been much critical discussion of the principles, and "principlist" bioethicists are well aware of them. This has resulted in endless tinkering with the principles—further specifications and various attempts at ranking their priority as well as efforts to make them compatible with other theories or to make them more internally coherent—in successive editions of *Principles of Biomedical Ethics* and in other articles by the authors.

The most obvious problem for any bioethics that is based on a checklist of "principles," no matter how carefully they are chosen, is the ambiguity that could result in the relationship between the principles: that the principles (1) lack theoretical coherence and (2) do not provide substantive normative guidance because they are too abstract.[51]

As to the first criticism, coherence, one answer is that one should simply agree that there is no coherence, but pragmatically speaking, the "*search* for broad coherence between considered judgments, accepted norms and endorsed values on different levels and in various contexts" is the best tool for solving conflicts.[52] Attempting to find a more substantive answer, Beauchamp argues that what justifies morality are the objectives of "*promoting human flourishing by counteracting conditions*

---

50. Evans, *Playing God?*, 88–89.
51. See Clouser and Gert, "A Critique of Principlism."
52. Schöne-Seifert, "Danger and Merits of Principlism," 116 (emphasis mine).

that cause the quality of people's lives to worsen."[53] And so we come to a new ambiguity: the meaning of "human flourishing." The slippery idea of "quality of life" employed here, particularly when considered materially, has a bad history. Disabled groups have long argued that ideologically influenced "quality-of-life" arguments established by healthy elites lead to the conclusion that certain lives represent, as the Nazis put it, "life unworthy of life."

Richard John Neuhaus, who before his death was pastor of a parish in Brooklyn, found the quality of life concept "intuitively disturbing."[54] In an obituary on Neuhaus, George Weigel wrote,

> Neuhaus was also concerned with elitism and its corrosive effects on the poor people he served. He often spoke of his experience of reading an early essay on "quality of life," back in the embryonic days of what would eventually come to be known as bioethics. The author described "quality of life" in terms of income, education, recreational opportunities, and so forth; then, as Neuhaus told the story, "I got into my pulpit on Sunday, looked out at the congregation, and realized that not a single person there had what was being described as 'quality of life.'" Something was seriously wrong; and so the dignity of every human life, not its alleged "quality," became the conceptual basis on which he entered the bioethics struggles that now define such a significant part of the national agenda.[55]

Defending the unique dignity of every individual person and creature cannot be achieved through concepts such as "flourishing," to which we will return.

The defenders of principlism say the second criticism, the abstract emptiness of the principles, is misguided; the principles may begin as empty, but they are specified *in context*, "the progressive filling in and development of principles and rules, shedding their indeterminateness and thereby providing action-guiding content."[56] Once again, this begs the very question at issue; the notion of "action-guiding content" can mean anything and the problem remains unaddressed. Everyone is in favor of beneficence, non-maleficence, justice, and respect, but their meanings may be in complete opposition.

---

53. Beauchamp, "Defense of the Common Morality," 260 (emphasis mine).
54. Neuhaus, *America against Itself*, 125.
55. Weigel, "Remembering Father Neuhaus."
56. Beauchamp, "Principlism and Its Alleged Competitors," 183.

For example, Lysaught traces the devolution of the principle of "respect," which in the Belmont Report began as substantive, inclusive of all persons, *both* promoting autonomy *and* protecting the vulnerable: "Persons with diminished autonomy are entitled to protection."[57] Under Beauchamp and Childress, respect for persons was dropped in favor of respect for *autonomy alone*.[58] That respect became "non-interference" and applied only to "autonomous" individuals: "Our obligations to respect autonomy do not extend to persons who cannot act in a sufficiently autonomous manner."[59] They excluded the "immature, incapacitated, ignorant," and infants specifically.[60] The unborn, the mentally deficient, those in a coma, and many other vulnerable individuals, or persons simply deemed irrational by their doctors, were no longer due this "respect." As Pierre Mallia explains,

> If one deems that a patient's refusal is irrational, claiming therefore it is non-autonomous, one may over-rule it. Conversely one may reason that although the choice is irrational, the patient is competent and therefore autonomous. Both can claim they are respecting the principle of autonomy.[61]

Moreover, "autonomy" is problematic even for rational adults. "Informed consent"—the *sine qua non* of bioethics—is based on autonomy, but it too can be compromised:

> The practice of informed consent shapes patients by persuading them (or coercing them, since most medical procedures will not be performed without a signed document) to locate themselves under the rubric of autonomous consent, to understand their relationship with the physician as somewhat contractual (based on a signed document, one which waives many of their rights), as consumers who are "choosing" a particular course of medical treatment, having weighed the advantages and disadvantages of the options.[62]

Finally, in a report of the Ethics Advisory Board of the United States, respect is decoupled from persons and reduced to an abstract notion. Lysaught concludes that the patchwork of philosophical and

---

57. *The Belmont Report*.
58. See Lysaught, "Respect," 665–80.
59. Beauchamp and Childress, *Principles of Biomedical Ethics*, 65.
60. Beauchamp and Childress, *Principles of Biomedical Ethics*, 65.
61. Mallia, *Nature of the Doctor–Patient Relationship*, 12.
62. Lysaught, "And Power Corrupts," 105.

moral views that had passed for bioethical rigor simply collapses into one principle, that of utility: "Under the rhetoric of the principle of respect for persons—wherein persons ought to be seen as ends only and never solely as a means to others' ends—we find instead the principle of utility."[63] Regarding the Ethics Advisory Board's statement that the human embryo is entitled to "profound respect," but could still be created or destroyed as needed, Callahan famously observed: "Those embryos that stand in the way of research are to be sacrificed—as nice a case of the ends justifying the means as can be found."[64]

Many ethicists would deny being guided *strictly* by the cold concerns of utilitarian calculus, and we have no reason to doubt them. But it is hard to resist utilitarianism when the "social good" is equated with material well-being and the greatest good for the greatest number, and when cost/benefit analyses translate ends into monetary value. The social, political, and market forces tending toward utilitarian efficiency and affordability are unremitting.[65] Furthermore, the meaning of everything else is up for grabs in service of this shadow principle, so that "respect," for example, "unleashed from its philosophical and religious moorings . . . now functions as simply a placeholder: fill it with your own content."[66] It is difficult to disagree with Lysaught when she says: "Given that the notion of respect fails to do any real theoretical work . . . one cannot but conclude that it is invoked for its significant rhetorical power. A potent carrier of meaning, the word 'respect' can effectively sway public opinion."[67]

Consensus within Pluralism

A problem internal to the technological paradigm is the instrumentalization of "consensus" in policy-setting debates, which can

---

63. Lysaught, "Respect," 677. Notably the same is true in the so-called free market: "The product-market metaphor relies on the self-interested utility-maximizer view of human agents that is congruent with neoclassical economics, in which individuals make choices based on their perceptions of what will benefit them most" (Malone, "Policy as Product," 18).

64. Callahan, "Puzzle of Profound Respect," 40.

65. A paradigmatic case comes from Oregon where, in 2008, a woman's health insurance company denied coverage for medicine that would treat her illness but offered to cover the $50 cost of drugs for "physician-assisted death" (Donaldson, "Death Drugs").

66. Lysaught, "Respect," 680.

67. Lysaught, "Respect," 667.

only be an admirable goal if it is not coerced.[68] That coercion can consist of demanding a "reduction of one's cultural and narrative particularity to something fundamentally indifferent,"[69] that is, asking the parties to divest themselves of their most deeply held beliefs. The resulting agreement is at best illusory, and thus does not provide a basis for true dialogue.

While true consensus based in solidarity is a good to be pursued, if the clash is at the level of comprehensive worldviews, then debates become ideological power struggles. Coming up with a consensus on, for example, which technological fix for a contaminated piece of land would be the most efficient is one thing; when the disagreements move to ultimate values like the dignity of human life, things are quite different. David Casarett, a proponent of consensus, is quite clear about the nature of "consensus-based" proceedings:

> Consensus is fragile and is easily disrupted when one or more participants hold tenaciously to a principle or value. The fragility of consensus requires that all participants, including the ethics consultant, be willing to reconsider their own normative claims. . . . *Ethical deliberation requires participants to examine deeply held values such as the sanctity of life, the primacy of autonomy, and the commonly held view that lives do not have a dollar value.*[70]

This is riddled with assumptions, including the belief that one's deeply held beliefs on an issue are just something to which one "tenaciously" clings. Note that Casarett does not include those beliefs that reflect his own ideology among those that might require reexamination: the *non*-sanctity of life, or the flexibility of "autonomy" according to the state, or the utilitarian view that lives *do* have a dollar value. Consensus-based decisions often work for less consequential evaluations but for graver matters, for example euthanasia, too often nothing held by one's ideological disputant is sacred; everything must fall to consensus, and it is assumed that the consensus will be governed by strictly formal rationality, including the monetizing of human life.

Moving beyond Casarett's tyranny of the majority, the authors of an article in the prestigious *New England Journal of Medicine* argue that

68. Bioethicist Edmund Pellegrino has argued that the patient's good, not consensus, should be the primary concern. In this he included the medical good of the patient as a human being, the patient's own perception of the good, and the spiritual good. See Pellegrino and Thomasma, *For the Patient's Good*.

69. Hart, *Beauty of the Infinite*, 428.

70. Casarett et al., "Experts in Ethics?," 9.

those whose views are out of step with the ruling regime should simply be told to abandon the debate entirely. Those professionals unwilling to accept this should either select an area "that will not put them in situations that conflict with their personal morality or, if there is no such area, *leave the profession.*"[71] This argument is becoming more prevalent as the "solution" to the problem of moral disagreement: *conscientious objection on ethical issues, even if protected by law, would itself be declared "unethical"*[72] and should have no place in moral debates.

We will return to dialogue later, but here we can readily see that this is the opposite of real dialogue.

A Reply to Foucauldian Criticisms

Classical Liberals are not unaware of this Foucauldian critique; in fact, Moreno points out that Foucault's "biopolitics" must be expanded from control over bodies to control over "tissues" to include stem cells, for example. He admits that liberal values such as neutrality can "conceal certain presuppositions that have very substantive consequences," such as that the debate participants may be co-opted, or that the way the procedures are institutionalized "can help ensure that the status quo, which may be patently unjust, is largely impervious to fundamental change."[73] He goes on to point out that "so long as ethics consultants agree to 'play nice' according to the civilized procedural values endorsed by liberalism, not only are they no danger to corporate interests, but, these critics would argue, they actually serve those interests by providing ethical cover."[74]

What should bioethicists wishing to maintain the status quo do in the face of this devastating critique, he asks? First, ethicists should be self-aware of their own privileged positions, understanding that they may be in morally compromised positions, such as being dependent for a job on a certain status quo. Then he comments on only three possible alternatives: either Sartre's existentialism that claims that all moral choices are irrational, though one *must* choose, or an absolutism that demands a foundation, or what he defines as cultural "relativism." He says modern bioethicists reject existential absurdity because their very purpose is to uphold the fact that there are indeed better or worse moral choices. They

71. Stahl and Emanuel, "Physicians, Not Conscripts," 1383.
72. Stahl and Emanuel, "Physicians, Not Conscripts," 1384.
73. Moreno, "Can Ethics Consultation Be Saved?," 30.
74. Moreno, "Can Ethics Consultation Be Saved?," 31.

reject absolutism without qualification. And finally, they reject cultural relativism because, while culture is important, in the final analysis, all morality is not context-dependent. What remains is the liberal emphasis on procedural rather than substantive values and a reflective equilibrium: "the paradigmatic gloss on American liberal thought, the naturalistic empiricism of the . . . pragmatists,"[75] for in the end, he says, "experience has a way of solving philosophical problems."[76] And so he simply returns to the only way he can imagine avoiding getting bogged down in unending debates: the pragmatic position of proceduralism.

However, one of the major critiques of procedural liberalism has been the inadequacy of pragmatism, or making practical results the criterion of truth. We have discussed the ambiguity of the phrase "it works." "Works" is a vacuous placeholder, a fill-in-the-blank. As a result, we only have a fragmented sense of what "it works" entails. In the empirical interpretation of knowledge derived from Locke, it is enough to grasp immediate connections to proximate causes without needing to understand how those connections bear on the whole. D. C. Schindler points to an example of a pragmatic solution to overeating, with its concomitant health problems:

> If a drug could be invented which simultaneously eliminated at one stroke all the bad effects of overeating, technology would deem that problem solved, when in fact the problem has not even been considered. Is gluttony merely a problem concerning the location of matter? Whatever the answer to this particular question, technology is incapable of raising it.[77]

The sociopolitical critique would ask, "Pragmatism to what political end?" while a reflection based in the metaphysics of gift would point to the key presupposition of pragmatism: the only measure of the truth of a practice is its "success," thus detaching the truth from the good, which we will discuss in the third part of this chapter.

Before turning to the root of the problem in metaphysical relativism, it is important to note that this answer offered by Moreno—pragmatism, experience, and formal proceduralism—doesn't give us much hope for conflict-free resolutions considering recent events in bioethics. The case of Alfie Evans—the British child with a never-diagnosed brain disease

75. Moreno, "Can Ethics Consultation Be Saved?," 33–34.
76. Moreno, *Body Politic*, 173.
77. D. C. Schindler, *Plato's Critique*, 18.

who in 2018 was unplugged from his ventilator against his parents' wishes by order of the British Court, which also refused to allow him to be moved (at no cost to the hospital) to Italy for treatment—horrified much of the world. This case was not an anomaly; it was the inevitable end game of liberalism.[78]

Moreno has stated that "this kind of critique of classical liberalism . . . goes well beyond an attack on ethics consultation, to the core of the liberal world view itself."[79] If that "core" is taken to be the *self-subverting presuppositions* that undergird the worldview, rather than any *state of affairs* (such as peaceful, rational debates, which everyone desires), Moreno may very well be correct. The discussion of principles and consensus reveal how deeply the kind of underlying presuppositions that metaphysicians of gift would reject have been encoded.

One of the central underlying presuppositions is that of "indifferent freedom." As both the sociopolitical account and the metaphysics of gift point to the coercion that results from liberalism's view of freedom (albeit for different reasons), we must define it and look more closely at how this takes place.

How the "Freedom of Neutrality" Becomes Coercion

Insofar as they adopt the juridical notion of freedom . . . Western democracies . . . cannot but affirm as their sole "truth" in the official-public arena that all claims to truth are merely the expressions of private or individual or "subjective" preferences.[80]

Proceduralism demands a juridical concept of freedom marked by the absence of coercion, but it subverts this ideal by virtue of its own constitution. The technological order cannot be neutral because science has its own implicit ontology; so also the ideas of a neutral public space, of a consensus based on a limited notion of agreement, and of the separation of choice from the good that liberalism uses to carry out the programs of the technological paradigm. All require a specific *ontology of freedom*, what Servais Pinckaers calls "freedom of indifference"—"a

---

78. The standard deferred to was the "best interests of the child," which was left undefined in the court's written decision. See Brugger, "The Agonizing Case of Alfie Evans."

79. Moreno, "Can Ethics Consultation Be Saved?," 31.

80. D. L. Schindler, *Ordering Love*, 63.

freedom defined in terms of a self-determination that initially excludes being determined by anyone or anything, one that looks on initially determining factors as intrusions upon, rather than as intrinsic to, the proper and most basic activity of the will."[81] That is, it views freedom as an active power "that produces effects as a result of self-originating energy rather than receiving determination from outside of itself."[82] It privileges the will in isolation, favoring autonomy over heteronomy so that "relationships are not taken to precede the individual will and thus suffuse that will, from the first, with responsibilities, . . . but are now reinterpreted, even if in reality they precede the will, as products of rational choice and consent"[83] in the form of contracts. Finally, it does not see human goods as ends that are intrinsically bound to the nature and destiny of persons, and sees the means to attain ends as an array of merely neutral options.

Those who agree with Moreno accept this truncated view of freedom, which sees pragmatic concerns alone as determinative, with the political order being further reduced to little more than a regulator to preserve, even if by coercion, a "neutral" space. Contrast this with the three dimensions of a more complete vision of freedom, which would involve the metaphysical (a question of the mode of *being*) as primary, and only then the moral (the use of the *will*) and the political (concerning the configuration of *power*).

Reconceiving Bioethical Practice

> *In the end, we can form proper ethical judgments with respect to biotechnological science . . . only insofar as we can recover adequate notions of nature and human-organic life as gift. And this recovery comes about only as we ponder biology, anthropology, and theology in all their ontological breadth and depth.*[84]

The Foucauldian critique reveals the inadequacy of the liberal view in its collapse into power and coercion but does not provide a way out of the morass. Instead, we find ourselves constrained to the political level, to

---

81. D. L. Schindler, "America's Technological Ontology," 266.
82. D. C. Schindler, *Freedom from Reality*, 147.
83. D. C. Schindler, *Freedom from Reality*, 148.
84. D. L. Schindler, "Biotechnology," 629.

questions of the *configuration of power* and thus, *regulation*.[85] Critiques of bioethics that stay within the terms set by proceduralism or within the notion of sociopolitical power, to borrow from Lysaught, "end up being little more than attempts to make a kinder and gentler Leviathan. But Leviathan it remains."[86] Those who defend a purely procedural stance towards bioethics do so out of a fear that the only alternative to its pragmatic approach is some sort of dogmatic authoritarianism. Yet, as we have seen, it becomes its own kind of authoritarianism because of a faulty implicit ontology, the answer to which is necessarily a more adequate one.

Like the Sophists discussed above, for whom "to purify" meant to cleanse form of content, proceduralism claims its method is ontologically "neutral," but we must recognize that neutrality itself is one of the myths of modernity, and proceduralism is one of its prime expressions. Proceduralism has a definitive shape and thus molds both those who wield it and those upon whom it is wielded, a truth known to all who understand that "the medium is the message."[87] Claiming neutrality may sometimes be a mistake borne of ignorance, but it seems there is something disingenuous about it, a disingenuousness that inevitably follows its own assumptions: "The technological society cannot submit its own metaphysics to rational scrutiny, and thus must conceal it.... Philosophical presuppositions are rarely, if ever, stated openly; of course they exist, but they are always expressed in indirect, and thus mystificatory, ways."[88]

However, Moreno argues that an approach founded on pragmatic trial and error and neutrality toward the good is "the only alternative to mere authority, whether its source is metaphysical, theological, or political."[89] Following the positivistic prejudice that the language of ethics must be either scientific (reduced to "neutral conditions of verifiability accessible to anyone"[90]), or purely private and subjective (escaping the

---

85. If procedural liberalism (supposedly) cannot say anything substantive about what freedom is (only that it is freedom from coercion), then it can only speak about how it *functions*, and finally how it is *regulated*, because "a purely negative freedom will always be encroached upon by the now purely positive—that is, essentially arbitrary—apparatus of regulation" (D. C. Schindler, *Freedom from Reality*, 361).

86. Lysaught, "And Power Corrupts," 112.

87. See McLuhan and Fiore, *The Medium Is the Massage*.

88. Lancellotti, "Augusto Del Noce," 326.

89. Moreno, *Body Politic*, 31.

90. Dell'Oro, "Theological Discourse," 133.

criteria of science), a narrative is set up that pits "liberal, rational science" against "tyrannical, irrational religion." But as Carlo Lancellotti notes,

> They are the two inseparable mythical agonists of the technological society . . . ; it needs both of them, because their opposition is essential to its self-definition. In fact, the dichotomy of science and religion conceals the elimination of a third factor: philosophical/metaphysical reason, which is replaced precisely by the human sciences.[91]

It is, in other words, a deliberate dichotomy with an ideological purpose. Its followers might be surprised to find that the metaphysics of gift does not fall into this trap and that there is agreement on many issues—though for quite different reasons. David L. Schindler, for example, has repeatedly noted his respect for and appreciation of the achievements of the Enlightenment in general and the American system of government in particular: he defends the separation of church and state, peaceful dialogue, the protection of individuals as free and rational beings, and that "freedom, equality, and rights as affirmed in the Declaration of Independence represent a significant historical achievement."[92] Regarding these achievements, Schindler says,

> Their ambiguity is such that, within America's positive achievements themselves, there remains an ontological vulnerability to nothing less than what we have referred to as . . . a totalitarianism of the "strong" over the "weak," rooted in a technological idea of human being and action. These achievements thus stand in need not only of perfecting moral or supernatural addition, *but of inner ontological re-formation*, if their just intentions are to be truly secured.[93]

In other words, the sociopolitical critique of the inevitable degeneration into coercive power is true but ultimately incomplete: the deeper problem is that the hidden metaphysical logic of the technological paradigm subverts the good that is intended. How are we to move beyond a sociological critique to a more adequate one? In his masterful study of Plato's *Republic*, D. C. Schindler notes that the central epistemological problem of the *Republic* is how one "gets outside" a purely relative perspective. The discussion of book I "takes place in the cave, that is,

---

91. Lancellotti, "Augusto Del Noce," 325.
92. D. L. Schindler, *America's Technological Ontology*, 243.
93. D. L. Schindler, *America's Technological Ontology*, 277 (emphasis mine).

within an inadequate horizon that cannot allow the whole truth to be seen."[94] In order to reveal the inadequacy of this dominant ideology, the horizon must be broadened beyond the Liberal/Procedural "cave." Bioethical critiques that remain subject to procedural terms, or to the notion of sociopolitical power, or that attempt to mitigate the problem through the use of the Kantian regulative principle, in any of its many iterations, to undergird the logic of pluralism do not qualitatively change the problem at hand.

And so we turn to the metaphysics of gift, which rejects a privileging of parts over the whole, the technologization and instrumentalization of reason, and a positivistic idea of culture and ethics. These all stem from a "tacit adherence to the good as indifferent freedom for the achievement of preferences and for self-definition."[95]

Individuals, Community, and Constitutive Relationality

Both modernism and postmodernism are characterized by dualisms, pairs conceived as oppositions, at every level: mind and body, subject and object, appearance and being, ideal and real, faith and reason, individual and state, and so on. Modernism affirms them and postmodernism either rejects them entirely for a "holistic" position or holds them in an unresolved tension. While there are some who argue for an extreme "rugged individualism" and others who would subsume everyone's individuality into the needs of the community, the procedural paradigm of liberal bioethics does not deny the reality of relational communities; in fact, its *raison d'être* is the perceived need to resolve the conflict between the autonomy of the individual and the needs of the community. However, its failure to understand the *constitutive relationality* that lies at the ontological core of the human person means that relationships are only understood as secondary or accidental features to be dealt with socially or politically. Individuality and community do not oppose each other, but presuppose each other, in the same way that parenthood and childhood do. While not denying the importance of relations, liberalism "*fails to grasp what is implied in their constitutive character. It fails to recuperate*

---

94. D. C. Schindler, *Plato's Critique*, 36.
95. Crawford, "Recognizing the Roots," 409.

the community that anteriorly conditions, and thus helps intrinsically to form, self-identity in its original and abiding meaning."[96]

The metaphysics of gift observes that relationality is *ontologically intrinsic*, reaching the inmost depths of the person, and that there is a mutual *polarity* between the above-mentioned pairs, such as individual-community, rather than a Hobbesian opposition or violent tension. This is important because it is at the metaphysical level that the self-identity needed for true autonomy is formed. The abstract individual imagined by the liberal paradigm "leaves self-centeredness in the objectionable sense intact."[97] Liberalism emphasizes the self-determination of human action, which is of course valuable, but "stripped of the original relation to the other(s) that alone could give the self's identity an originally other-centered orientation,"[98] concrete relational goods become pure choice abstracted from the reality of preexisting relationships. The empirical facts can be affirmed as "good," but good in that liberalism holds them to have an essentially functional purpose (for example, the need for society to reproduce itself):

> This means that the "basic empirical facts" will be at the mercy of the interminable tension endemic to liberalism between a positivistic understanding of law (hence, what a legislature or court makes them to be) and the self-positing of the individual through freedom understood as abstract choice (and hence, what that individual makes them to be). The solution will inevitably be a procedural ethics of choice limited only for the sake of maximizing further choice.[99]

This functional regard toward the other is the root of utilitarianism, alienation, and commodification. The technocratic paradigm, in its efforts to produce "well-being" and increase efficiency, fragments and extrinsicizes a person's relations to others. The liberal self is considered to be *ontologically indifferent* to the other (even if socially or emotionally attached). The way such a self engages the other is primarily by acts of self-interest or by seeing community exclusively as a voluntary association. Such relationships are by definition contractual, seeming to entail that there are no moral duties to persons who cannot participate in a social

96. D. L. Schindler, "'Homelessness,'" 370–71 (emphasis mine).
97. D. L. Schindler, "'Homelessness,'" 371.
98. D. L. Schindler, "'Homelessness,'" 371.
99. Crawford, "Recognizing the Roots," 399.

contract defined by rational self-interest, like the unborn, the mentally ill, and the disabled.

Conversely, to say that relations are *constitutive* implies that they are not first constructed or contracted but "given," that they are presupposed in all of a person's acts, and that they reveal the person as structurally dependent on others "in the very independence (creativity, self-determinateness, and the like) of his actions as entailed by his individuality."[100] *Relationality* and *individuality*, then, are related as poles, not as antagonistic opponents. This classical observation is so elemental that, though rejected for a time by modernity, distinguished postmodern thinkers such as Gianni Vattimo and Carmelo Dotolo have come to recognize its unavoidable reality and necessity for any reflection on human nature, affirming a "communal constitution to our existence that we cannot deny. . . . This is a pre-conceptual, pre-theoretical fact and, for this very reason, it is impossible to deconstruct."[101]

Failing to understand that "constitutive openness to the other is a primordial fact"[102] and failing to understand the person as an individual-in-community leads to a notion of autonomy that, as Edmund Pellegrino observes, fostered the emergence of the negotiated contract model in which

> the notion of a universally applicable set of principles beyond autonomy is irrelevant: doctor and patient may pursue any course they wish, provided it is mutually agreed upon. That which is agreed upon is no concern of third parties. It might include active euthanasia, assisted suicide or an advance directive that calls for involuntary or non-voluntary euthanasia.[103]

The liberal paradigm says that we start out dependent upon others, and then mature into an autonomy that leaves this dependence behind. True autonomy, however, is something different, something deeper than the biological/psychological/social state that follows childhood. David L. Schindler argues that "we bear this relation of dependent belonging in the core of our being, however much, as we move from infancy to adulthood, there is a progressively deeper capacity for recuperating this

---

100. D. L. Schindler, "'Homelessness,'" 355.

101. Vattimo and Dotolo, *Dios: La posibilidad buena*, 57 (English translation mine).

102. Prades and Cantos, "Postsecularism, Postmodernism and Pluralism."

103. Pellegrino, *Philosophy of Medicine Reborn*, 190.

relation in freedom."[104] The key to the metaphysics of gift is an adequate sense of constitutive, original givenness and of each person's (in fact, each creature's) relation to others. As we will see in depth in the next chapter, this givenness and relationality is born from the "generosity" of being itself, at the deepest level of reality.

What follows in our discussion—reason, freedom, and the reorientation of principlism—all builds on this constitutive relationality to reach a comprehensive yet open understanding of reality as a whole.

Reason and the Good

Formal rationality, as we have noted, prides itself on excluding certain content. When reason is thus formalized, and not founded upon and ordered to the Good—a hallmark of the metaphysics of gift—it loses its own reason for being, its reasonableness. D. C. Schindler describes this reality in the thought of Plato:

> Plato's founding of truth and reason on the idea of the good . . . . ultimately seeks to show that, without being so ordered, reason finally loses its rationality. Reason cannot be reason proper outside of a love of the good. . . . To say that reason is grounded in the good means that reason has its proper place within a context that exceeds it.[105]

Schindler's study of Plato's *Republic* serves as a critique of procedural relativism, shows the limits of the Foucauldian critique, and builds up the metaphysics of gift. Questions about the meaning of justice—the ostensible topic of the *Republic*—turn into questions about the meaning of the good and end in questions about reality and the relation between being and appearance. A central insight of the *Republic* is the essential connection between a thing's intrinsic meaning, its goodness, and its objectivity, or having a measure that goes beyond the individual. Denying this means that the individual is taken as having its measure only in itself, without intrinsic relation to a larger whole. Epistemological relativism, which holds that truth is relative to perception, results from this partial perspective, which in turn reflects a certain metaphysical view of reality: "If it is true that perception is essentially relative to the individual, that knowledge is essentially relative to perception, and that reality is

104. D. L. Schindler, "'Homelessness,'" 355.
105. D. C. Schindler quoted in Tyson, "Reasoning within the Good," 323.

essentially relative to knowledge, then the being of things is constituted by their being perceived."[106]

However, if there is no way to reach reality except through each individual's perception, "the only available mode of communicating is to impose one's relative perception on another from the outside. . . . To persuade comes to mean to lend prevailing force to a particular appearance."[107] In book I of the *Republic*, Plato focuses on the conflict between two views of reason, that of Socrates and that of Thrasymachus, a Sophist. Understanding that "violence" refers not only to physical force but also to imposition and coercion, Schindler reveals that the ontological root of Thrasymachus's violence is a result of his relativism, which abstracts from the whole and denies any subordination to the Good. Schindler explains convincingly,

> If an individual is taken simply and exclusively on its own terms, as having its measure nowhere but in itself, and thus as lacking any intrinsic relation to the whole . . . that would necessarily subordinate it to something larger than itself, *it has no choice but to relate to everything outside itself in the mode of manipulation.* Again, while we tend to associate dogmatism with authoritarian assertions of power, Thrasymachus shows us that *argument by violent imposition is the final outcome of skepticism.* There is a link between the epistemological position that being cannot be distinguished from appearance and the reduction of relation to reactionary demonstrations of power. . . . Thrasymachus can only pour his ideas over others' heads like so much bathwater; imposition from above or from outside follows the logic of his notion of truth.[108]

The metaphysical problem reverberates in the ethical problem and cannot be separated from it. Schindler points out that Thrasymachus's problem is not simply one of moral character "as it is, more fundamentally, a problem with what he takes to be most real";[109]

> We tend to think of violence most fundamentally as a moral issue; that is, violence is a way of characterizing behavior rather than, say, a person's understanding of the nature of reality and truth. . . . We would interpret Thrasymachus's championing of

---

106. D. C. Schindler, *Plato's Critique*, 58.
107. D. C. Schindler, *Plato's Critique*, 60.
108. D. C. Schindler, *Plato's Critique*, 80 (emphasis mine).
109. D. C. Schindler, *Plato's Critique*, 56.

power as independent of his epistemological presuppositions—what it means for him for something to be true. If we wanted to challenge him, we would urge him, for example, to respect others and develop a concern for the dignity of the individual. We would not talk about the structure of reality. But Plato does. [He sees] goodness, truth, and being . . . ethics, epistemology, and metaphysics as inseparably bound up with one another. This interconnection would mean that the ethico-political problem of violence . . . *is at root also an epistemological and metaphysical problem*.[110]

Despite what is seen as a zero-sum game between dogmatic authoritarian imposition and the relativism of procedural liberalism, *both* reveal a radically impoverished conception of reason. Both have a fragmented and partial view of reason that never reaches the heart of the matter; while dogmatism absolutizes the relative by making particular claims definitive in isolation from the whole "within which that claim would have its reasonable and sense-giving ground," relativism evinces its dogmatism by making each perspective "a kind of self-contained totality, which is therefore on its own terms incontrovertible and thus definitive."[111] In both cases, reason is instrumentalized and abused. In neither case is truth or goodness the goal, for without intrinsic relation to the good, reason becomes a power of persuasion, and sometimes the very violence liberalism deplores. Thus, once again, it subverts itself.

Freedom and the Good

Human freedom is often portrayed as a territory that modern society is always striving to expand. The only limits to one person's freedom are the borders of another's. In the case of conflict, liberalism has found ways to expand the freedom of some by denying the freedom of others, such as the unborn, the comatose, the terminally ill, or anyone who needs more care than the average person, such as those with Down Syndrome or the elderly.

However, the question that is not asked frequently enough is: how do we, as a society, understand freedom? From a metaphysical perspective, an adequate approach requires that freedom be understood as essentially *connected to and obedient to the Good* and that it see *relation to others*

110. D. C. Schindler, *Plato's Critique*, 55–56 (emphasis mine).
111. D. C. Schindler, *Plato's Critique*, 14–15.

as intrinsic to its meaning. To put it another way, freedom is only good when it recognizes and upholds the inherent goodness of others and the entire ecological community as well. These are interconnected, for it is the *priority of the good* that makes freedom "a reality that is more than merely moral or voluntary insofar as it precedes the deliberate activity of the agent," and at the same time, "this priority entails a subordination of the will to what is other, so that a recognition of otherness of a particular sort as intrinsic to freedom is a condition for the continuing affirmation of the priority of the good."[112]

On the other hand, we have the modern vision of "freedom of indifference." In proceduralism, freedom is not considered ontologically; it stems only from the will, by which a self-determined individual makes "autonomous choices." Freedom is seen as an empty, "indeterminate potency"[113] to choose whatever is willed; naturally, it will end in the political, in questions of the *configuration of power*. If under procedural liberalism we (supposedly) cannot say anything substantive about what freedom is (only that it is freedom from coercion), then we speak only about how it *functions*, and finally how it is *regulated*, because "a purely negative freedom will always be encroached upon by the now purely positive—that is, essentially arbitrary—apparatus of regulation."[114] The Foucauldian critique reveals the inadequacy of the liberal view in its collapse into coercion, but goes no further.

The classical conception of freedom says that every action aims at a good, and those goods in turn are directed towards an ultimate good, which indeed may be different for different people. Plato suggested that they all distill into one of three categories that mirror the three parts of the soul (mind, spirit, and appetite): "love of wisdom, love of honor, and love of gain."[115] That ultimate good is pursued in every particular good that determines each of our particular acts, and so that ultimate good imparts its own particular quality to all of those acts. Similarly, when people act together, they act in accordance with a common good that lends a particular quality to their community: "The common good is not necessarily a different thing from an individual good, but rather what we might describe as a more profound way of representing any good,

---

112. D. C. Schindler, *Plato's Critique*, 3–4.
113. D. C. Schindler, *Plato's Critique*, 149.
114. D. C. Schindler, *Plato's Critique*, 361.
115. D. C. Schindler, *Plato's Critique*, 51.

whatever it might be. The key question is whether we take something as good in itself, as true, or we functionalize it or otherwise relativize it to something particular."[116]

This is a metaphysical notion of the good rather than a reduction of the common good to a collection of individual goods—a new iPhone update used by millions, for example. That "coincidence of private goods"[117] is a hallmark of contractual, extrinsic relationship, rather than metaphysically intrinsic relationality, in which others are conceived instrumentally as means to obtain some personal good, and extrinsically because their goods are not intrinsic to our own. The metaphysical notion of the common good is also transcendent; that is, it is a good that is truly common to all, especially insofar as they are members of a community.

This is a far cry from what results from proceduralism, when the liberal conception of freedom becomes a *substitute for the good*, the *summum bonum*. When this happens, freedom subversively collapses into various natural, ethical, and political determinisms:

> This substitution comes to expression not just in our explicit discussions of freedom, but more generally in our institutions and "values," and in a variety of other cultural phenomena; and, finally, that this substitution entails a fundamental logical incoherence, which is to say that it both expresses and gives rise to patterns of fragmentation and contradiction. . . . An eclipse of the good from the horizon that defines the operation of the human will entail a radical shift in perspective that tends to hide the very problems this incoherence generates, or to cast them as irrelevant for all intents and purposes. . . . To reflect properly on what is at issue and what is at stake requires, among other things, a resistance to this tendency, which may be characterized in this context as a reduction to pragmatic or political concerns as finally determinative.[118]

At this point, a proceduralist might interject that persons have the capacity to imagine different means to achieve an end, and that that is precisely where freedom comes in: there is no absolute necessity to choose any particular means.[119] But proceduralism's separation of the

---

116. D. C. Schindler, "Enriching the Good," 650.
117. D. C. Schindler, "Enriching the Good," 651.
118. D. C. Schindler, *Freedom from Reality*, 2.
119. In fact, the technological paradigm makes means the end in itself; as we have seen, the procedural process becomes the goal.

means from the end implies that human goods are seen as pure choices abstracted from the concrete reality of preexisting relationships.

We must relearn the truth that means have a determining effect on the end achieved. There is an intrinsic, participatory relation between means and ends; the various means point beyond themselves and in a sense are *presupposed* in the end, despite the end's radical difference. Gandhi provided a compelling example:

> If I want to deprive you of your watch, I shall certainly have to fight for it; if I want to buy your watch, I shall have to pay you for it; and if I want a gift, I shall have to plead for it, and, according to the means I employ, the watch is stolen property, my own property, or a donation. Thus we see three different results [ends] from three different means. Will you still say that means do not matter?[120]

Metaphysics of gift goes even further. When a means is chosen, "a mode of the relation between means and ends" is also codetermined at the same time.[121] Mary Taylor points out that not only the *ends* but also the *persons* and the *relationships* in Gandhi's story also change: the persons involved become extrinsically related as thief and victim and the relation is one of coercion;[122] or they become extrinsically related as buyer and seller and the resulting contractual relation is one of consumerism; or the relationship may be one of *gift*, of intrinsic, covenantal friendship in recognition of a common good and destiny. In the third case, utility is not rejected, but is rather *caught up* into the gift relationship and the usefulness of the watch takes on new meaning. The act is revelatory of how means relate to ends and also of the deeper meaning that transcends the particular end achieved in the moment.

While it is true that we live in a pluralistic society and people will have different conceptions of the good, authoritarianism is not the only alternative to modern liberal proceduralism. Goodness is an ethical concern "because it is more basically a metaphysical reality, an actuality that is fruitfully present to all things as their ultimate source and destination."[123] The alternative is the metaphysics of gift, with its

---

120. Gandhi, *Indian Home Rule*, 67.

121. D. C. Schindler, *Freedom from Reality*, 196.

122. "A dictator or bureaucrat can hold a real or metaphorical gun to your head to get what he wants" (Mary G. Taylor, "Ecology on One's Knees," 644).

123. D. C. Schindler, *Freedom from Reality*, 359.

ontological and substantive conception of freedom rooted in reality, in the *actuality* of the perfection of the given form and in the good. This is not to say there are any easy answers to bioethical debates. Reflection on the common good and dialogue infused with the hope for solidarity in a shared vision may be complex, but they are not impossible.

Principles and Pluralism Reoriented to the Good

Much of the internal criticism of proceduralism is intended to shore up the current model. An approach based in the metaphysics of gift does not reject principles, consensus, respect for different perspectives, or the value of science, but argues that questions about, for example, the lexical ordering of the principles or sociological analyses of the power behind state-coerced consensus are insufficient, and do not address the root of the problem. Some tasks cannot be undertaken by the social sciences alone; the sociopolitical critique *begins* to show what happens when the ontology and anthropology behind the technologization of bioethics are inadequately understood, leading to the technological modeling of medicine and ecology on contractual relationships and the concomitant dehumanization of persons under the market/consumption models of human relationships.[124] We will take two examples in which the themes of intrinsic relation, reality, the whole, and rootedness in the Good intertwine.

Principles Reoriented within Virtue and Agency

The point crucial to virtue ethics is that there can be no human practice, which is always collective, unless we are aiming for the good.[125]

Edmund Pellegrino has defended the notion of "virtue" in bioethics. In response, Beauchamp writes that his theory is "compatible" with virtue, although he does not see virtue as foundational. On the whole, the language of principles and procedures has replaced that of the virtues. Principles are instrumentalized, reduced to a material sense. As we've mentioned, Beauchamp said that "the objectives of morality, I will argue, are those of promoting human flourishing by counteracting conditions

---

124. On the contractual model, see Veatch, *Hippocratic, Religious, and Secular Medical Ethics*.
125. Milbank and Pabst, *Politics of Virtue*, 5.

that cause the quality of people's lives to worsen."¹²⁶ But this is a functional view of material goods, not the good of the person-in-community as such, a good that perfects. That good is the aim of what has been called "virtue ethics," but of a specific kind; the term "virtue ethics" has suffered from an ambiguity of meaning. Ethicist Holmes Rolston III rejects an interpretation of virtue ethics:

> Environmental virtue ethics, taken for the whole, is a misplaced ethic, a displaced ethic. It seems unexcellent—cheap and philistine—to say that excellence of character is what we are after when we preserve these endangered species.... It is virtuous to recognize the rights of other persons, but the motivating force is their rights that I appreciate, not my self-respect.¹²⁷

Yet, virtue ethics as individual "self-respect" is precisely what metaphysicians of gift do *not* have in mind. As with everything else, the truth lies in a much deeper whole. *All* human activity—at every level, including the economic, political, and social—is grounded not in amoral neutrality, but in the reality of the good, "regarded as the real factual and valuative object of human pursuit."¹²⁸ Hence, virtue ethics is "less moralistic than either liberal consequentialism (the imperative of happiness) or liberal deontology (the imperative of duty to preserve freedom). For it assumes that the ethical is a normal and essential ingredient of human action."¹²⁹

Thus, virtue ethics is situated within the whole arena of human relationships and activities, not simply within each individual's character. Matthew Crawford distinguished genuine *agency*, epitomized by the practitioner of a *technê*, from the technological ideal of "freedom" construed as isolated autonomy. True individuality in all its fullness is expressed in activities that connect one to others in a shared world:

> Such a sociable individuality contrasts with the self-enclosure that is implicit in the idea of "autonomy," which means giving a law to oneself. The autonomy denies that we are born into a world that existed prior to us. It posits an essential aloneness; an autonomous being is free in the sense that a being severed from all others is free. When the conception of work is removed from the scene of its execution, we are divided against one another,

---

126. Beauchamp, "Defense of the Common Morality," 260.
127. Rolston, "Environmental Virtue Ethics," 70, 68.
128. Milbank and Pabst, *Politics of Virtue*, 4.
129. Milbank and Pabst, *Politics of Virtue*, 5.

and each against himself. For thinking is inherently bound up with doing, and it is in rational activity together with others that we find our peculiar satisfaction.[130]

Proceduralism's "autonomy" abstracts the person from the world around him and from others, as his concern is centered in his own interests. As with all analogical pairs, autonomy, when split off from a kind of heteronomy that considers others, is like an unstable isotope that cannot be sustained without collapsing. What is needed is a kind of convergence of the two poles that transforms both. Each person can be conceived in analogical relationship to the other and can only become truly himself or herself when seen in and through his or her intrinsic counterparts. Ontologically richer than proceduralism's "freedom as autonomy," this notion of agency, based on the "both/and" of the person as an "individual-in-community," requires an appreciation of what has been given, of one's place in the whole and in relation to others.

Pluralism Reoriented in Perspectives, Consensus in Solidarity

For Balthasar, "truth is symphonic"—a "plurality of centers of interest which can coexist happily as so many perspectives in mutual collusion."[131] Truth is not private but is a synthesis formed in community. Truth is certainly objective, but that objectivity can only be reached through an interweaving of many perspectives. The difference lies in Balthasar's view that "all play from the same score which transcends and embraces them."[132] The reason we need the plurality of perspectives is *not because perspectives are all we have*, as Nietzsche believed, and all we can do is make arbitrary choices among them, but because *the truth is inexhaustible*. The individual who is always part of the community and the community that transcends the individual exist not in competitive antagonism, but as mutually nourished and embraced within the larger whole. As D. C. Schindler noted, "The truth of things, their complete sense, is not something first possessed by the individual knower, but by the individual-transcending community, and is also possessed by the individual to the extent that he is immersed in the community."[133]

---

130. Crawford, *Shop Class as Soulcraft*, 207–8.
131. Nichols, "Balthasar's Aims," 117.
132. Balthasar, *Glory of the Lord II*, 22.
133. D. C. Schindler, *Dramatic Structure*, 252.

It is important to note that the sharing of perspectives is generative and fruitful, not a static statement of one's position, nor an uneasy "consensus" formed by negotiations that generally leave at least one party feeling pressured or strong-armed. In the face of multiple claims to truth, the adequate response is not shutting down dialogue that comes from a different perspective, culture, religion, moral view, or rationality, thus forcing it into a coercive monologue, but defending the freedom to seek the truth. Genuine respect for others, says David L. Schindler, "is safeguarded most properly and profoundly, not by detaching the right to freedom . . . from the truth, but on the contrary by situating that right to freedom within the truth that alone can in the end really liberate: the truth of freedom as love."[134]

The difference between proceduralism and the metaphysics of gift, then, is that the former operates under a truncated reason, and the latter is truly open to the whole.

A Richer, Deeper Foundation

Freedom is rooted in a pattern of life that has its center in the truth of reality, a truth that gets amplified through the generative diversity of analogy, through relations and activities that reflect gratitude in their basic form. The energy of origin is thus communicated, and it is crucial to see that this communication depends in some respect on genuine presence, on contact with real things.[135]

In the end, there is no denying the value of mechanical technologies or of formal rationalism, only a need to recognize their limits and to understand that they are always mediated by "deep, often unarticulated metaphysical assumptions about the ultimate natures of persons and things."[136] There is no denial of effective instrumentality, only a recognition that a moralistic or instrumentalist conception of human action is secondary to a fundamentally ontological conception. There is no denial of the aspirations of bioethical debate to a respect for pluralism and in favor of the deepest freedoms of those involved in the outcome, only the

---

134. D. L. Schindler, *Ordering Love*, 61.
135. D. C. Schindler, *Freedom from Reality*, 361.
136. Hanby, "Medicine after the Death of God."

realization that we must work to recover the presence of a richer, deeper notion of the good, of reason, and of freedom.

The technological paradigm is not only inadequate in regard to freedom, nonviolence, and the like, but as we have seen, its methods often subvert the very freedom at which it supposedly aims, undermining the very things ostensibly marked for protection. While seeking to avoid every determinism, it collapses into determinism nonetheless. As Milbank put it, "the metacrisis of liberalism" reveals itself "in its full nihilistic scope," specifically in its tendency of abstraction from reality, the prior, the given, leaving us with a violent Hobbesian state of nature or Rousseauian conflict-ridden association that "requires the remedies of coercive state control" and that rests on a "violent ontology and pessimistic anthropology."[137] Repeatedly, what is advertised as "freedom" is delivered as coercion, or worse, tyranny. "Dignity" for critically ill children devolves into the power of the state and money; the "choice" of euthanasia devolves into a demand that others (objecting doctors and nurses) be deprived of their own rights not to take a life and into a demand that the ill person allow himself to be killed for the "greater good" (to mitigate a financial burden). Ultimately the questions of human action, including the moral questions dealt with in bioethical debates, are always based in epistemological questions that require metaphysics for their resolution. Thus, human action, human knowledge, and the many other facets of reality cannot be abstracted from each other. These unified dimensions of the acting person can only be seen as intimately connected from an adequate ontological perspective, and so we turn now to examine the work of the primary exponents of the metaphysics of gift in greater depth.

---

137. Milbank and Pabst, *Politics of Virtue*, 3.

4

Thinking through Gift

Contemplating Nature's Splendor

The beginning of mindfulness is an original wonder before the givenness of being. Such wonder is often recognized but its significance is not always plumbed.[1]

THE OBJECTIVE OF THIS chapter is to unfold the metaphysics of gift, to show that it is not merely a constellation of sentimental feelings or poetic language; it is a true ontology in itself as well as one better suited for evaluating and valuing our relationship with the natural world. This chapter begins with being and ends with wonder, which David L. Schindler included as part of the ontological foundations of reason. In the metaphysics of gift, wonder and gift are "onto-logically inseparable," for they are "the same reality viewed, respectively, subjectively and objectively."[2]

The Theme of "Gift" in Recent Discourse

The theme of "gift" has become more prevalent in recent years, both theoretically and as a way to view contemporary economic, social, and political problems: "Ever since Marcel Mauss, anthropologists, sociologists, and historians have come more and more to realize that human society

---

1. Desmond, *The Intimate Strangeness*, 5.
2. D. L. Schindler, *Given as Gift*, 87.

as such is composed by gift-exchange before it is further cemented by state authority and economic contract."³ Essentially, there have been two opposing ways to understand "gift":

(1) Discourse on gift in the social sciences and history usually includes a requirement that there be *a return or exchange*; gift is seen in a *relational* context.

(2) On the other hand, many philosophers point instead to the gratuitousness and non-obligatory nature of gift, leading them to conceive of an abstract and idealized notion of *pure gift*: "Modern philosophy has been much concerned with the 'givenness' of reality and has sometimes understood this givenness as 'gift', either in ontological or phenomenological terms," frequently specifying that a true gift "cannot assume any return or even reception, nor genuinely exist within a context of preestablished relationship."⁴

Neither seems quite right. In the first case, if we think more deeply about "gift," it soon appears that it is *not* a proto-economic contract. The social version conceived after the model of economic exchange easily becomes extrinsic and contractual, evolving into obligatory "business" gifts, and perhaps even bribes. Kenneth Schmitz points out that there are societies in which a gift is expected in return for any gift given. The gratuity of the gift is lost and it becomes "an exchange of 'presents' undertaken out of social duty, for social advantage, or even as part of a commercial transaction."⁵

In the second case, it is true that the very notion of gift comprises a non-obligatory nature (it is neither compensation nor transaction). But while a gift is indeed "a free endowment upon another who receives it freely, so that the first mark of a gift is its gratuity,"⁶ it does not seem right either that is should be "a *unilateral* purism"⁷ outside of any idea of relation. A gift that is not received is not a gift at all but something

---

3. Milbank, "Foreword," ix. He is referring to Mauss's "An Essay on the Gift: The Form and Reason of Exchange in Archaic Societies," originally published in *L'Année Sociologique* in 1925.
4. Milbank, "Foreword," ix.
5. Schmitz, *Gift*, 45.
6. Schmitz, *Gift*, 44.
7. Milbank, "Foreword," ix (emphasis mine).

incomplete; and beyond that, the reception of a gift *simultaneously* establishes a relationship.[8]

In the *Republic*, Plato has Socrates say that the highest good is neither the good chosen *purely* for its own sake, with no regard to its effects, nor is it the good chosen for the effects it brings about; instead, the highest good encompasses *both*. That is, the intrinsically-good/instrumentally-good dichotomy is not sufficient, and there must be a wider truth in which both aspects are integrated. As D. C. Schindler notes, while we can distinguish between absolute good in itself and relative good in relation to extrinsic benefits, "Plato goes on to designate a third sense of goodness that is absolute in a manner *inclusive of* rather than *exclusive of* the relative."[9]

And so we come to a third way to think about gifts: they are not a one-way donation but an interplay of reciprocity and relationality, understood in terms of an intrinsic gratuity. Rather than entering an extrinsic contractual obligation, the giver entrusts himself to the receiver in such a way that the giver is made present to the receiver in his gift: "The thing given is not simply a detachable item, an independent thing in its own right; nor is it to be understood as an external substitute for the giver. It is a *token* of him; that is, it is not only *his*; it is *he*."[10] In addition, the reciprocity is non-obligatory, as free and gratuitous as the original gift, bringing it to completion. Milbank adds, "A giver cannot give unless he is first already himself a recipient."[11] David L. Schindler says the same thing, seeing "the creature as gift, that is, as one who *gives* but only as always *first given*."[12] In this understanding, a gift is truly given. The giver and receiver are not only being brought into a relational communion with each other, but in a participatory generosity (the gift being "passed on" to others) the whole community of being is encompassed.

It is clear here that not only does the metaphysics of gift provide a different understanding of gift from those in the social sciences, but its "recovery" of metaphysics is vastly different from the recoveries discussed in chapter 1. It is not a nostalgic return to an outdated classical metaphysics, as some critics have suggested. This third way, says Milbank, both

---

8. See Schmitz, *Gift*, 11.
9. D. C. Schindler, *Plato's Critique*, 89.
10. Schmitz, *Gift*, 59.
11. Milbank, "Foreword," x.
12. D. L. Schindler, "Being, Gift (Part Two)," 412.

reinstates a premodern realist focus in metaphysics, while at the same time "incorporating what is valid in the modern turn to the subject,"[13] including insights from phenomenology and hermeneutics (without a reduction to phenomenon or to the subject alone).

A gift, then, is not simply something that passes from the ownership of one person to that of another. That is merely the "physics of transference"; instead we must turn to the "metaphysics of the gift itself," which is the subject of this chapter.[14]

The Meaning of the Original Gift of Being

In one and the same act of creation, the gift of being is given to the receiver along with everything that proceeds from this gift. The receiver is actualized (and not simply actual) by means of the very gift of being in its givenness.[15]

The "original gift"—also known as *creatio ex nihilo*—is that from which all others derive their meaning, leading as it does to the transcendental aspect of generosity. Schmitz called his seminal 1982 work *The Gift: Creation*. The original gift of creation refers not to an event in the distant past, but a constant act, which is at the heart of the very structure of being itself.

Too often talk of "creation" brings to mind some kind of singular event such as the Big Bang, or, from the perspective of a literal interpretation of Genesis, denies any kind of natural evolution. Thus a discussion of the giftedness of creation has no place in the study of philosophical metaphysics. But *creation*, according to Aquinas, is not *change* (passing from potency to act), but a relation of cause and effect that brings about something entirely new. This radical newness of creation is qualitatively greater than and necessary for all other forms of causal relationship. Aquinas's discussion of *esse* allows believers and nonbelievers alike to speak of creation: "Simply put, to see each irreducible, concrete act of existence is to *see* creation, for to see the being-in-itselfness, the gratuitous novelty—in short, the beauty—of every concrete act of existence, to see

---

13. Milbank, "Foreword," xi.
14. Schmitz, *Gift*, 58–59.
15. Oster, "Thinking Love," 675.

the infinite existential difference between every cause and effect and the irreducibility of the latter to the former, is to *see* this surplus."[16]

Confusion surrounds the meaning of the "original gift" of being in the metaphysics of gift and a subsequent misunderstanding of the consequent and analogous use of "gift" *between* beings. We cannot move to the level of, for example, seeing human interactions in the light of "gift" in economics, bioethics, or politics without first understanding its significance on the ontological level and seeing the similarities and differences between the original gift and subsequent gifts in the social spheres.

The notion of an original gift, the gift of existence, is clearly problematic. On the one hand, it seems that substance must precede being, because there must be something there to *receive* being. On the other hand, it seems that being must precede substance, or it could not "be" at all. Gilson stated the objection this way:

> The proposition that creation is a gift of being is also misleading, since how can you give something to someone who does not exist? It hardly improves matters to say that creation is a reception of being, since how can something that doesn't exist receive anything? Let us by all means, if we must, speak of creation as a sort of reception of existence. But let us not claim to be able to form any idea of what this means.[17]

Is the idea of a "gift of being" misleading? David L. Schindler admits that the double assertion (being prior to substance, substance prior to being) is paradoxical; the question then is whether the language of paradox is unreasonable or irrational. Schindler says it is neither; in fact, paradoxical language alone is adequate to address the question, because "the language of paradox is rightly judged unreasonable or irrational in principle only if the truth about being requires a denial of relationality in the original constitution of creaturely being—which is precisely the point in dispute."[18]

In speaking of the communication of gift, says Schmitz, it is useful to bring in the notion of "privation." For Aristotle, accidental changes require two things: there must be a subject undergoing the change and a *privation* before or after the change. "Privation is the absence of a due

---

16. Hanby, "Creation as Aesthetic Analogy," 374.
17. Gilson, *Le Thomisme*, 143 (English translation by Stefan Oster).
18. D. L. Schindler, "Being, Gift (Part One)," 239n5.

good," one "appropriate to a definite subject," and, for Aristotle, by that definition privation could only be applied to an existing subject.[19] For example, a sick man is one who has been deprived of health. Anselm, however, seeks to go further. He points out that the question at hand addresses not an accidental change, but an absolute one; creation *ex nihilo* refers to an *absolute* privation, where there is no subject and so nothing is owed or due. The gift is *absolute gratuity* and "strictly speaking: not called for."[20]

Here, the concept of gift, of gratuity, opens up a new horizon. A gift that is truly given gratuitously, that is not owed to the recipient *per se*, can be considered good and appropriate to the recipient, but only in retrospect. In an analogous way, when speaking of the *absolute* gift of creation *from nothing*, it is only in retrospect that we can qualify the previous state as a complete privation that points to a radical newness "that must be traced back, not to the recipient at all, but to the donor, to the giver rather than the receiver."[21] Thus, while the act of the gift of existence is not owed to the creature in any way, clearly it means everything for the creature after the fact.

Schmitz illuminates this reality analogically by analyzing gift giving in its metaphysical sense, beyond the mere "physics of transference" involved, when one is truly commending oneself to another:

> The giver does not hand over something "outside" himself but under his control; rather he builds up the thing into a gift by loaning it his own conscious intention as he attends to the receiver. In the act of endowment the giver makes himself present to the receiver; and in this attentive presence he does not only give what is his, he commends himself.[22]

All acts of true gift in the interpersonal realm reflect back on the metaphysical reality of being as gift, not metaphorically, but analogically. In the end, the confusion in the objections with which we began is based

---

19. Schmitz, *Gift*, 31.
20. Schmitz, *Gift*, 32.
21. Schmitz, *Gift*, 34–35.
22. Schmitz, *Gift*, 59. On the same page, Schmitz quotes Emerson: "The only gift is a portion of thyself. Thou must bleed for me. Therefore the poet brings his poem; the shepherd, his lamb; the farmer, corn; the miner, a gem; the sailor, coral and shells; the painter, his picture; the girl, a handkerchief of her own sewing. This is right and pleasing, for it restores society in so far to its primary basis, when man's biography is conveyed in his gift" (Emerson, *Essays*, 291).

on a *univocal* interpretation of the term "gift." The gift of being we are talking about is a unique use of "gift," distinct from the strictly defined giftedness that would apply to other interactions in our world. Neither does "gift" have an *equivocal* meaning, as in representing something entirely different. It is, rather, *analogical*, and the tension between the analogous uses must be kept in mind: the originary gift, *ex nihilo*, as the structure of being, and the gifts within the interactions of the world. Though there will always be an ever-greater difference between the gift of being—creation *ex nihilo*—and any gift we can give, there is a similarity such that we can indeed call creation "gift."

Schmitz employs an example to illuminate the structure of reality created, through the gift of being, *ex nihilo*: The child depends on his parents for everything, including the means to give them gifts. Nonetheless, the parents value their child's gift as a token of the child himself. It can even be interpreted as an expression of gratitude for his own existence. Here we have a situation of *relative inequality* between the parents and the child, but let us consider a situation of *absolute inequality*, in which the original donors are the founders of the entire order in which the gift takes place. This second situation is that of creation *ex nihilo* because *esse* brings a being (*ens*) into existence through a donation of itself (which is *esse creatum*) that effectively *allows the being to be its own subject*, and thus to have true autonomy from its source.[23]

The truth about creation, which also resolves the paradox of creation as gift, is that

> *esse creatum* and the concrete substance-subject [*ens*] come into existence *simultaneously*. This simultaneity necessarily implies a distinct (mutual if asymmetrical) priority and posteriority of *esse* and substance in their original unity *qua ens*, which alone properly exists as a creaturely subject. This is what may appropriately be termed the paradoxical structure of being as demanded by creation *ex nihilo*. It is this structure that alone accounts for the original constitution of the creature.[24]

It is our goal to flesh out the significance of this reality and circle back to it with a deeper appreciation of its consequences with the help of those brilliant minds that have already done so.

---

23. "*Esse*, you might say, causes, not by itself being the *creative* subject of creatures' existence, but by letting *them* be the *created* subjects of their own existence" (Walker, "Personal Singularity," 470).

24. D. L. Schindler, "Being, Gift (Part One)," 239.

Five Exponents of the Metaphysics of Gift

Of course, reflection on the notion of gift began long before the social scientists of the twentieth century; that the world, our existence, and all creation are a gift goes back at least to the Hebrew Scriptures. We will start, though, in the Middle Ages. The five metaphysicians we will concentrate on are arguably the most influential, and formative of others, though they are not the only ones to deal with metaphysics of gift. They are not only philosophers, but also theologians. However, philosophy and theology are not related as dualistic competitors but as interrelated poles—that is, though they illuminate each other, each has its own autonomy. For these thinkers, the originary giver of *esse* is God, not an impersonal "force," a "negative capability," or, in a recent version, the "infinitely small quantum foam of the singularity before the Big Bang,"[25] all of which mistake cosmology with ontology. As this is a philosophical and not a theological study, some preliminary comments are necessary.

None of these thinkers, as theologians, would concede that God is "extra," or "added-on" to a metaphysics that would otherwise function equally well without him; God for them is foundational, the Giver of the gift of existence, *a trinitarian circle of reciprocal self-giving and receiving, extended to all creation through the generous donation of being.*[26] But none would deny that the metaphysics of gift, even conceived philosophically, is far more adequate than other paradigms and unfolds in beneficial applications to every field. That the "gift of being" has theological roots does not lessen its philosophical value.

First, many other concepts have entered philosophical discourse from the same theological origin. Take, for example, the notion of "person"—for the Greeks (*persona*), a mask worn in dramas—which was developed during the christological and trinitarian debates of the early church in the fourth and fifth centuries. This is when the person came to be seen as something deeper than merely the "individual." The term, clearly, is now central in philosophy.

In addition, metaphysics of gift has proven especially fruitful for philosophy. Caldecott noted that it restores dimensions stripped away by nominalist philosophy and its successors: "It re-establishes the priority

---

25. Dastidar, "Stephen Hawking."

26. "I take the demand that a metaphysical argument be free of the influence of faith, or the claim to be able cleanly to abstract what in such an argument is a matter purely of nature or purely of reason, to be in the end Cartesian rather than, say, authentically Thomist" (D. L. Schindler, *Ordering Love*, 14–15).

of relationship over object, of person over thing, and therefore a sense of natural interiority, of true metaphysical depth, and the wonder that is the root of philosophy."[27] He also observed that the ontology of gift can restore important dimensions to the social sciences, for example in economics, overturning the model of the person we inherit from the Enlightenment:

> That model turns man into a solitary and conflictual actor in the market, an isolated and docile subject of the state, pursuing his own survival, pleasure, and power. The alternative . . . recognizes man as "originally in-relation," . . . whose needs and therefore self-interest involve social goods founded on gift and specifically self-gift—trust, generosity, altruism, friendship, co-operation, and charity.[28]

So although we are dealing with theologians, they are also philosophers who "think through the most urgent cultural problems to their deepest metaphysical roots."[29] "We do our thinking *de facto*," says D. C. Schindler, "and whether or not we are believers, within a horizon that has definitively been stamped by Christian revelation [and] cannot in principle exclude the possibility that our most basic philosophical concepts have been colored in profound and subtle ways by revelation."[30] Balthasar saw Przywara's metaphysics as standing in "intimate contact with the mysteries of revelation" without ever abandoning the "strictly philosophical domain."[31] That point and the following apply to all the metaphysicians of gift.

However, in the current philosophical climate, clarifying the autonomy of philosophy from theology is not enough. It is not only faith that is problematic in the intellectual sphere, but reason also, which falls under a "hermeneutics of suspicion" that counters the Enlightenment's worship of reason, claiming that we require a restraining of reason or limits to reason as a response to "the rational domination of nature in science and technology that acknowledges no boundaries, on the one hand, and the violence of absolutist claims, on the other."[32] In chapter 1

27. Caldecott, "The Divine Benefactor."
28. Caldecott, "The Divine Benefactor."
29. Schindler and Healy, "Introduction," xi.
30. D. C. Schindler, *Catholicity of Reason*, 301.
31. From a letter Balthasar wrote to Ulrich, quoted in D. C. Schindler, *Catholicity of Reason*, 302.
32. D. C. Schindler, *Catholicity of Reason*, x.

we noted that a hallmark of the metaphysics of gift is an *openness* to the totality of reality rather than a claim to have captured and circumscribed that totality: the metaphysics of gift sees the *wholeness* of reason not as a circle that tries to enclose everything, but rather as a sailor looking out towards the horizon, or an "open parabola" situated in a context that exceeds it.[33] As Przywara put it, philosophy must be in the "middle," separate but open to scientific reason and to theology, otherwise it leads to totalization, solipsism, and ultimately, nihilism. One's philosophy cannot make any theological claims without betraying itself, because a philosophy built on any theological presupposition (whether that be strict atheism or theism) is not philosophy at all, but theology in the guise of philosophy. Thus, philosophy cannot demand a belief in God, but neither can it deny it. This preserves openness to mystery, as is essential for true philosophy.

On the other side, if metaphysics were to be defined as excluding (or including) any sort of faith or revelation, it would become dependent on this theological assertion. Claiming that "revelation will be irrelevant to the meaning of God as the cause of being cannot be determined prior to revelation. To make that determination, then, presupposes revelation."[34] A deeper look at the fact that reason and faith are irreducible to each other and at the same time intrinsically though asymmetrically related is beyond the scope of this book.[35] It is perhaps enough to say here that all the metaphysicians of gift reject any reduction of human thought and experience to purely discursive reason, closed to mystery, and see theology and philosophy in an analogical rather than oppositional relationship.

This perspective is not a modern invention. Thomas Aquinas, though a theologian, spoke often as a philosopher without direct recourse to theology. For example, the entire text of *De Unitate Intellectus contra Averroistas* is a philosophical argument against an erroneous interpretation of Aristotle's conception of the intellect upheld by Siger of Brabant, at the end of which Aquinas declares, "This then is what we have written to destroy the error mentioned, using the arguments and teachings of the philosophers themselves, *not the documents of faith*."[36] But if someone were tempted to think that Aquinas saw the faith as

---

33. See Ratzinger, *Dogma and Preaching*, 386.
34. D. C. Schindler, *Catholicity of Reason*, 300.
35. Expertly presented in D. C. Schindler's *Catholicity of Reason*.
36. Aquinas, *De Unitate Intellectus*, cap. 5, n. 124 (emphasis mine).

something that could be opposed to philosophy, he scolds his opposition for falling into this very absurdity.[37] In fact, he affirmed the importance of a sound philosophy regarding the natural world in its own right as necessary to preserve a proper theology:

> The consideration of creatures is further necessary, not only for the building up of truth, but also for the destruction of errors. For errors about creatures sometimes lead one astray from the truth of faith, so far as the errors are inconsistent with true knowledge of God.[38]

Thus Aquinas, and all the thinkers here discussed, take their philosophy as seriously as they do their faith.

After Aquinas, we will discuss the work of Erich Przywara, who reintroduced Aquinas's *analogia entis* to the twentieth-century philosophical and theological worlds. It had not died out completely; it was kept alive in the Neo-Scholastic schools, though essentially ignored elsewhere. As with Aquinas, Przywara's view has its origin in the Christian understanding of creation. *Analogia entis* refers to the seminal difference between God and the world, but—analogously—can be applied "intra-worldly." The dialectical theology that the *analogia entis* answered (in which God is diametrically opposed to all that is created) cuts God off from creation, reducing it to essentially nothing, while God is everything; it "fails to register the 'both-and' . . . of divine immanence and divine transcendence" (hence ruling out any sort of divine immanence within the beauty of the world); it "overrides human nature and reason, making them strictly passive with regard to the divine"; it denies any natural knowledge of God (hence the resulting backlash against blind fideism being an equally truncated and blind rationalism); and renders "null and void the revelation of creation."[39]

As with Przywara, Ferdinand Ulrich's work ultimately finds its fullness in theology. It is God who is the ultimate giver, and created *esse* is the non-subsistent similitude of the love of God. Because the circumstances of history are so important, Ulrich believes that philosophers must pay attention to Christian thought whether they are believers or not (just as those writing today cannot write as if Hegel and Heidegger did not exist). As D. C. Schindler explains, "To the contrary, one

---

37. See Aquinas, *De Unitate Intellectus*, cap. 5, n. 123.
38. Aquinas, *Summa Contra Gentiles*, lib. 2, cap. 3, n. 1.
39. See Betz, "Translator's Introduction," 18–19.

would thereby inevitably build what Ulrich refers to as 'theologoumena' [private theological opinions] into one's thinking, but precisely without recognizing them as such."[40] Therefore, even those without religious belief must be at least cognizant of the philosophical dimensions of faith. The paradox for Ulrich is that "it is precisely faith that first makes philosophizing (or reason) radically philosophical (or reasonable) in the proper and ultimate sense of the term."[41] Why? Because his metaphysics of gift leaves room for things to have their own autonomy: "The fact that created being is a gift . . . means that it is in very deed *totally given*. It is radically finitized, hence, nondivine; it is not that divine Person who brings us revelation in the strict sense. Only so, indeed, is it totally transparent to the Giver precisely in its 'natural,' created character."[42]

Hans Urs von Balthasar too was first and foremost a theologian, for whom everything converged in Christ, the "concrete analogy of being."[43] Yet Balthasar understood both the autonomy as well as the deeper relation of theology and philosophy. As with Przywara and Ulrich, for Balthasar, philosophy must at the very least be open to mystery and the awareness that there is always "more" to be discovered: "*Invenire quaerendum*: to find everything is only a discovery by someone invited to seek further."[44]

Finally, David L. Schindler, one of the greatest living thinkers and teachers of metaphysics of gift, follows in the path marked out by those listed above. Nearly all of his work hinges on the judgment that "love is the basic act and order of things," a judgment he draws from the correspondence between "the Christian understanding of creation" and "a rightful understanding of the 'ontological difference.'"[45] To him, distinguishing the two is an obvious requirement of a sound metaphysics, but there is no separating the two in life, which is Schindler's primary concern, as they both point to love.

40. D. C. Schindler, "Grace of Being," 152.
41. Oster, "Thinking Love," 663. And according to Martin Bieler, revelation "helps philosophy to maintain the unity of its vision of created being as *completum et simplex, sed non subsistens* instead of yielding to the temptation—out of angst—to close the gap between the finite and the absolute in a move toward univocation, which then must be counterbalanced by equivocation. . . . The movement into the finite by *esse* has as its most perfect theme the gift of existence to the human being" (Bieler, "*Analogia Entis*," 336).
42. Oster, "Thinking Love," 673 (emphasis mine).
43. Balthasar, *Theology of History*, 69n5.
44. Przywara, quoted in O'Meara, *Erich Przywara*, 61.
45. D. L. Schindler, *Ordering Love*, 1.

In the end, metaphysics of gift, by its own principles, not only allows but requires philosophical autonomy because it understands all things as being true gifts, *radically given*. Only total givenness assures autonomy, not only of human beings and thus their actions, but of the non-human forms of nature as well. Contrast this conception with that of emanation (an extension of what came before rather than an expression of creative freedom), or an evolutionary idealism that deprives creatures "of any intrinsic value by reducing them to mere stepping-stones toward a perfection that lies solely in the future."[46] While it is beyond the scope of this book to delineate the latent dualism inherent in any view of "autonomy" as strict, neutral independence, it is sufficient to note that the philosophy presented here is accessible to anyone.

Thomas Aquinas

> *St. Thomas's metaphysics begins with a gift, a certain plenitude. The world of things is received as manifest actuality; and the task of metaphysics is to refer everything the mind encounters—things themselves, their forms, matter, qualities, relations and movements—back to the fullness first manifest in and through the judgment that things are.*[47]

We begin with being, which is, according to Aquinas, that which is most familiar to us because it is what the intellect first conceives.[48] This is because being is, as D. C. Schindler explains, "a notion that is universally accessible; it is universal accessibility itself, and does not depend for its intelligibility on any particular historical situation or condition."[49]

In Greek philosophy, "being" was essentially a synonym for "intelligible form," which for Aristotle must be understood in connection with the act/potency distinction, the quintessential example of which is the hylomorphic composition of form as act and matter as potency. Thus, act as form or essence was the highest perfection.

Aquinas developed a radically different view. Form does actualize the potency of matter, but that is only part of the story, and not sufficient to explain the existence of things. If form were enough, then form and

---

46. Healy, *Eschatology*, 67.
47. Schmitz, *Gift*, 100.
48. See Aquinas, *De Veritate*, q. 1, a. 1.
49. D. C. Schindler, "'Unless You Become a Philosopher,'" 91.

existence would coincide and everything that truly existed would exist necessarily and eternally.[50] But it is self-evident that creatures are not responsible for their own being. Instead there is *another* distinction, in which something else—*esse*, the "actuality of every form or nature"[51] and the "actuality of all acts"[52]—actualizes the form–matter composite itself. While Aristotle's highest actualizing principle was form, Aquinas "discerned at the heart of reality a *transformal* principle of actuality.... This transformal principle accounted not just for a substance being this or that, but for its being at all."[53]

The Latin word *esse*, the verbal infinitive meaning "to be," is usually translated as "being." Thomas speaks of finite beings' participation in *esse* in three ways: 1) they participate in the uncreated *esse subsistens* (God); 2) they participate in the created "act of being" that all beings participate in, or *esse commune*; and 3) they participate in the specific created act of being which they each receive, or *actus essendi*. That which receives *esse* results in *ens*, "that which is." There is a distinction between subsistent *esse* (in which *esse* and essence coincide, and Aquinas identified with God) and substances or entities (*ens*), which also subsist, but with a real distinction between their *esse* and essence. In what follows we are considering the second and third instances above, non-subsistent *esse*.

Being as gift is clearly present in Aquinas's work; he says "*creare autem est dare esse*" [to create, however, is to give being], and "*universaliter autem omnes substantias creat, dans eis esse*" [but he creates all substances, as their universal cause, by giving them being].[54] Within these statements we see the foundational point that existence is given as a gift, stemming from the distinction, unknown to the Greeks, between existence and essence. Aquinas's understanding of analogy based on real causality and participation follows from the insight that the tension between existence and essence is a sign "not of irreconcilable opposition, but of inherent complementarity and potential integration,"[55] and not just as a manner

---

50. This was the position held by Plato and Plotinus, for whom "the One generates without freely willing it" and so is bound by necessity (López, "Eternal Happening," 219n13).

51. Aquinas, *Summa Theologiae*, I, q. 3, a. 4.

52. Aquinas, *De Potentia Dei*, q. 7, a. 2, ad. 9.

53. Healy, *Eschatology*, 27.

54. Aquinas, *I Sententiarum* 37, 1, 1, and *De Divinis Nominibus* 4, 3 quoted in Oster, "Thinking Love," 669n34.

55. Jameson Taylor, "A Defense," 558.

of predication. Instead, along with the "real distinction," we have a "real analogy," one that says something about how the world really is. While we cannot treat the complex debates on these topics in the depth they deserve, we hope to express some of the radical newness of Aquinas's vision.

The Real Distinction

> *To say that beings do not "come from" themselves requires the recognition of a mysterious and real distinction between the essence and existence of every being.*[56]

That essence and existence can be distinguished from each other and neither can be reduced to the other shows that they constitute not merely a nominalistic separation, but a *real distinction*.[57] The real distinction between *esse* and essence as distinct ontological principles that constitute any given being needs clarification. *Esse* is not exhausted in any given being, and beings (*ens*) participate in being and continue to receive being as a gift throughout the duration of their existence. The danger is in conceiving *esse* as something—some *thing*—"added" to the essence to form a composite of similar things, that is, of constituent elements of the same order. That which receives being is not an abstract, nonexistent essence alone, but the *entire substantial being*. Aquinas says, "Creation does not mean the building up of a composite thing from pre-existing principles; but it means that the *composite* is created so that it is brought into being at the same time with all its principles."[58] Gilson puts the matter this way:

> Since they represent irreducibly distinct modes of causality, essence and existence are irreducibly distinct, but the reality of their distinction presupposes the actual reality of the thing. Essence is not distinct from existence as one being from another being, yet in any given being, that whereby a being both is and

---

56. Balthasar, *Love Alone Is Credible*, 78.

57. Some philosophers distinguish "real distinction" and "ontological difference," with the former referring to the internal constitutive principles of an existing thing, while the latter refers to being's difference from the existing thing. Others use the terms interchangeably.

58. Aquinas, *Summa Theologiae*, I, q. 45, a. 4, ad 2.

actually subsists is "really" other than that whereby it is definable as such a being in the order of substantiality.[59]

Thus, there are many *things*, but "being" is not one of them. There are starfish and stars, cats and catamarans; all things are different, but they all "are." Neither is *esse* the subject of being: "*Esse* is not what is created, it is not the subject of creation; instead, the terminus of the act of creation is the concretely subsisting *ens*."[60] In summary, the unity achieved between being (*esse creatum*) and essence in every creature must be understood as equally primordial dimensions of each and every thing that comes into existence.

ESSE SIGNIFICAT ALIQUID COMPLETUM ET SIMPLEX SED NON SUBSISTENS[61]

Neither the esse *nor the creatures who participate in it are sufficient to ground themselves. Of its own inner necessity, then,* esse *is internally open and constitutively related to a gift from beyond itself.*[62]

We now turn to a specific characterization that Aquinas makes, one that we will return to repeatedly. He says, "*Esse significat aliquid completum et simplex sed non subsistens*," *esse* signifies something complete and simple, but non-subsistent.

The person who runs participates in running, but "to run" does not itself run; similarly, the thing that exists participates in being, but being does not itself "exist"—it is *non subsistens*. Non-subsisting *esse*, the act of existence, is complete and simple (that is, not a compound of constituent parts) and hence, "perfect." *Esse* as act is infinite, in some sense, but at the same time the act of existence as *esse creatum*—within the created order—is finite, since *esse* does not subsist in itself, but only in that which exists. As Nicholas Healy explains,

> The gift of *esse* is the source of all the perfections within every created entity, and yet, paradoxically, created *esse* is itself dependent upon essence to attain subsistence.... Thus, while *esse* as act points to an inexhaustible fullness and supra-essentiality at

---

59. Gilson, *Being and Some Philosophers*, 172.
60. D. C. Schindler, "What's the Difference?," 19.
61. Aquinas, *De Potentia Dei*, q. 1, a. 1, ad 1.
62. Hanby, "Creation as Aesthetic Analogy," 364–65.

the heart of created reality, as non-subsistent it is "affected" by the otherness of essence without for all that losing its "simple completeness."[63]

Esse non subsistens will be important for the later metaphysicians of gift in its role as that which mediates;[64] that is, things exist by participating in being, but their participation in being is itself caused by *esse subsistens*. Non-subsistent *esse* mediates between the ultimate cause of all things and the things themselves. Because of this, we are able to affirm that things possess their own existence and goodness:

> Essences can have a positivity that is distinct from that of *esse* without however having that positivity except from within their sharing in *esse*. . . . However overly subtle and abstract this distinction may seem, it has crucial implications. . . . *It allows us therefore to affirm the difference of creatures as ultimately and essentially good*; and it allows us to affirm the overcoming of dualism as Plato does with his notion of participation, without depriving the material cosmos of any reality of its own.[65]

Aquinas's account stands in stark contrast to the modern concept of what beings are: "Objective, unitary instantiations, not *participating in being* but standing forth as punctiliar substances, *devoid of analogical tension within themselves*, and as discrete 'entities' embraced within the empty and abstract category of being or—more properly—existence."[66] It stands in contrast to any monist concept, whether inspired by Eastern philosophies or various Western traditions, of the ultimate unreality of beings, in which entities are dissolved into merely temporary, illusory nodes in the flow. It stands in contrast to all forms of oppositional dualism, to a Gnosticism that says that the material world is evil, and to any philosophy that cannot ultimately account for beings having their own goodness and freedom. For Aquinas, beings are not illusory, or a fall from purity, or autonomous instantiations of an abstract category, but rather true, good, and beautiful in themselves, while at the same time participating in the fullness of being, in communion with all other beings.

---

63. Healy, *Eschatology*, 25.

64. Non-subsistent fullness is "a mediator that is no-thing in itself, and so is pure mediation"; to call it a mediator would be to make an act a *thing*. D. C. Schindler, *Companion*, 48.

65. D. C. Schindler, "What's the Difference?," 21.

66. Hart, *Beauty of the Infinite*, 230.

The real distinction is the foundation for the radical understanding of participation in the metaphysics of gift, which is best expressed as analogy.

Analogy

> *Thomist analogy, therefore, permits the expression of a concrete universal that shows a Totality in which there are, simultaneously, community and alterity.*[67]

Analogy allows us to see unity-in-distinction, the simultaneity of community and difference. Though Aquinas wrote no formal treatise on analogy, it is present throughout his work.[68] We must begin where he did: with the "analogy of being" (*analogia entis*), which concerns the infinite difference between the Creator and the creature. While Plotinus's "One" is beyond being, beyond human knowing and naming, for Aquinas the One is not beyond being but is rather Being Itself—utterly transcendent and deeply mysterious, yet at the same time, though he cannot be "known" by the human person, he can make himself known, can manifest himself. "Being" is not a genus under which both Creator and creature fall. As we saw above, for Aquinas only God is *esse subsistens*. Because God and worldly entities exist in such divergent fashions, only analogical language is possible. However, the flip side of this affirmation is that because the difference is not complete, analogical language can be used truly. It is the context of the "divine names" of God that is the main occasion for Aquinas's deliberation on analogy.[69]

Aquinas says that not just the essence of God, but the essential principles of *things* are unknown to us.[70] In the case of created things and their constitutive character of *esse*/essence, there is also a deep mystery at their heart, that is, not an unknowable darkness, but "an abyss of light,"

---

67. Beuchot, "Limits of Cultural Relativism," 160.

68. "Any attempt to understand the analogy of being in Aquinas has to come to terms with the simple fact that the topic of analogy is present from the very first moment of Thomas's written work. . . . There is simply no instance in Thomas's work where analogy is not tacitly presupposed or being treated without being named or simply being silently at work in the exercise of the *sacra doctrina* itself" (Hütter, "Attending to Wisdom," 214).

69. See Aquinas, *Summa Theologiae*, I, q. 13.

70. See Aquinas, *Aristotle's* De Anima, lib. 1, l. 1, n. 15.

an intelligibility that the human mind cannot fully fathom.[71] The gifted "being" of a thing is really distinct from its essence. Yet at the same time he says, "*intellectus vero penetrat usque ad rei essentiam*," the mind truly penetrates to the essence of things.[72] Here there is not an absolute, dualistic distinction between Being and Appearance, as in Kant's noumenal/phenomenal split. Being *appears*, is truly revealed in things, and what appears in those things is truly *being*, not some phenomenal illusion. As with Being Itself (*esse subsistens*), analogical understanding means that what we know of the things of nature we can know truly, though not exhaustively.[73]

In moving from God to created things, from the origin of analogy in the *analogia entis* to analogy's application to the things of the world, we have moved from a purely theological discussion to a general philosophical one. Analogy illuminates a similarity within a greater dissimilarity, and as Aquinas is able to speak about the analogy between Being Itself and created *esse*—both *esse commune* and the *actus essendi* of each particular entity—so can we speak of the topic of analogy analogously *within the world* as unity-in-difference.

Analogy is connected to the problem of the One and the Many because the explicit use of analogy arose as part of the attempt to reconcile the positions for which "Parmenides" and "Heraclitus" are shorthand: whether all is being or all is becoming.[74] On the one hand, we appear to have a philosophy of absolute difference (championed today by postmoderns like Gilles Deleuze), and on the other, a monistic philosophy of absolute identity. Both Plato and Aristotle sought to salvage common sense by affirming both the reality of changing, finite things, as well as an enduring intelligibility that somehow lay behind that change, but it was Aristotle who first discussed analogy in a technical philosophical sense. In book 4 of his *Metaphysics*, he says that "being" is predicated of different things in multiple ways that cannot be reduced to one form or definition, and he discusses analogy as a way of relating disparate things; the flip side

---

71. Pieper, *The Silence of St. Thomas*, 96.

72. Aquinas, *Summa Theologiae*, II, q. 1, a. 31, 5.

73. See Aquinas, *Summa Theologiae*, I, q. 12, a. 1; and I, q. 13, a. 1. Aquinas explains that God is knowable and nameable, though not exhaustively, because God can be known through his effects.

74. See Palmer, *Parmenides*, 39–44. "Both Plato and Aristotle understood Parmenides as perhaps the first to have developed the idea that apprehension of what is unchanging is of a different order epistemologically than apprehension of things subject to change" (Palmer, *Parmenides*, 44).

is that one cannot abstract a single genus, "Being," from the multiplicity of things. "Rather, the very plurality of beings must be integrated into a differentiated unity of being by way of an analogy of proportion."[75]

Aquinas begins to develop his notion of analogy following Aristotle. He describes three ways of predicating: univocally, where a word is predicated of several objects in the same way, with the same meaning (snow is white, swans are white); equivocally, where the meaning is different (a pitcher is a vessel for water, and a baseball player); and analogically, a middle term between the first two signifying a unity-in-diversity or similarity-in-difference (a river has its origin in a spring, and a thought is said to "spring from" another thought). The "analogy of proportion" in the above quotation concerns two things that are similar in a proportional manner to two other things (branch is to tree as arm is to body). In a second form of analogy, "*pros hen*" analogy or analogy of attribution, one or more things are related to a third which is primary, as when things are predicated "differently but not equivocally."[76] The most familiar example is that of "healthy," which is rightly predicated of living things. Food and blood may be said to be "healthy," and are analogically ordered to man: they are signs or causes of health, but predicated in different ways. In either case, analogy provides a mean or middle ground between equivocity and univocity.[77]

One objection might be that while we have moved from talk about God to talk about things in the world, isn't it still just *talk*? There are those who argue that in Aquinas, analogy remains within the realm of logic, never rising to metaphysics, to causal relations in *reality*. As Richard Hütter puts it, they claim there is no transition from the "logic of predication to the metaphysics of ontological participation."[78] In a cogent critique, Hütter argues that for Aristotle and Aquinas logic *depends* on metaphysics, not the other way around,[79] and as Lawrence Dewan notes, it follows from logic's dependence on metaphysics that "it is the metaphysician who defines analogy, and does so in terms of the foundation in reality for the modes of discourse."[80]

75. Hütter, "Attending to Wisdom," 216.
76. See Betz, "Translator's Introduction," 47.
77. Aristotle describes it as a "geometrical proportion." See Aristotle, "Nicomachean Ethics," V, 3, 1131b14 (1007).
78. Hütter, "Attending to Wisdom," 227–28.
79. See Hütter, "Attending to Wisdom," 225–26.
80. Dewan, *Form and Being*, 94.

The dialectical opposition of thought and being reveals the morass of representational epistemology, wherein one puzzles about how to "link up" one's "inner and outer worlds," after having first performed a Cartesian separation between "ideas in the head" and "reality."

> In contrast to the tendency to separate reason and experience in modern thought and the tendency to collapse them into each other in postmodern thought, the classical tradition affirms a relationship between them of unity-in-distinction. Truth and being in this tradition are understood to be perfectly coextensive, if formally distinct, and human reason is essentially embodied, so that its perception of the truth of being will always occur by way of embodied experience. In this case, intelligibility is in being, it is not a conceptual construct that is then applied to or imposed on experience, and to know is therefore to be intimate with reality in a manner that can only be distantly imitated by physical contact.[81]

Thought is not opposed to or beyond reality but is a deepening into it in the most real way. We will return to this point later on but here it is necessary to show how analogy is not simply a conceptual tool but is rooted in the realities of causality and participation.

Causality

The mechanical interaction of bodies is, of course, necessary for things to be the way they are, but it does not account for them, it is not what explains them or reveals what they are. . . . What principally characterizes cause . . . is the communication of form.[82]

Following Galileo, "cause" was no longer the communication of form, but became synonymous with (or reduced to) physical motion, as when one billiard ball strikes another and *force* is communicated; nothing is shared other than the empirical coordinates of time and space.

One of Aquinas's well-known formulas is: "The effect is assimilated to the cause, for every agent produces something like itself."[83] It indicates that everything is, in some way, similar to its cause by participation

---

81. D. C. Schindler, "On Experience and Reason," 261–62.

82. D. C. Schindler, *Catholicity of Reason*, 124, 132.

83. "Effectus assimilatur suae causae, quia omne agens agit sibi simile" (Aquinas, *Summa Theologiae*, I, q. 3, a. 3, ad 2).

without becoming identical to it. Aquinas provides a concrete example in the similitude between cause and effect—between giver and receiver: the sun communicates likeness in the greening of plants, but a plant does not resemble the sun nor behave like the sun. Yet there is a communication of likeness between them, "for if we remove the plant from the sunlight, it whitens and dies. The greening disappears, for if the cause fails, the effect fails."[84] This is not similitude in any ordinary sense of the term, "in any strict sense of figural resemblance," but rather a "life-line that communicates a presence [and] establishes an analogy of community."[85]

The state of all created things being "ontological siblings" derives from the fact that all entities share in act, that by which something comes into being, and by participation through the communication of likeness. The sun's very real (not metaphorical) "gift" to the plant is a *causal likeness*—a relation of likeness within greater unlikeness, which is the very meaning of analogy.

Participation

To speak of metaphysical participation is to say that one thing ... has its reality, in other words, by virtue of something other than itself. ... It would be only a slight exaggeration to call participation, for good or ill, the metaphysical idea par excellence.[86]

Participation too, via causal likeness, is at the very heart of analogy: "There obtains a strict correspondence between the structure of analogy and the structure of participation, with analogy as the way of predicating the unity of being and participation as the real unity of being."[87] When something participates in something else, it somehow "shares" in another without exhausting the other. This could be in terms of *intelligible content* as *logical participation* (the notions of the specific and the generic, as the concept "man" participates in "animal"). At the same time, metaphysics grounds logic and not the other way around, so logical notions can be "stand-ins" for metaphysical conceptions; logical notions can be used to define real things (*res*).[88] Here we are interested in *real* or *ontological*

---

84. Schmitz, *Gift*, 124–25.
85. Schmitz, *Gift*, 125.
86. D. C. Schindler, "What's the Difference?," 1.
87. Hütter, "Attending to Wisdom," 236.
88. See Dewan, *Form and Being*, 86.

participation central to the metaphysics of gift, clearly explicated in D. C. Schindler's article, "What's The Difference?" We draw on it for part of what follows.

Ontological participation holds that "the physical existence of any individual thing is a derived (though transitory) particular manifestation of deeper, transcendent, archetypal metaphysical reality.... The notion of 'participation' holds that concrete existing individuals are dependent for their existence upon transcendent powers of being."[89] And it is true that for Aquinas, ultimately, this means God. At the same time, however, "to participate is to have partially what another is without restriction,"[90] and as Aquinas repeatedly said, all effects are similar to their causes. He also says,

> Now it is by its essential principles that a thing is fully constituted in itself so that it subsists; but it is not so perfectly constituted as to stand as it should in relation to everything outside itself except by means of accidents added to the essence, because the operations by which one thing is in some sense joined to another proceed from the essence through powers distinct from it. *Consequently nothing achieves goodness absolutely unless it is complete in both its essential and its accidental principles.*[91]

Therefore, we can turn to an *intra-worldly* application, applying Aquinas's participation of things in their being and Plato's theory of participation of substances in their accidents. D. C. Schindler suggests seeing "whiteness," for example, as analogous with being, in that whiteness "does not subsist in itself any more than *esse* does, but subsists only within the substance in which it inheres."[92] He suggests a fruitful continuation of the relation:

> That a transposition of this view of participation to the substance-accidents relation is possible in the first place stems from the similarity that effects necessarily have to their causes. It follows that formal act cannot be without some analogy to existential act. We would expect, then, that as form is actuated by *esse*, it would reflect the self-diffusive character of *esse* within the order proper to it. Indeed, Aquinas affirms that "it is the nature of every actuality to communicate itself as far as possible."[93]

89. Tyson, "Post-Secular Approach," 140.
90. Hütter, "Attending to Wisdom," 230–31.
91. Aquinas, *De Veritate*, q. 21, a. 5 (emphasis mine).
92. D. C. Schindler, "What's the Difference?," 21.
93. D. C. Schindler, "What's the Difference?," 21–22.

We will return to accidents later on, but first, recall the Greeks: negatively speaking, privileging the One or the Many seems to *create* problems. If participation is understood as meaning that the universal form, the "One," is the true reality, then the sensible entities do appear to be deprived of any reality (or are merely derived, and granted a provisional reality). The physical world appears to be a temporal illusion without its own autonomy, something to be escaped if one is to reach the truth. Or if the particular instances, the Many, are ultimately real and any concept of a universal form "behind" them is a fiction, then any real relation between really existing things is also illusory. Positively speaking, privileging the One or the Many seems to *solve* problems. No particular person embodies the whole reality of all of humankind, nor the universal term "humanity," and it does seem that the One is the higher reality since all else is a partial reflection. On the other hand, the particular, individual things alone are what we confront "in reality" and thus seem to be the primary meaning of being, and appear to be higher than any universal form.

Plotinus sought to resolve this conundrum with the notion of a continuous chain of being emanating from the One to the concrete particulars of the world, the Many, as a fountain flows down and is continually renewed. He reaffirms, against the gnostics, the material world as good, but can he sustain the *difference*—that these things don't merely dissolve back into the ultimate reality of the One? Multiplicity from unity in Plotinus, says D. C. Schindler, seeks to preserve and valorize both qualitative and quantitative difference, but as manifestations of the goodness of the One, are they truly good simply *in themselves*?[94]

Here we confront the philosophical root of the Thomistic difference regarding the subject of participation. In the Greek view, instances of anything are relative to the absolute and subsistent reality of the Form. This could explain how the many were actually one but could not account for the gift of their autonomy. Aquinas achieves something very different— the notion of participation that "includes *an affirmation of the difference of that which participates, and thus opens the world to its transcendent source without thereby making the world something insubstantial.*"[95] He does so by affirming a radical composition at the heart of beings, radical because first, the *esse*/essence distinction means that-which-is (*ens*) is "in

---

94. D. C. Schindler, "What's the Difference?," 14.
95. D. C. Schindler, "What's the Difference?," 15 (emphasis mine).

some sense more real than *esse*, because it alone subsists," but at the same time, "its reality is due wholly to the act of existence." *Esse*—in which particular beings participate—is *complete, simple, and perfect*, but that perfection does not subsist in itself, as in Neoplatonism, but only in its other, "which is not therefore merely a negative derivation of *esse* but has something positive to contribute to the very act that lets it be."[96] Aquinas says that every substance participates in *esse*, but every participant is further composed "of that which participates and that in which it participates, and the participant is in potency to that in which it participates."[97] The composition of beings can be seen as mutually, though asymmetrically, participatory.[98]

> In a word, the Thomistic insight into the non-subsistence of being allows a full integration of the metaphysics of participation while at the same time "leaving room" for the genuine positivity of difference: of the variety of essences within the existential order, and of the variety of material instances within the essential order. In Aquinas's words, "the cause of being insofar as it is being must be the cause of all the differences of being and consequently of the whole multitude of beings."[99]

Thus, we encounter goodness not merely in looking *past* things to their ultimately good source, "but also in looking *at* them, in celebrating their intrinsic solidity and their irreducible uniqueness."[100] An adequate metaphysics of participation must affirm both, and in Aquinas, we reach the "both/and" so crucial for the metaphysics of gift: seeing the reality of both the One and the Many, the goodness of both the source and its effects, and the truth of both unity and difference.

---

96. D. C. Schindler, "What's the Difference?," 22.

97. Aquinas, *Aristotle's* Physics, lib. 8, l. 21, n. 1153.

98. "Thus, while the act of being actualizes the corresponding essence principle of a given entity and makes that entity actually exist, simultaneously the essence principle receives and limits the act of being. Neither preexists as such apart from the other, and each enjoys its appropriate priority in the order of nature (not in the order of time) with respect to its particular ontological function within a given entity" (Wippel, *Metaphysical Thought*, 129–30).

99. D. C. Schindler, "What's the Difference?," 24, quoting Aquinas, *De Potentia Dei*, q. 3, a. 16, ad 4.

100. D. C. Schindler, "What's the Difference?," 3.

Conclusion

What we see in these essential elements of Thomas's thought—the real distinction, *esse* as *completum et simplex sed non subsistens*, and analogy encompassing causality and participation—"is a pervasive and inexorable polarity in the core of worldly being, which we might say represents its deepest truth."[101] Instead of the antagonistic opposition of various dualisms (mind and body, immanent and transcendent, human and nonhuman, universal and individual), in polar relations "each aspect contains the other (asymmetrically), and so they can be understood only with respect to each other."[102] Both nominalism and realism inadequately comprehend Aquinas's thought:

> Nominalism is right to deny the reality of the forms considered in themselves, and realism is right to insist that the forms nevertheless exist. Both aspects are true: Humanity is "nothing" in comparison to a particular human being, but this does not invalidate the complementary affirmation that the totality of existing human beings will never fully exhaust what it means to be human, i.e., that the universal remains in some sense "higher" than the particular.[103]

We turn next to Erich Przywara, who brought the Thomistic *analogia entis* back into the philosophical discussion of the twentieth century and further developed a dynamic understanding of this polarity, which might be seen as analogy in dramatic motion, simultaneously distinguishing and relating.

Erich Przywara

The being—Sein—which all philosophies take to be the primordial question and primordial datum with respect to everything else, does not (subsequently) "have" analogy as an attribute or as something developing from it; rather analogy is being, and thus thought is . . . analogy. As this primordial dynamic, analogy is a rhythm—just as, according to Pythagoras, the cosmos vibrates with a resonant rhythm.[104]

---

101. D. C. Schindler, "What's the Difference?," 22.
102. D. C. Schindler, *Dramatic Structure*, 79.
103. D. C. Schindler, "What's the Difference?," 23.
104. Przywara, *Analogia Entis*, 314.

Iterations of the problem of the One and the Many in the twentieth and twenty-first centuries, not just in philosophy but also in fields like ecology, were expressed in Enlightenment-inspired dualism, an almost pantheistic monism, or a postmodern indiscriminate pluralism. All suffer from a refusal of mediation best answered by analogy, especially Erich Przywara's ontology of the "suspended middle" in the dynamic interplay of the *esse* and essence of Aquinas's real distinction.

Przywara (1889–1972) was a philosopher and theologian born in what is now Katowice, Poland. He was a committed and public anti-Nazi, whose editorial offices were closed by the Gestapo. Przywara entered into dialogue not only with theologians, but with philosophers *as* philosophers, particularly Husserl and Heidegger. He greatly influenced other philosophers like Edith Stein (she credits him in the preface to her *Finite and Infinite Being*); his *Analogia Entis* "clearly pointed the way from phenomenology to metaphysics, given that (as metaphysics) it begins precisely with phenomenological questions."[105] Describing his homeland as a place where interacting opposites united, such as Romanticism and technological innovation, he also appreciated this theme of unity within the rhythmic interplay of opposites in polyphonic musical forms.[106]

Przywara's unique contribution to the metaphysics of gift was the development of the doctrine of the *analogia entis*'s unity-in-difference as a living, vital polarity, not a static one, and showed it to be *the formal principle of metaphysics as such*. This dynamic understanding of analogy is extended to many other relationships in crucially important ways; for example, in the "suspended co-belonging"[107] of being and consciousness, neither is the privileged point of departure. It is this contribution that we will focus on here, first commenting on its original religious context and then briefly on its dynamism. Finally, we will trace Przywara's application of the *analogia entis* to metaphysics as such.

Philosophy and Analogy

For Przywara, "The shape of philosophy can be defined more precisely in light of its standing with regard to science and theology."[108] Science inves-

---

105. Betz, "After Barth," 42.
106. See Betz, "Translator's Introduction," 12.
107. Gonzales, "Why We Need Erich Przywara," 161.
108. Przywara, *Analogia Entis*, 401.

tigates the inner order, coherence, and lawfulness—*logos*—of particular regions of reality; hence "bio-logy" and "psycho-logy." Whether it examines material data (positive facts, in the extreme becoming positivism) or it seeks a pure form or structure of its given area (constructive science, in the extreme becoming constructivism), it proceeds from "below to above." Theology proceeds from "above to below," its subject matter being, among other things, "the being and history of the entire world as it derives from God."[109]

Philosophy, he says, occupies the middle ground. Its very name—*philo-sophia*—means both the love of and the seeking of wisdom, and reveals its "transitive" nature: "Only itself in participating in what is other to itself, namely Wisdom . . . . as participatory loving-towards."[110] It is the role of philosophy to "unfold the coherence and meaning of being and history."[111] What emerges from it is "a philosophy of the intrinsic *ontological correlation between existence and essence*: an ontology or metaphysics of creaturely being."[112] Przywara distinguishes between "fallen" philosophy, which seeks absolutes it cannot attain, and "redeemed" philosophy, which points beyond itself not only to this analogical *esse*-essence distinction *within entities*, but all the way to the "incomparably greater analogy,"[113] the ontological relation between the entity and God. The sign of redeemed philosophy, its inner form, is the "analogy of greater dissimilarity in every unity."[114] Hart says,

> At its most elementary, what Przywara calls the *analogia entis* is simply the scrupulous and necessary rejection of two opposed errors, each the mirror inversion of the other: the equally reductive and equally "metaphysical" alternatives of pure identity and pure dialectic. To the degree that any metaphysics remains confined to the oscillator between total otherness and total identity, it can conceive of no "resolution" of the difference between the absolute and the contingent that is not in some sense tragic; for—as both Western and Eastern philosophies attest—such a metaphysics must affirm either the "necessary" violences of

---

109. Przywara, *Analogia Entis*, 402.
110. Gonzales, "Why We Need Erich Przywara," 163.
111. Przywara, *Analogia Entis*, 405.
112. Przywara, *Analogia Entis*, 407.
113. Przywara, *Analogia Entis*, 408.
114. Przywara, *Analogia Entis*, 403.

historical dialectics or the final nothingness of perfect identity or the perfect void.[115]

We will see that, for Przywara, analogy is both dynamic and is the formal principle of metaphysics as such—that is, beyond all particular metaphysics and for all metaphysics.

Analogy as a Musical Dynamic

Przywara continued to develop what first appeared in Aquinas: that analogy was not simply about verbal predication, nor about one or another attribute of being; rather, *being itself was analogical*. What was innovative in Przywara's thought was that he saw analogy as having more in common with music; not only was analogy not mere words, but it could barely be captured in words. Analogy was not an immobile equilibrium or fixed midpoint. He said that it is in no way a principle "that is fundamentally static from which everything else would be deduced or to which it would be reduced. It is essentially the basic dynamism in which the intra-created oscillates."[116] The word translated as "oscillates" is "*schwingend*," which "indicates a vibrant—and ultimately musical—swinging and swaying back and forth."[117] Betz explains that "understanding Przywara's *analogia entis* is not simply a matter of seeing the notes of a musical score, . . . but of hearing with a musical ear the proper *stress* of its rhythm."[118] As Przywara said, "Only in the sense of such a rhythm and such a measure is analogy a 'principle.' Ontically as being and poetically as thought, it is 'principally' the mystery of the primordial music of this rhythm—as with the fugues in Bach's 'Art of the Fugue,' which, interweaving one another, pass beyond themselves into 'great silence.'"[119]

---

115. Hart, "Destiny of Christian Metaphysics," 401.

116. Przywara quoted in O'Meara, *Erich Przywara*, 80.

117. Przywara, *Analogia Entis*, xxiin6. The terms "oscillate," "polar," "tension," etc. are used analogously when speaking intra-worldly and when speaking of God and creation.

118. See Betz, "Translator's Introduction," 86.

119. Przywara, *Analogia Entis*, 314.

Analogy as the Formal Principle of Metaphysics as Such

STAGES

The emergence of analogy from philosophy as the principle of metaphysics as such is covered in the four stages in the first section of the *Analogia Entis*. In it, Przywara attends to the evident tensions between a transcendental philosophy of consciousness (the question of essences) and a philosophy of being (the question of being and our historical-existential being-in-the-world).[120]

In §1, Przywara notes that today we take for granted an opposition between the physical and the mental, between being and consciousness, between "realism" and "idealism,"[121] between the problem of metaphysics as a problem of the structure of being or of the structure of thought. This dualistic worldview obscures the origin of metaphysics, which was something very different for Aristotle. For him, the relation of the two is not opposition, but is simply the relation between "the more universal to the particular."[122] *Physis* is the more universal term, the mode of being whereby an entity has within itself the principle of movement and rest,[123] while *psyche* is the more particular and "more exalted form of this power of self-grounding," the place of definitions and ideas.[124] Metaphysics, then, is the "going behind into the back-grounds of the being proper to *physis*, whose highest instance is *psyche*."[125]

Having lost this original unity, the problem that issues forth is the notion of a "neutral duality" between "the act of cognition, which questions, and the object of cognition, at which its question is directed."[126] The interrogation can take many forms: Heidegger's "My question is the self-expression of being, which questions"; German idealism's "My question is the question of consciousness concerning being"; the Scholastic "My question proceeds through consciousness and beyond it to being"; and modern philosophy's (from Descartes through Kant and beyond)

---

120. Betz, *After Barth*, 59.
121. Przywara, *Analogia Entis*, 119.
122. Przywara, *Analogia Entis*, 119.
123. See Aristotle, "Physics," II, 1, 192b (236–37).
124. Przywara, *Analogia Entis*, 120.
125. Przywara, *Analogia Entis*, 120.
126. Przywara, *Analogia Entis*, 120.

"My question is more originally the question concerning being in the consciousness that questions."[127]

And so the methodology, Przywara says, is either "meta-ontic" (beginning with being) or "meta-noetic" (beginning with consciousness). In reality, however, the "either/or" is between "a meta-noetics that provides a point of departure for a meta-ontics and a meta-ontics that finds its reflection, at the last, in a meta-noetics."[128] Meta-noetic questions about acts of knowledge immediately move backward to ontological categories; the meta-ontic "moves backward in self-critique" toward the meta-noetic, which "transcends itself, in a forward intentionality" toward the others. Their mutual implication is manifest in Aquinas's statement that the first object on the *intellect* is *being*—a receptivity toward that-which-is. *Both meta-ontics and meta-noetics appear to be necessary, and yet at the same time impossible*, impossible because neither one can retreat into "an enclosure of its own purity"—each is already pervaded by the other.[129]

The metaphysics of creatures, then, is a suspended tension between being and consciousness, and so the real question to ask is, which one is primary; which one provides the originary point of departure for the other?[130] He concludes that the meta-ontic is the *objectively* prior and comprehensive category, and the meta-noetic is *methodologically* prior; the dynamic epistemological tension is

> rooted in a dynamic *ontological* tension between essence and existence, which is ontologically prior to any methodological considerations. In other words, *for Przywara, the epistemological instability that manifests itself in the ineluctable back and forth between a meta-ontics and a meta-noetics is ultimately a reflection, at the level of method, of the inherent instability of creaturely being as such.*[131]

Creaturely being is "unstable" because no creature is the source of its own existence. While the essence, as is normally understood in philosophy, makes the creature what it is, at the same time, "essence and existence are related in the creature in such a way that the essence of the creature is never fully given—that is, never identical or reducible to

---

127. Przywara, *Analogia Entis*, 120.
128. Przywara, *Analogia Entis*, 121.
129. Przywara, *Analogia Entis*, 121.
130. Przywara, *Analogia Entis*, 121.
131. Betz, *After Barth*, 60 (emphasis mine).

its existence—but is always on the horizon of its existence as something to be attained."[132] The "formally constitutive basic formula of creaturely metaphysics," Przywara concludes in §1, is "essence in-and-beyond existence."[133]

The tensions back up to the transcendentals—truth, beauty, and goodness.[134] For Aristotle, he says, *nous* (from which "noetic" is derived) designates the crowning of a hierarchy that includes "scientific, ethical, and artistic modes of consciousness" that aim at the true, the good, and the beautiful,[135] and *on* (from which "ontic" is derived), rather than indicating a "purely factual presence," is synonymous with the "proper being" of the transcendentals.[136] The tension between a meta-ontics and a meta-noetics is revealed as a tension between a classical "transcendental metaphysics," which primarily begins with meta-ontics, and the "metaphysical transcendentalism" of modernity (as in Kantian transcendentalism), which primarily begins with meta-noetics and which looks at a convergence of the logical (the true, "pure reason"), the ethical (the good, "practical reason"), and the aesthetic (the beautiful, "synthesizing judgment") towards being.[137]

The question is whether, in the unity of metaphysics and transcendentalism, the transcendentals are determined by the noetic (the immanent metaphysics of Kant and his followers) or by the ontic (unfolding the philosophies of Plato and Aristotle). Once again, after a dense and detailed argument that ranges through the history of philosophy and even meta-mathematics, Przywara finds no stable resolution: instead, the two points of departure[138] lead to a threefold path of reflection:

> The meta-noetic (as the first problem of metaphysics) will thus have to commence from a general problematic of consciousness,

132. Betz, *After Barth*, 60.
133. Przywara, *Analogia Entis*, 124.
134. Przywara, *Analogia Entis*, 125.
135. Przywara, *Analogia Entis*, 125. In fact, Przywara states unequivocally that "noetic, naturally, means Truth-Beauty-Goodness, in the fullest sense" (*Analogia Entis*, 198n1).
136. Przywara, *Analogia Entis*, 125. Also "energetic" in the act–potency relation.
137. Przywara, *Analogia Entis*, 126.
138. Transcendental metaphysics starts with a "pre-transcendental, pure comprehension of being" and moves toward a comprehension of being's threefold truth, beauty, and goodness and its unity, while metaphysical transcendentalism comprehends the threefold truth, beauty, and goodness and aims at a comprehension of being in its unity (Przywara, *Analogia Entis*, 130).

from which the threefold radiance of the transcendentals will be gradually abstracted in order thereby to guide this general problematic to its proper depth. Likewise, the meta-ontic (as the second problem) will allow a general problematic of being to evolve from within into a consideration of being in its transcendental aspect, and thus into its most precise form. And finally, in an explicit meta-physics (as we may well denominate the third problematic of the correlation of consciousness and being), it is this very correlation (of the "world") that must proceed along the same path: from its most general shape, to an explicit recognition of its fully transcendental dimension (i.e. the correlation of the noetically and ontically transcendental) to its ultimate formal structure.[139]

And so, Przywara is brought back to the open tension of "essence in-and-beyond existence" now seeing "the greater scope of its domain."[140]

The tensions continue in his examination of a deductive *a priori* metaphysics "with its emphasis upon the purity of a transcendental subject and its alleged capacity for timeless, superhistorical truth" and an inductive *a posteriori* metaphysics, "which takes history, the senses, tradition, and embodiment seriously as that through which any superhistorical truth is discerned."[141]

Analogy functions for Przywara not only in the God–world relation but also in the intra-worldly tension of essence and existence within each *ens*, preserving the tension between philosophies of existence and philosophies of essence that in the modern world mutate into an oppositional either/or "between an abstract, universal, and ultimately sterile rationalism disconnected from history and tradition (characteristic of the Enlightenment) and a radical, individualistic voluntarism that can make out no rational norms and terminates in the historicism, relativism, and will to power of Nietzsche."[142] One deprives history of any real truth; the other dissolves truth into history.

In the end, like meta-ontics and meta-noetics, *a priori* and *a posteriori* metaphysics are both necessary and both impossible (in pure forms).

---

139. Przywara, *Analogia Entis*, 131. In German, "problematic" can mean stimulating or provocative, not simply "questionable." See O'Meara, *Erich Przywara*, 61.

140. Przywara, *Analogia Entis*, 131.

141. Betz, *After Barth*, 64.

142. Betz, *After Barth*, 50–51.

Each metaphysic is irreducible to the other and at the same time not separated, and each one deepens the other; hence, they are analogical.

After *a priori* and *a posteriori* metaphysics, Przywara discusses philosophical and theological metaphysics in §4, which will not be reviewed here. We will take the next sections out of order, first looking very briefly at §7, on philosophical history, followed by §5 and §6, on the basis of analogy in the foundations of logic.

History

Przywara's stated task was to show that the *analogia entis* is the actual principle of "metaphysics-as-such."[143] He says that this is further evidenced by the fact that the nonhistorical reflections converge with the historical analysis of the tradition, "from the antithesis between Heraclitus and Parmenides, to the interplay of emphases between Plato and Aristotle, and to the further interplay of Platonic and Aristotelian emphases between Augustine and Thomas," as well as in the search to secure a starting point: Descartes's "mental act in the enclosure of the *cogito*"; Kant's "form of the act as such (the transcendental)"; for Husserl, "the ultimate irreducibility of the objective and intentional forms of the mental act."[144] Yet, every attempt to establish a starting point either means that point is simply *posited* as the starting point, or the attempt to establish it as such ends in a circle. The problem has always been how to hold the two poles together, and the solution is analogy.

That the *analogia entis* is the formal principle of metaphysics as such can be seen in the way that the formal and historical considerations converge, "as it is decisively figured in the problematic of the principle of non-contradiction."[145] We now turn to that principle.

Logic

If there were any doubt that analogy is the radical—at the root—principle of metaphysics, one need only look at the tension within logic itself. The foundational principle of logic is the principle of noncontradiction, formulated by Aristotle to encompass both the meta-noetic and the

---

143. Przywara, *Analogia Entis*, 307.
144. Przywara, *Analogia Entis*, 308–9.
145. Przywara, *Analogia Entis*, 307.

meta-ontic: "For the same attribute cannot, in the same way, both belong and not belong to a thing. . . . for it is not possible to believe something both to be and not to be."[146] Noncontradiction, then, says Przywara, is the foundation of the *analogia entis* and "the most basic and most formal ground of the interpenetration between the meta-noetic and the meta-ontic . . . . the most fundamental possibility for the activity of thought itself."[147] Analogy is the metaphysical premise and expression of noncontradiction, which serves as analogy's foundation within logic. The *analogia entis* is thus distinguished from both pure logic and pure dialectic, by which Przywara affirms: "We have hereby certainly (despite and amid all our historical reflections) achieved the standpoint proper to a superhistorical *objective problematic.*"[148]

As shown by Aristotle, noncontradiction, with its interpenetration between the meta-ontic and meta-noetic, is *formal*, "a formal position that precedes even the most elementary position regarding material content."[149] It is also *negative* in that it contrasts with the *positive* Principle of Identity (in the meta-ontic form, "what is, is"; in the meta-noetic form, "what is valid, is valid"). Finally, it is negative in a *reductive* sense: "Even if one denies everything, one cannot deny 'this.'"[150]

The principle of noncontradiction as the "most fundamental possibility for the activity of thought as such"[151] is found in the three basic modes of thought: in the logic of identity ("pure logic"), in the contradiction of dialectic, and in the mode of analogy. By tracing the history of philosophy, Przywara shows that while philosophies of identity continually seek a more basic logic (an X = X), and dialectical philosophies aim at pure contradiction, only in analogy is noncontradiction preserved as "negative reductive formality." He takes Heraclitus and Parmenides as paradigmatic for the first two modes and shows that neither a

---

146. Przywara, *Analogia Entis*, 198–99n3, Przywara is quoting Aristotle's *Metaphysics*, IV, 3, 1005b19–24. In the same context, he also quotes *Metaphysics*, XI, 5, 1061b36–1026a20: "The same thing cannot simultaneously be and not be [and hence] it is impossible to make contradictory true assertions regarding the same thing," which also shows the tension between being and knowing.

147. Przywara, *Analogia Entis*, 199.

148. Przywara, *Analogia Entis*, 238.

149. Przywara, *Analogia Entis*, 199.

150. Przywara, *Analogia Entis*, 199. He continues, "In this regard it was Augustine who gave the principle its sharpest formulation: 'the doubt that doubts everything still cannot doubt that it doubts'" (*Analogia Entis*, 199).

151. Przywara, *Analogia Entis*, 199.

philosophy of "the Many" nor of "the One" can maintain the principle of noncontradiction; the term "unstable" is quite accurate, as in the instability of radioactive elements whose nuclei quickly decay.

Consciousness and being are "a constantly surging flux of oppositions, which suggest being lost upon a chaotic sea."[152] Science attempts to capture the origin and end, either moving from hypotheses to conclusions ("from a multiplicity of streams to their *one* confluence") or from hypotheses to principals ("from multiplicity back to the *one* origin").[153] Still, "pure opposition seems to be the final word," yet even Heraclitus is forced to envision a logos, recognizing an "utterly beautiful harmony of differences."[154] For Parmenides's thought, in which the oppositions are "merely vain echoes," not truth, the denial of change "leads one to take truth and falsity, being and non-being as the same, and thus noetically and ontically to eliminate the principle of noncontradiction."[155] For Heraclitus, if everything changes, there is no truth (the true can turn into the false) and no being (being can turn into nothing). "Consequently there is no longer any ultimate difference between true and false, being and non-being, and the principle of noncontradiction, noetically and ontically, is done away with once again."[156]

Conclusion

The comprehension of analogy as dynamic is seminal for the metaphysics of gift, which in turn will affect everything else. To take just one example, in a discussion of Przywara's understanding of the "suspended" ontological position, the immanent oscillation and asymmetrical reciprocity between *esse* and essence within the creature, Michael Hanby notes that the analogy internal to the creature preserves *legitimate* scientific abstraction and *legitimate* scientific autonomy by avoiding the metaphysics of positivism, which evacuates the things of the world of their interior meaning and novelty, emptying the world of wonder and mystery. With the erasure of the real distinction, with the loss of all formalizing and finalizing activity, with causality reduced to

152. Przywara, *Analogia Entis*, 203.
153. Przywara, *Analogia Entis*, 203.
154. Przywara, *Analogia Entis*, 204.
155. Przywara, *Analogia Entis*, 204–6.
156. Przywara, *Analogia Entis*, 206.

nothing more than "pushing and pulling," with the invention of a concept of "matter" as "a fully actualized status apart from and prior to form, natures, or relations, which have been deprived of ontological status,"[157] the world is reduced to an assemblage of extrinsically related parts and their interactions, which leads inexorably to an ethic of mere utility. To recover the truth of analogy is to recover the unique individuality of every single existing thing, not only in its givenness as studied by science, but in its giftedness, as a being defined not by its separateness from other things, but by the relations that constitute it. To recover analogy is

> to "save the appearances" by recovering the world as subject of its own being . . . with its own irreducible mystery always pressing toward expression as form, a mystery that is neither the opposite of truth and knowledge nor the unknown awaiting discovery just beyond their boundaries but an immanent feature of them. Indeed . . . *it is precisely this coincidence of mystery and truth in the being-in-itselfness of the world exhibited in the "interplay" between essence and existence that makes real knowledge possible, inasmuch as it protects the actuality of the world from the homogenizing violence of technological abstraction.*[158]

The tensions uncovered and illuminated in Przywara's reflections are all founded on the same dynamic. Each instability is shown to be a result of creaturely instability flowing back to the distinction between essence and existence. In the end, it comes down to what Balthasar called Przywara's metaphysics of action and what Casarella called the metaphysics of pilgrimage. Przywara has presented a dramatic interpretation of Aquinas's real distinction for which creaturely being is an "inherently between, sojourning, wayfaring, relational being,"[159] always in tension between being and becoming, always open to transcendence.

Ferdinand Ulrich

Ulrich is best read as judging all things from the perspective of love. . . . Because love lies ultimately at the source of all things, the world is an expression of love, it has love as its form and purpose, or in short: love is the meaning of being.[160]

---

157. Hanby, "Creation as Aesthetic Analogy," 353.
158. Hanby, "Creation as Aesthetic Analogy," 369–70 (emphasis mine).
159. Gonzales, "Why We Need Erich Przywara," 162.
160. D. C. Schindler, "Grace of Being," 150.

Ferdinand Ulrich (1931–2020), the "unavoidable reference point for a metaphysics of being as love and freedom as gift,"[161] was born in what is now the Czech Republic. Philosopher Gerd Haeffner said that Ulrich was the one who found the principle that modern philosophy, "torn between immanentism and extrinsicism . . . sought in vain. In vain because it failed to rethink Greek metaphysics . . . in the light of a more original starting point: the question of being, intertwined with the experience of absolute being as love."[162] At the heart of his thought is the giftedness of all things; where there is instead "the impossibility of perceiving being as 'gift,'"[163] philosophical thought goes awry. It is radically *giving away* in a generosity that grants the recipient its own goodness and autonomy (so that it may in turn become fruitful when reenacted in community with others), that constitutes love. It was Ulrich who first brought the account of being as love into the philosophical discourse in *Homo Abyssus*.[164]

Metaphysics of Gift as Love

The Interplay of Wealth and Poverty

The "poverty" of love is in fact nothing but the ultimate seal of its superabundant wealth.[165]

Earlier we spoke about "gift" as an ontological truth that refers by analogy to the dynamic of giving and receiving at every level of existence.[166] Love too must be seen in all its ontological depth, and since it is "ontologically inscribed," love in this sense is the primary analogue from which other loves derive their meaning. Love as the meaning of being is not self-evident. We tend to think of love as acts of affection, freedom, and will; these acts appear to apply only to relations between persons, and hence do not reach the ontological foundations.

---

161. Oster, "Thinking Love," 664–65n15.

162. Haeffner, review of Ulrich's *Gegenwart der Freiheit*, in *Theologie und Philosophie* 51 (1976), cited in Oster, "Thinking Love," 661.

163. Ulrich, *Homo Abyssus*, 30.

164. Published in 1961 and translated into English in 2018 by D. C. Schindler.

165. Ulrich, *Homo Abyssus*, 372.

166. This includes physical and chemical transference of energy, stimulus and response in physiology, and the mutual exchange of commerce, etc. See Schmitz, *Gift*, 77.

Like Heidegger, Ulrich thought we must begin with being, but unlike Heidegger, he did not reject Aquinas.[167] Instead, he brought Aquinas's metaphysics of being into dialogue with modern and postmodern philosophy. For Ulrich, the importance of Aquinas's "*esse significat aliquid completum et simplex sed non subsistens*"—*esse* is complete and simple, but not subsistent—cannot be overestimated. This statement "designates the very core of his philosophy,"[168] though, as noted earlier, it appears to contradict itself. But according to Ulrich, the two aspects of *esse* do not contradict each other: they represent a single phenomenon understood from two perspectives, as both the Morning Star and the Evening Star refer to the planet Venus. They only appear in opposition if we forget *esse*'s self-diffusing power into the full being, *ens*, that-which-is, and imagine it juxtaposed to the things it "makes be." For Ulrich, as for Aquinas, *esse* is the similitude of God's goodness,[169] and goodness, in turn, is self-diffusive, self-giving.[170] In the really existing thing we can hold on to both the tension and resolution of the paradox:

> Think of *esse* as the sheer act of giving oneself away, or letting be. In this respect, *esse* is indeed perfect, but it, so to speak, *has its perfection only in that which is other than itself*, i.e., in the beings it makes be. Its own perfection is always already given away, or more adequately, possessed as having been given away. Thus, the perfect wealth of esse is coincident with a complete poverty.[171]

Unlike the purely empty being of Heidegger, which is the most universal of concepts, the non-subsistence of *esse* is a perfection, not a

---

167. "For Thomas, being, *esse*, is neither simply identical with entities . . . nor, again, is it (the content of) a purely univocal concept that supposedly enables us to punch through the wall of finitude to reach God (under the guise of 'being' in its 'absolute' form), and which, in so doing, perverts metaphysics into a formalistic tool of what Heidegger chastised as onto-theology" (Oster, "Thinking Love," 667–68).

168. Bieler, "*Analogia Entis*," 322.

169. "*Esse est similitudo divinae bonitatis*" (Aquinas, *De Veritate*, q. 22, a. 2, ad 2).

170. "*Bonum dicitur diffusivum sui esse*" (Aquinas, *Summa Theologiae*, I, q. 5, a. 4, ad 2).

171. D. C. Schindler, "What's the Difference?," 19 (emphasis mine). Martin Bieler discusses the giver and gift in Ulrich's *Leben in der Einheit von Leben und Tod* (*Life in the Unity of Life and Death*): "Presence and separation include each other, for only by separation is the presence for the other realized. Only if the giver himself is present in the gift does the separation of the gift carry something valuable across to the other. True giving is always both: presence and separation, presence *through* separation" (Bieler, "*Analogia Entis*," 332).

deficiency. Thus Ulrich avoids two extremes. First, he does not focus on *non-subsistence*; thus we resist "positivism's temptation to bury being in the things-that-are, which then become the empty material out of which a loveless science forces concrete subsistence to emerge as the result of its own autonomous experiment."[172] Second, he does not hypostatize being's *simplicity and completeness* so that it can be subsumed into human conceptualization; thus we avoid the onto-theology postmoderns reject.

Analogy

> *Only analogy is the true expression of the givenness of esse, because in analogy the* completum et simplex *and the* non subsistens *of esse are saved at the same time. Analogy shows that esse is fully present inside the limits of ens, because esse is poured out (*non subsistens*) without losing its unity (*completum et simplex*). So in analogy the individual appears as a mode of being to whom the gift of being (esse) is really given.*[173]

Bernard Montagnes remarked that "the structure of analogy and that of participation are rigorously parallel: they correspond to each other as the conceptual aspect and the real aspect of the unity of being."[174] Ulrich considers the two forms of participation that Aquinas distinguished: participation *per compositionem* (by composition) and participation *per similitudinem* (by similitude).[175] Participation by composition is based on a duality between the receiver and that which is given (hence the composition of two different elements; the first receives the second in a limited manner). To participate is essentially to possess the gift received, and the receiver "limits" the gift in direct proportion to his capacity to receive, as a dog receives training from his master in a manner limited by its mode of being. In participation by similitude, two things share a form, but one is imperfect in contrast to the perfect form on which it depends; this creates a hierarchy. By similitude, the dog and his owner participate in life, but in a hierarchical manner, along with fish, flowers, and algae. Both aspects are necessary, interconnected, and indispensable:

---

172. Oster, "Thinking Love," 691.
173. Bieler, "*Analogia Entis*," 333–34.
174. Montagnes, *Doctrine of the Analogy of Being*, 91.
175. Ulrich, *Homo Abyssus*, 127.

> If one of the aspects is given up, the analogy is destroyed. If there was only a *participatio per similitudinem,* the result would be univocation. If there was only a *participatio per compositionem,* the result would be equivocation. . . . The aspect of univocation in metaphysical thinking corresponds to the overemphasis of the *completum et simplex,* whereas the overemphasis of the *non subsistens* of *esse* leads to equivocation. The *modus medius* of analogy is reached only if one maintains the unity of the *completum et simplex* with the *non subsistens,* of presence and separation.[176]

If "univocity" means that finite being is just an extension of absolute being, as in Neoplatonic emanation (the gift is not truly separated), and "equivocity" denotes an absolute difference (there is no presence of the giver in the gift), then "analogy" reveals that *"truly everything* is given (presence of the giver in the gift through loving separation of the gift with respect to the receiver)."[177]

To see, then, that love is the meaning of being requires a deeper understanding of the truth about gift. In true gift there is a real separation from the giver, although the presence of the giver is still within the gift. The gift *mediates the presence of the giver, without compromising the gift's goodness as a gift*; this double character of given and mediation preserves the real distinction. Recall that pseudo-gifts would include those that are really just transactions, without the presence of the giver (the gift is totally separate from the giver), or the giver might give the gift while expecting something in return. The paradoxical nature of the true gift is that it is "only in giving *gratuitously,* in a generous *letting go* of the gift" that the giver truly gives himself.[178]

Thus Ulrich interprets Aquinas as touching on the mystery of created being as love. "Being is wealth, unity, plenitude, light, life, goodness: pure, simple act (*completum et simplex*). Nevertheless, as such it is always given away radically. In this sense, it can be thought of as poverty, refusal to cling to self, expropriatedness, emptiness (the emptiness of love)."[179]

---

176. Bieler, "*Analogia Entis,*" 333–34.
177. Bieler, "*Analogia Entis,*" 334.
178. D. C. Schindler, "The Grace of Being," 153.
179. Oster, "Thinking Love," 672.

Being as Love and Action

> *If we ... no longer recognize the other and indeed one's own freedom as gift, then the healthy structure of the relationship between giver and gift as the giver's generous separation of the gift from himself (which precisely allows him to remain present in the gift) collapses, and so does the receiver's reception of the gift that extends the generosity.*[180]

The notion of *generosity* Ulrich highlights is central to the metaphysics of gift; it is at the heart of relationship, community, and solidarity with others, and hence of all action as it plays out socially, ethically, and politically. For Ulrich, logical distinctions in the structure of being are related to human freedom, and "so can be described both conceptually and in terms of a disposition or way of relating."[181] His critique of modernity is not merely an intellectual critique, nor simply a moral critique; rather, modernity is a failure of love (understood comprehensibly) to encompass both the will and the intellect, at once and inseparably.

In the view of that metaphysics, original creaturely being (that-which-is) is not a mere continuation of prior being (as in emanation/emergence); it is really distinct, and preserves the real difference. It is *given* in the reception of *esse*. "The gift of being is the gift of ontological freedom; it is the liberation into one's own subsistence."[182] It is the person, where substance/subsistence becomes conscious of freedom, in whom the gift character of reality and being-as-love is most truly re-created; for persons, the "fundamental *operatio* proper to [their] nature ... is their own affirmation of the communication of *esse*."[183] Substantial being is structured as generous in the manner of gift: of what gives only as first given, and only then is able to participate in this generosity by passing it along, reenacting the giving/receiving that characterizes being as love.

At the beginning of this chapter, we discussed an alternative view of gift: one that neither compels nor excludes reciprocity. If gifts requiring a recompense collapse into mere transaction, and gifts that bar reciprocity are an abstraction from the community of being, this alternative is a composite, a relational hylomorphism of mutual freedoms: a generous overflowing, both ontologically inscribed *and* in relation as an interior

---

180. Bieler, "Introduction," xliv.
181. D. C. Schindler, "Grace of Being," 151.
182. Oster, "Thinking Love," 683.
183. Bieler, "*Analogia Entis*," 329.

bond. This gift is a sign of the paradox of *esse* (which is not a contradiction but a distinction seen in contrast) as both non-subsistent and complete, or as both "poverty" and "wealth"; the paradox of true gift is that the giver "empties" himself, the gift is both generously "let go of"—truly given—*and* the giver is still present in the gift, open to receiving in turn. So there is "no opposition in principle between the in-itself reality of the gift, and its relatedness, its transparency to the giver."[184] The gift can be a gift in itself as well as establish true, relational communion to another who is also a being given in freedom.

What is the metaphysical basis for this third way? Ulrich applies a rigorous philosophical analysis to this question in *Homo Abyssus*, showing how creaturely acts and potencies are structured according to the logic of gift; we return once again to Aquinas's insight into *esse* as a similitude of divine goodness:

> Divine love did not allow him to "remain in himself without fruit," that is, without the production of creatures, but love "moved him to operate" according to a most excellent mode of operation according as he produced all things in being (*esse*). For from love of his goodness it proceeded that he willed to pour out and to communicate his goodness to others, insofar as it is possible, namely by way of similitude, and thus his goodness did not remain in him, but flowed out into others.[185]

As a similitude of the good, "natural things have a natural inclination not only towards their own proper good . . . but also to spread abroad their own good among others, so far as possible."[186] Furthermore, in *De Veritate*,

> A thing is called a being inasmuch as it is considered absolutely, but good, as has already been made clear, in relation to other things. Now it is by its essential principles that a thing is fully constituted in itself so that it subsists; but it is not so perfectly constituted as to stand as it should in relation to everything outside itself except by means of accidents added to the essence, because the operations by which one thing is in some sense joined to another proceed from the essence through powers distinct from it. Consequently *nothing achieves goodness*

---

184. D. C. Schindler, "Grace of Being," 154.
185. Aquinas, *De divinis nominibus*, cap. 4, l. 9 quoted in Healy, *Eschatology*, 27–28.
186. Aquinas, *Summa Theologiae*, I, q. 19, a. 2.

> *absolutely unless it is complete in both its essential and its accidental principles.*[187]

The highest good is both good in itself and good in its effects; it reaches its fullness not only absolutely but in relation, in both being and acting. Ulrich agrees, repeatedly emphasizing that "not the reality, the mere *substantia*, is the final aim of creation, but the *substantia* bringing forth accidents: the *substantia* acting in freedom. Far from being static, the analogy of being shows how being and action are inseparable."[188] As Ulrich puts it, the sense of being is "revealed in the good . . . through the substance's procession into the accidents and its self-communication to them."[189] The communication of being and of freedom are simultaneous, as the creature is given its own autonomy to act. D. C. Schindler looks in more detail at the meaning of the movement into the accidents and is worth quoting here in full:

> [For Ulrich], *esse* is really distinct from essence in all created being, so that it can be said to transcend all things that are without itself being either an existing thing in its own right, or a mere logical concept. As we saw, this is only non-dialectically possible insofar as being is understood as pure mediation or radical generosity. . . . The "to be" can be said to *belong* properly to things; it is so radically given away to things and subsequently so deeply received by them, it can be said in fact to be the *result* of a being's constitutive principles. But if the gift of being is so deeply inscribed in things as to be in some sense the things themselves (an *ens* is an *esse habens*), it means that *the essences of things cannot be thought of as self-enclosed quantities ("essence-blocks," as Ulrich puts it), but are themselves forms of generosity in their own order.* Substances concretely subsist as poured out, so to speak, into their accidents, living beings subsist in their proper operations by which they enter the world and the world enters them, and human beings have the actuality of their essence in the ecstatic and "redditive" acts of intellect and will in which they affirm the meaning of being and bring that meaning to fruition.[190]

---

187. Aquinas, *De Veritate*, q. 21, a. 5.
188. Bieler, "*Analogia Entis*," 329-30.
189. Ulrich, *Homo Abyssus*, 289.
190. D. C. Schindler, "The Grace of Being," 156-57 (emphasis mine). Accidents are here understood in the Aristotelian sense: interior to and constitutive of substance.

In terms of gift, accidents and operations are the way that gift is transmitted; as *esse* gives itself away in concrete, substantial beings, so those beings give themselves away through their agency. To illuminate Ulrich's interplay of gift, freedom, and love in the concrete situation of interpersonal relations, Oster presents the analogy of someone recognizing an undeveloped musical gift in a child and teaching the child to play the piano. A true teacher awakens within the child his own love of music, "a creative capacity of his own freedom, which he thus experiences as gift . . . at once totally received and totally the child's own."[191] The proposal precedes the child by being in the freedom of the teacher, and at the same time it was "in" the child as a "presupposition of the educator's love" (as with Kierkegaard, love presupposes that which it brings forth in the other is already, in some sense, "there").[192] This is a unity of free giving and free receiving and not a kind of forced teaching by coercion in a mechanical cause–effect relationship (though of course at first *some* imposed discipline is necessary before the child's desire is awakened). In this second case, the child,

> who is no longer loved as a unique, unmanipulable other, but is only the passive object of the educator's self-assertive will, confirms negatively the value of successful pedagogy. And when we transpose that positive value back into the metaphysical contemplation of being as love with the negative case in mind as a foil, we glimpse what it means to say that creation is a donation of being that lets the recipient of the donation be. We also begin to understand why that letting-be must include the gift of freedom, which liberates the other in the uniqueness and fruitfulness of its own self-being.[193]

Conclusion

Ulrich beholds the world in light of the gift of being, but, since the gift can be found and "touched" as such only in the concreteness of finite entities, Ulrich's contemplative gaze has a built-in attentiveness to the real world.[194]

---

191. Oster, "Thinking Love," 679.
192. Oster, "Thinking Love," 679.
193. Oster, "Thinking Love," 680 (emphasis mine).
194. Oster, "Thinking Love," 662.

In Ulrich's work, the mysterious interplay of the *esse*/essence distinction, the key ontological insight of Aquinas, becomes analogous to love between persons, a dynamic encounter of giving and receiving, of asymmetrical, reciprocal generosity, and a source of wonder. Recall that the science that followed Galileo had a mechanical view of causality, seeing it not as that which accounts for something, but rather that which produces an effect through direct contact. Causality is *communication* (primarily, communication of form), and communication means the unification of communicants by that which is shared. The gift of self—self-communication—is at the heart of love: "It belongs to the very essence of goodness to communicate itself to others."[195]

Hans Urs von Balthasar

Balthasar's point is simply that, unless hard thinking is awakened and sustained by wonderment over the splendor of being as love, it cannot ever see the point of going all the way to the bottom of any problem.[196]

Hans Urs von Balthasar (1905–88) was a monumental thinker, one who fits under no label. Immensely gifted, he was immersed in culture, music, and literature; his work engages with almost every great theologian, philosopher, and literary figure in history. However, his retrieval of past thinkers was never as one concerned simply to revive their work. Rather, he engaged with them as one who knew that their work could both take on new light from, and shed new light on, dialogue with current questions.

Balthasar was well aware of the dangers of losing sight of true metaphysics and the attempts to naturalize it. The true "point of origin for philosophy," he said, was "metaphysical wonderment," a wonderment that is "constantly on the point of turning into a marveling at the beauty of existence as a whole . . . of that order and orderliness . . . which the individual sciences are only too keen to enquire into."[197] Marveling only at the order of existence touches the *what* but never truly reaches the *why* of reality. The former is *natural wonder*, which lacks the radical surprise that things exist at all and cannot respond to the primary metaphysical question. Only in appreciating both *what* things are and *that* they are

---

195. Aquinas, *Summa Theologiae*, III, q. 1, a. 1.
196. Walker, "Love Alone," 37n42 (emphasis mine).
197. Balthasar, *Glory of the Lord V*, 646–47.

as "mutually implicatory aspects of a single phenomenon"[198] can natural things of the world maintain their unique integrity and enter into a relation with persons via *love* rather than control. The philosophical act lives from both Being and love.[199] Balthasar explains, "Love loves Being in an *a priori* way, for it knows that no science will ever track down the ground of why something exists rather than nothing at all. It receives it as a free gift and replies with free gratitude."[200]

Balthasar was deeply affected by the other philosophers we have discussed. Undoubtedly, he was led to being as love through Ferdinand Ulrich, "to whose views I owe so much" he said.[201] Further, he was "impressed by Przywara's dialectical interpretation of St. Thomas' real distinction,"[202] which he called "the source of all the religious and philosophical thought of humanity."[203] He saw that the expression of the human condition is already the metaphysical question illuminated by that distinction: a person recognizes his contingency ("I am, but I could also, however, not be") and sees that he is "a limited being in a limited world, but his reason is open to the unlimited, to all of Being."[204] He was also influenced by Przywara's re-introduction of Aquinas's *analogia entis* and its application to the history of philosophy, for Przywara "taught Balthasar to interpret the pathos of modern philosophy according to how it reacted to the doctrine of analogy. He made him see, in other words, the dilemmas that human thought runs into when it abandons the tensions represented in analogy."[205]

Heidegger had said that the distinctive crisis of Western metaphysics was the forgetfulness of Being. Balthasar said that Aquinas "is in harmony with Heidegger, with whom he shares the insight into the transcendence of Being, and into the fundamental distinction between Being and existent, which is fundamental for all thought," but, he continued, "even though their respective understandings of the nature of this distinction diverge from the first point on."[206] What the history of

---

198. D. C. Schindler, *Perfection of Freedom*, 23.
199. Balthasar, *Glory of the Lord V*, 645.
200. Balthasar, *Glory of the Lord V*, 647.
201. Balthasar, *Our Task*, 38.
202. Balthasar, *Our Task*, 38.
203. Balthasar, *My Work*, 112.
204. Balthasar, *My Work*, 112.
205. Oakes, *Pattern of Redemption*, 36.
206. Balthasar, *Glory of the Lord V*, 435.

philosophy has lost, and what Heidegger failed to attain, is a vision of Being that preserves wonder at its ever-deeper mystery while at the same time comprehending it in light of its transcendental attributes, its beauty, truth, and goodness. As Balthasar said of philosophy: "The apparent duality connoted by the word *philo-sophia*, when looked at profoundly enough, could ultimately be resolved in a living unity—and would thus, in its own distinctive way, display the analogy of worldly being which is said to be identically 'wisdom' and 'love.'"[207]

What is most pertinent to the metaphysics of gift is Balthasar's understanding of the real distinction and of the structure of the analogy of being as a relation of giver and gift, which will be most perfectly revealed in the concrete methodology of the "fourfold distinction" introduced in chapter 1. We will examine his thought on polarity as the solution to the enduring problem of the One and the Many, address the appearance/being duality in the encounter between subject and object, and then revisit his reflection on the Mother and Child as it informs metaphysics, epistemology, and ethics.

Polarity

The mystery of being for Balthasar is not the murky night of ambiguity in which being and man dissolve into one another, but instead the translucent joy of genuine mutuality.[208]

In regard to the problem of the One and the Many, Balthasar says that limited, finite creatures participate in the One in a *polar* manner. He developed his insights into polarity in concert with Aquinas and Przywara—the structure of reality is polar in the "real distinction"[209]— and also with Goethe, who spoke of polarity as that which first made itself known through observation and experience of the things of nature, such as electromagnetism and the systole/diastole of the cardiac cycle.

---

207. Balthasar, *Theo-Logic I*, 9.

208. D. C. Schindler, *Dramatic Structure*, 6.

209. The "real distinction" between essence and *esse*-existence "itself eludes univocity" and pervades "every last fiber of all finite being ... between the individual and the universal within unity; between "form" [Gestalt] and 'light' within beauty ... between obedience and freedom within ethics; between finite and infinite freedom, where the former attains its realization precisely by surrendering itself to the latter" (Balthasar, *Theo-Logic I*, 8–9).

Polarity, however, goes beyond natural processes. Oppositions in the form of various dualities have been found compelling from ancient times to the present. They manifest themselves in political and ecological oppositions, such as conservative versus liberal, or biocentrism versus anthropocentrism. But polarities have features that dualities do not. Dualities may cancel each other out; they may sit side by side in juxtaposition, often antagonistically; or, one may absorb the other. Polarity is not contradiction, in which "opposites are affirmed of one and the same thing at the same time and in the same respect,"[210] nor is it paradox characterized as irrational. What characterizes a polarity is that the two poles, while resisting identity, *are integral to each other*, and yet each is always irreducible to the other in a mutual reciprocity. Balthasar's "identity-in-tension" is the "unity-in-distinction" we have been addressing. Subject and object, universal and particular, immanent and transcendent, giving and receiving, thought and action, all are best understood in a polar manner, which *opens into true wonder:*

> The existence of such polarities gives finite being the consistency, vitality, and dignity that elevate it beyond mere facticity and make it the object of an unquenchable interest, indeed, of *a reverent, astonished wonderment*. For the more deeply the knower delves into these structures, the more they unveil themselves to him and, at the same time, withdraw behind the veil of their mystery.[211]

Regarding solidarity with others (whether socially or ecologically), rather than the acid bath of reductive monism, or the cutthroat competition in a zero-sum game between irreducible dualities (persons vs. nature, the individual vs. the collective), or the "murky ambiguity" of postmodern hermeneutical pluralism, there is polarity: "the translucent joy of genuine mutuality."[212] Relations can never be truly understood by taking one side in isolation from the other, or even accepting both in an uneasy truce; a polar relationship is a "both/and," "a unity that is not monadic and a duality that is not dualistic," one in which "each aspect contains the other (asymmetrically), and so they can be understood only with respect to each other."[213] Irreducibly different, yes, but as a mutual

---

210. D. C. Schindler, *Perfection of Freedom*, 23.
211. Balthasar, *Theo-Logic I*, 9 (emphasis mine).
212. D. C. Schindler, *Dramatic Structure*, 6.
213. D. C. Schindler, *Dramatic Structure*, 79.

interdependence, each side making a positive contribution to the other, they are inseparably one.

Polarity is essential to the metaphysics of gift, for which the original gift of being (the polarity of wealth and poverty within each existing thing) points to a greater mystery beyond, a mystery that each pole expresses "accurately but still inadequately,"[214] truly but not exhaustively. In the ultimate sense, Balthasar's polarity finds its source in the ontological level: one pole is being, which appears and expresses itself in the concrete particular, the other is the expressed form, which both reveals and conceals the inner mystery of being. This reflection brings us to the polarity between being and appearance, which has troubled philosophers for millennia.

Being Appears: The Dramatic Encounter of Subject and Object

In contrast to Heidegger, who connects truth to the mystery of being as something lying in darkness beyond particular beings, Balthasar shows that the mystery of being is revealed, that is, made immediately apparent, in and through the mediation of the encounter of particular beings in their simultaneous unity and difference.[215]

The tendency in philosophy to oppose being and appearance had its scientific roots in Galileo's opposition between empirical reason and subjective experience, the latter being untrustworthy at best. This ontological claim issued into an epistemological one and Descartes's turn to the subject, such that the human subject became an absolutized consciousness locked away in opposition to the external world. As Russell said, "Ideas become a veil between us and outside things."[216]

This led to skepticism about what could "really" be known, for how can we know if these ideas represent the world adequately? The responses to the privileging of epistemology took different forms, from Romantic "feeling," to Kantian transcendentalism, to the Nietzschean will. Postmoderns rejected the subject–object dichotomy, usually claiming ontological neutrality, but David L. Schindler points out that the claim of neutrality toward ontological content is just a disguised form of the

---

214. Balthasar, *Glory of the Lord V*, 625.
215. D. C. Schindler, *Dramatic Structure*, 6.
216. Russell, "Knowledge by Acquaintance," 119.

same dichotomy. Even in a world of quantum fluctuation, cybernetics, and chaos theory, the problematic ontology and epistemology are still with us; the postmodern rejection of modernism and mechanism leaves dualism intact:

> The body-machine in the meantime might have become the more subtle one indicated in computers, code-scripts, and "information"; and the arbitrary subject in the meantime might have been constructed more subtly in terms of depth psychology, a biogenetics of chance-based necessity, and sociology. The body (matter) nonetheless remains fundamentally mechanistic in character; and subjectivity . . . remains fundamentally adventitious, arbitrary, and chance-like. . . . The mechanistic conception did not so much die with the arrival of quantum theory as become statistical (probabilistic) in nature.[217]

In contrast to these efforts, Heidegger turned away from truth reduced to human subjectivity and human control, and towards *Being*, which he said had been forgotten since the pre-Socratics. Balthasar began from a different point of departure: "I have thus tried to construct a philosophy and a theology starting from an analogy, *not of an abstract Being, but of Being as it is encountered concretely in its attributes*."[218] He dealt with the ontological being/appearance question and the epistemological subject/object question as two sides of one coin.

First, the ontological question: we encounter the radiance of being through particular things, which are a unity of *esse* and essence. The both/and of polarity was a way to "privilege the 'existential' without thereby surrendering (or destroying) conceptual or 'essential forms'"[219] through the convergent notions of *Gestalt* and *drama*, each one central to the meaning of the other. Unlike the ancient Greek "form," which represented finitude in the sense of fullness, perfection, completeness, and necessity (being determined), *Gestalt* encompasses the sense of indeterminate freedom, and should be related not to necessity or fate but to *hope*,[220] that is, to an openness to the ever-greater, to mystery: "The appearance of the

---

217. D. L. Schindler, *Heart of the World*, 164–65, 173.

218. Balthasar, *My Work*, 115–16 (emphasis mine). "Categories have a finite content and so can be defined over against one another. The transcendentals, by contrast, are all pervasive and, therefore, mutually immanent qualities of being as such" (Balthasar, *Theo-Logic I*, 15).

219. D. C. Schindler, *Dramatic Structure*, 13.

220. D. C. Schindler, *Dramatic Structure*, 14.

form, as revelation of the depths, is an indissoluble union of two things. It is the real presence of the depths, of the whole of reality, and it is a real pointing beyond itself to these depths."[221] *Drama*, like analogy, is "the simultaneity of continuity and discontinuity" in that it both resolves and at the same time surprises;[222] it is an essentially *dialogical* encounter; and, most importantly, it expresses the structure of being in that "the meaning of anything, its being, *is revealed only in being's activity even while the activity is an interpretation or unfolding of the being. It is not the case that being 'essentially' comes first, and then merely manifests in action.* . . . *[But] being and action follow each other.*"[223]

Second, the epistemological question: the problem of the supposed dichotomy between reality and our experience of it is ignorant not only of the metaphysics of the real distinction, but also of the epistemology of participation and the polar relationship of subject and object. What is missing, says Balthasar, is the way in which "subject and object expand within each other, thus helping each other in a common discovery of the truth," the result of which is the failure to interpret positively the phenomenon of appearance, which "gives the thing in itself its integrity and plenitude."[224] The subject is neither a "finished product that . . . merely waits for the object's arrival," nor do objects represent a self-contained world—they do not "present themselves to the ego as if it were merely a spectator watching a sort of film about which he is supposed to make a judgment."[225] Rather, the drama of knowledge is that *the subject and object unfold together*. Entities do not exist merely as perceived by a subject, but rather in a polar *mutuality*: "The revelation of the object can occur only in the space provided by the subject . . . [and] the revelation of the subject can occur only in an encounter with the object."[226] Take the example of a tree:

---

221. Balthasar, *Glory of the Lord I*, 118. "We 'behold' the form; but, if we really behold it, it is not as a detached form, rather in its unity with the depths that make their appearance in it. We see form as the splendour, as the glory of Being. We are 'enraptured' by our contemplation of these depths and are 'transported' to them" (*Glory of the Lord I*, 118–19).

222. D. C. Schindler, "Surprised by Truth," 607.

223. D. C. Schindler, *Dramatic Structure*, 19 (emphasis mine).

224. Balthasar, *Theo-Logic I*, 65.

225. Balthasar, *Theo-Logic I*, 67.

226. Balthasar, *Theo-Logic I*, 62.

In reality, the objects of this world need the subject's space in order to be themselves. They do not merely emit distant signals of themselves into this space or send messages to proclaim the autonomous majesty of their existence, but rather they come in person to claim it for their most intimate purposes. A tree without its green, autumnal variety, the pink and white display of its spring blossoms, its fragrance, . . . is simply not a tree. It needs the sensorium as a space in which to unfurl itself. It unveils its color within an eye that sees color; it whispers only in an ear that hears sound. . . . The space of being that is opened and illuminated in the subject makes available to the object an opportunity to be itself in a way that the inferior space of inanimate elements does not. . . . The truth of the tree . . . is the unveiledness of its being, but the unveiling in which the truth is constituted calls for the joint operation of subject and object. . . . Subject and object expand within each other thus helping each other in a common discovery of truth.[227]

For Balthasar the "realm of forms of sub-human nature remains the singularly illuminating touchstone for the value of metaphysics,"[228] for what one believes about them will reverberate throughout all philosophical positions: anyone who explains animals or plants in a mechanical way—modern and postmodern materialists alike—"has already lost," as have those like Hegel who interpret them as stages of Absolute spirit, and like Heidegger, for whom sub-human nature "receives as little metaphysical interpretation as it does with the other thinkers."[229] None of these visions can explain the "superior and playful freedom beyond all the constraints of Nature" we observe in the world around us.[230]

One may *classify* plants and animals within the discourse of evolution; however, one must understand that such a classification does not

---

227. Balthasar, *Theo-Logic I*, 63–65.

228. Balthasar, *Glory of the Lord V*, 621.

229. Balthasar, *Glory of the Lord V*, 621.

230. Balthasar, *Glory of the Lord V*, 621. This freedom is present not only in the diversity and creativity of species but, analogously, in each individual creature. Darwin himself could find no other way to explain the myriad physical and behavioral adaptations in nature—particularly in birds—than to posit a second evolutionary force, beyond the utilitarian "survival of the fittest." Sexual selection proposes that *free* choice, usually by the female of the species, is a driving force in the evolution of life. This force evidently has a bias towards beauty that depends upon the complementary relationality inherent in the sexual difference. See Prum, *The Evolution of Beauty*.

exhaust their meaning.[231] Witnessing a plant blossom does not give us only the *appearance* of life; on the other hand, "no one ought to conclude that he has somehow inspected the whole essence of life or that he has penetrated to the mysterious center from which the plant's outward manifestations . . . emerged. He knows, simply by looking at these manifestations, that the possibilities of life are infinitely more abundant than what is actually on display."[232] Additionally, no single created entity can exhaust the meaning of being, which can be expressed only in the multiplicity of creatures.

Balthasar thus brings wholeness to the world of nature in a way that "holistic ecology"—which eliminates the ontological and axiological differences between persons and nature—never could, extending a solidarity to the non-human world that goes far beyond (and is qualitatively different from) both the demand that humans and nature be seen as ontologically identical, and the either/or dualism of the intrinsic/instrumental value of nature. It is a solidarity in which things present themselves to us *both* in all their concrete integrity and freedom, *and* in their deep and abiding relationality, hence solidarity and analogy are linked: "Analogy presents a principle of profound solidarity; the meaning of each being is tied up with the meaning of all other beings; each thing, in its concrete existence, makes a contribution to the meaning of the whole."[233]

The totalization that Markus Gabriel saw as going hand-in-hand with the "appearance versus reality" opposition would not occur if the polar relationships of form and being, subject and object, were acknowledged; again, being really does appear—we are not locked out of a "noumenal world"—but it does not appear exhaustively, and there is always the ever-greater openness to a reality that will never be captured. This is a long way from the lifeless and extrinsic relationships and the "knowledge by representation" epistemology of modernism, from the skeptical dualism of appearance/being, from the false dilemma between substance metaphysics and process metaphysics, from the "dissolving-into-identity," or from merely being able to hold the two sides of a duality in an irreducible tension of postmodernism. And it is a long way from despairing about the possibility of truth via eliminating being and letting

---

231. See Balthasar, *Glory of the Lord V*, 620–21.
232. Balthasar, *Theo-Logic I*, 86–87.
233. D. C. Schindler, "Ever Ancient, Ever New," 11.

in positivism, or reducing truth to function. Although there are polarities in truth, "these never justify dividing the truth of this world into two heterogeneous dimensions: a theoretical, rational truth of thought and a practical, vital and irrational truth of life."[234]

The best drama brings us both resolution and surprise, because drama, says Balthasar, is *the mutual implication of action and being—each reveals the other*. We will see in the Smile of the Mother, the paradigmatic instance of truth as dramatic, that the Thomistic "real difference" is broken open interpersonally and phenomenologically into a revelation, an analogy of love.

The Smile of the Mother: Seeing the Form

> *Since, however, the child . . . replies and responds to a directive that cannot in any way have come from within its own self—it would never occur to the child that it itself had produced the mother's smile—the entire paradise of reality that unfolds around the "I" stands there as an incomprehensible miracle . . . due to an original favor bestowed on him, something for which [he] will never find sufficient reason in himself.*[235]

Earlier we looked at the "Smile of the Mother" in the context of the "fourfold distinction," a re-visioning of Aquinas's "real distinction," to bring into sharper focus the mutual dependence of *esse* and essence, and hence their mutual gift-character, in the unity of being. Now, after travelling through Aquinas's distinction and his *analogia entis*, and their later developments, we can begin to see the penetrating insight of Balthasar's endlessly fruitful contribution. First, however, there is a possible point of confusion that must be clarified at the outset—that the image makes an anthropological claim alone rather than, first and foremost, an ontological one. With this reflection, Balthasar does not replace the ontological with the personal:

> Rather, he seeks to show that the experience of love between a mother and child cannot be *reduced* to anthropology or psychology, *but sheds light on the meaning of being, even as an*

---

234. Balthasar, *Theo-Logic I*, 254.
235. Balthasar, *Explorations III*, 16.

understanding of the meaning of being is essential to grasp the full implications and breadth of love between persons.[236]

Against the dialectical oppositions of modernity, and postmodernity's inability to reconcile them, the picture of the mother and child reveals a "clear separation of persons who are held together by love,"[237] constituting the paradigmatic image, that is, the "icon" (something real in itself that also transmits a meaning of which it is not the source) of analogy, of polarity, of unity-in-difference. For the mother and child smiling at each other *after* birth is a repetition of the bond they had *before* birth. The unity-in-love that exists while the child is in the womb, says Balthasar, "persists even when the mother's face smiles at the child at a distance," in the space in which "the miracle occurs that one day the child will recognize in its mother's face her protective love and will reciprocate this love with a first smile."[238] In this concrete encounter, *difference* enters the picture, yet at the same time, "the child will see clearly that love is realized only in reciprocity, in an oppositeness that *is encounter and not opposition, a relationship that is held together in its very difference by the spirit of love and that, far from being endangered by mutuality, is rather strengthened by it.*"[239]

Difference is not external to unity and neither destroys it nor sits juxtaposed to it in an uneasy tension. In polarity the poles, "even as they are in tension, exist strictly through each other,"[240] and this allows them to be seen as mutual gifts to each other, not as rivals in a zero-sum game.

The same is true of being and appearance. It is *being* that appears, and being truly *does appear*. Truth does not lie simply in the appearances, for without the point of reference behind them we cannot fully interpret their meaning; but the truth does not lie behind the appearances either, for no "pure background" is ever unveiled to us. Truth can be found "only in the floating middle," so to speak, "between the appearance and the thing that appears."[241] Balthasar says, "We add here that the epiphany of Being has sense only if in the Appearance we grasp the essence that

---

236. Healy, *Eschatology*, 63 (emphasis mine).
237. Balthasar, *Unless You Become*, 19.
238. Balthasar, *Unless You Become*, 17.
239. Balthasar, *Unless You Become*, 18 (emphasis mine).
240. Balthasar, *Theo-Logic II*, 182.
241. Balthasar, *Theo-Logic I*, 138.

manifests itself. The infant comes to the knowledge, not of a pure appearance, but of his mother in herself."[242]

The Smile of the Mother is not merely a metaphor for polarity or unity or the appearance of being, but the thing itself. The mother and child illustrate the nature of all polarities: rather than a closed circle, the image reveals an "ellipse"[243] with two interacting poles, one prior to the other. Rather than an either/or between being and appearance, or being and action, or subject and object, there is the both/and of mutuality. In what follows we will retrace wonder, metaphysics, epistemology, and ethics through the fourfold distinction, opening both Przywara's meta-noetics/meta-ontics (being and knowledge) and Ulrich's metaphysics of love.

METAPHYSICS OF BEING AS LOVE

As William Desmond has pointed out, "Openness to the gift of astonishment asks of the thinker that he or she become again as a child."[244] The child's initial experience provokes wonder that unfolds through all levels of the Fourfold Distinction. Initially, says Balthasar, "the fact that I find myself within the realm of a world and in the boundless community of other existent beings is astonishing beyond measure and cannot be exhaustively explained by any cause which derives from within the world."[245] That is, the experience is a wondrous gift, not a logical necessity, hence there must be something behind or beyond the existence of the totality. He noted that wonder at being is not only the beginning of thought, "but—as Heidegger sees—also the permanent element (*arche*) in which it moves. But this means—contrary to Heidegger—that it is not only astonishing that an existent being can wonder at Being . . . but also that Being as such by itself to the very end 'causes wonder,' behaving as something to be wondered at, something striking and worthy of wonder."[246] Reflection,

---

242. Balthasar, *My Work*, 114–15. He adds: "That does not exclude our grasping the essence only through the manifestation and not in itself" (*My Work*, 115).

243. "The 'Thou' of the mother is not the 'I' of the child, but both centers move in the same ellipse of love" (Balthasar, *Explorations III*, 15).

244. Desmond, *The Intimate Strangeness*, 109.

245. Balthasar, *Glory of the Lord V*, 615.

246. Balthasar, *Glory of the Lord V*, 614–15. Heidegger, says Balthasar, projected the fourth movement of the Fourfold Distinction into the second, turning the oscillation of Being and human existence, "which should remain open and pointing beyond itself,

Balthasar continues, must hold fast to primal wonder as it moves through the four stages, to which we now return.

As we said above, Balthasar saw Aquinas's real distinction as "the source of all the religious and philosophical thought of humanity,"[247] and within the same discussion he writes, "The infant is brought to consciousness of himself only by love, by the smile of his mother."[248] The intentional relationship between the two propositions leads Nicholas Healy to state that the substance of Balthasar's contribution to metaphysics lies in the insight that "the Thomistic distinction between *esse* and essence provides the foundation and framework, yet this distinction is reinterpreted through a concrete phenomenology of love."[249] The real distinction is best understood as love as a form of order.

Balthasar sees the "Fourfold Distinction" in the metaphysics of being as a single distinction which opens in four different ways.[250] First, if that which the intellect first conceives of is being, then the first being of which we are aware is (most often) the mother; here, *being has the personal face of love*, and at the same time, *the personal face of love has ontological depth*:

> In that encounter, the horizon of all unlimited being opens itself for him, revealing four things to him: (1) that he is one in love with the mother, therefore all being is one; (2) that that love is good, therefore all being is good; (3) that that love is true, therefore all being is true; and (4) that that love evokes joy, therefore all being is beautiful.[251]

This original intuition will never be left behind: "This first act, journeying toward transcendence, immediately touches the final end: there can be nothing more beyond the love which wakens me and shelters me, and which greets me in the smiling face of my mother. . . . Everything, without exception, which will follow later . . . must remain an unfolding of it."[252]

---

into the fixed and indissoluble form of a Sphinx, before which and for which man cannot live and cannot love" (*Glory of the Lord V*, 643).

247. Balthasar, *My Work*, 112.
248. Balthasar, *My Work*, 114.
249. Healy, *Eschatology*, 54.
250. Balthasar, *Glory of the Lord V*, 635.
251. Balthasar, *My Work*, 114.
252. Balthasar, *Glory of the Lord V*, 635-36, 616.

Second, it illustrates the dependence of each being on Being in the "real distinction" and the truth that "all other existents stand in the same relation to Being as I do myself. . . . although all existents partake in Being, yet . . . they never exhaust it."[253]

> We have all been permitted entry. Our mother too. And the animals with which I play. There is much that is real, and yet Being overarches everything, sublime and serene; nothing of all this had to be as it is. Everything stands in an open light which is greater and more glorious than the essence of this world with all its terror and beauty.[254]

And vice versa, the ultimate dependence of non-subsistent being on the existent: "Thus there is the third point: what would happen to this light if none of us existed to see it? Does it stand in need of us?"[255] To that question, Balthasar replies with a Thomistic "yes and no." "No," because even all together, all of creation, all those children, mothers, and animals, are not sufficient to explain being; "it is free to manifest itself in an infinite number of other ways and to be a light for an infinite number of other entities."[256] But ultimately, yes:

> Nevertheless: what would light be if there were no one to see it? Are we then both necessary to one another: Being to existents and existents to Being? . . . Is the permission to be, the being given entry, a beginning both for me and for Being? Does it become glorious only by virtue of its being in need? Is it serene only because it has been given entry—into us?[257]

But, asks Balthasar, once we are aware of these second and third levels, can we remain locked in this double dependence? The *ultimate* source of the gift cannot be one existent alongside all the others, nor the oscillation between *esse* and essence, "hardened into a mathematical necessity (as ultimately happens in Heidegger)"; it remains "the event of an absolute freedom."[258] And so comes the fourth opening, "beyond the still conditioned, mutually dependent freedom of the existent with regard to Being and the freedom of Being to shine unconstrainedly as a light

---

253. Balthasar, *Glory of the Lord V*, 618.
254. Balthasar, *Glory of the Lord V*, 635.
255. Balthasar, *Glory of the Lord V*, 635.
256. Balthasar, *Glory of the Lord V*, 635.
257. Balthasar, *Glory of the Lord V*, 635–36.
258. Balthasar, *Glory of the Lord V*, 625.

within the existent: an unconditioned freedom, ... an *actus purus*. ... which is posited in the first instance ... so that the individual entity is not submerged within the exigencies of a process of explication and Being does not lose its freedom in the same 'Odyssey' of its cosmic evolution towards itself."[259] That the finite entity is not closed in on itself but is open to the infinite reflects this ultimate and last difference, "uniquely grasped by Thomas Aquinas,"[260] and recalls Przywara's creaturely metaphysics, whose purpose was to break open both persons and philosophy "toward the influx of transcendence."[261]

Epistemology, the Openness of Reason

How we act (ethics) depends on what we know or believe we can know (epistemology), which in turn depends on what we take to be real (metaphysics).[262] In terms of knowing, for Balthasar, a child awakens to love as it awakens to knowledge: "*Knowledge (with its whole complex of intuition and concept) comes into play, because the play of love has already begun beforehand, initiated by the mother, the transcendent.*"[263]

Balthasar has said that he does not propose a system built on gift as an abstract, intellectual *concept*; the act of knowing is not a purely intellectual grasping of abstract essences, but arises within love that is open to the transcendent. "First principles cannot be abstract propositions, since it is precisely not on the basis of abstraction that we arrive at them: they must necessarily be concrete and immediate encounters, not only with the laws of being, but with being itself. ... That immediate encounter with being remains the basis that supports all discursive activity of the understanding."[264] Against subjectivism and Kantian transcendentalism he says:

> It is to have recourse to a violent solution—which in addition closes our eyes to the deeper reality—if, in the manner of Kant and his followers, we construct a concept of knowledge and science by first bracketing out the unknowable: our concept will

---

259. Balthasar, *Glory of the Lord V*, 636.
260. Balthasar, *Glory of the Lord V*, 446.
261. Gonzales, "Why We Need Erich Przywara," 160.
262. See D. C. Schindler, "Why Socrates Didn't Charge," 398.
263. Balthasar, *Love Alone*, 76 (emphasis mine).
264. Balthasar, "On the Tasks of Catholic Philosophy," 180.

then be necessarily finite and necessarily rationalistic. If our ruling idea is limited to what the cognitive subject is able to construe, then we wholly lose the phenomenon of objective self-manifestation, the self-revelation of the object from the heart of its own depths, and everything runs aground in a shallow functionalism.[265]

In contrast to Kant's vision, reason's "conditions of possibility" do not preexist as things that must be imposed on any encounter whatsoever; rather, those conditions of consciousness are "dramatically constituted in the gift of its participation in and with the reality the child's mother lovingly offers."[266] The Smile of the Mother underscores the open vision of reason introduced in chapter 1 as part of the metaphysics of gift, one in which reason need not impose limits on itself, but goes out to meet the other and to receive its limits from the other. That is, against the idea that the subject somehow constructs reality, *the object—whether the mother, other persons, or any natural entity, has its own mysterious giftedness that is prior to the subject's intellectual acts.* Those limits to reason, then, are not experienced as an imposition or obstacle: "Instead, these limits again and again bring to fulfillment what reason is in its most profound and original form: a generously appropriating encounter with its other . . . to think, in this case, is to pledge oneself, to be brought out of oneself in a way that precisely allows one to give oneself."[267]

Ethics and the Smile of the Mother

The origin of ethics also lies in this original encounter and in the attitude of receptivity, which Balthasar defines as "accessibility to another's being, openness to something other than the inner dimension of one's own subjectivity."[268] But there is a second movement: "Receptivity, however, not only implies this unlocking of the self to other beings but also expressly denotes the capacity to let itself be enriched with the gift of their distinctive truth. This capacity to receive truth is among the supreme values of existence."[269] That is, receptivity naturally unfolds into reciproc-

---

265. Balthasar, *Glory of the Lord I*, 447.
266. D. C. Schindler, "Hans Urs von Balthasar, Metaphysics," 111.
267. D. C. Schindler, "Hans Urs von Balthasar, Metaphysics," 111.
268. Balthasar, *Theo-Logic I*, 44.
269. Balthasar, *Theo-Logic I*, 45.

ity: "For the child it is natural to receive good gifts ... [and so] the child adopts the mother's giving attitude unquestioningly as the right one, and he gives spontaneously when he has something to give ... he wants to share because he has experienced sharing as a form of goodness."[270]

The community formed by the event expands beyond the mother to the rest of the world, both in how the child encounters the world and in the realization that his own giftedness (knowing that "I did not create myself") and experience of unifying love must be true of all other beings as well. Perhaps first among philosophers, Balthasar explicitly opens this philosophical dynamic of being as love to natural entities:

> Whoever grasps this can also open himself receptively to subhuman nature and, thus, learn things from natural beings—from landscapes, plants, animals, stars—which a purely cognitive ("scientific") attitude never discovers. The depth of the significant shapes of nature, the meaning of its language, the extent of its words of revelation can only reveal themselves to one who has opened himself up receptively to them.[271]

The ethics, then, inherent to the original human encounter unfolded by Balthasar are marked by an openness and receptivity to the good of the other such that we may discover this goodness as a good-for-myself. This is the only way to become the kind of people that treat others, and all of nature, according to love.

Conclusion

In the penultimate chapter of his *Realm of Metaphysics in the Modern Age*,[272] Balthasar summarizes the history of the dual loss of Being as Love and its effect on gift that stems from the rejection of the simultaneously personal/ontological birth of consciousness presented in the "Smile of the Mother." Balthasar says that in transcendental philosophy, the other is no different from myself, as an aspect of the absolute subject; in empirical terms the other is merely provisional, not worthy of any absolute commitment; in the biological and evolutionistic systems the other is merely a cell within the whole, and "all human life thus becomes animal life"; in materialistic and economic processes, consciousness is a material

---

270. Balthasar, *Unless You Become*, 22.
271. Balthasar, *Man in History*, 94.
272. See "The Light of Being and Love," in Balthasar, *Glory of the Lord V*, 635-45.

product "which can be transformed at will and made into something else ... so there is nothing better for consciousness to do than to ready itself at the outset for its own elimination."[273] When love has been debased in this way, "then no other value can compensate for this loss, human existence itself lacks all radiance and meaning, and there is no longer any reason why it should be better that something exist rather than simply nothing at all. What kind of gift can the other person be for me?"[274]

The desire to give a purely scientific or otherwise reduced account of things; the effort to lock everything within the subjective consciousness alone; the attempt of Kant and his descendants to imagine that we can break away from pure subjectivity while having the mind "construct" something "objective" elsewhere; and the drive in Romanticism and Idealism to counter fragmentation with a wholeness that ends in subsuming the individual into pantheism or other identity theories: all are signs of the inadequate comprehension of the structure of being as manifested in the world. That miscomprehension overlooks the mystery of the integrated whole, the concrete singular, which the real distinction reveals as inexhaustibly rich and open, not self-enclosed but encompassed within an open ellipse together with the community of being. In this miscomprehension, the essence of gift then appears as a contradiction between matter and form, act and potency, body and soul, subject and object, mother and child: "Gift is understood in either univocal or equivocal terms and precludes reflection on either the distinction or the unity between the giver, the gift, and the receiver."[275] Reflecting on the "Smile of the Mother" icon and archetype of polarity, analogy, and ultimately, Being as Love, we can say with Balthasar, "I understand and receive myself as an expression of being as a whole, as a gift put in my own hands, a gift that I did not give myself."[276]

David L. Schindler

David L. Schindler[277] is one of the preeminent living expositors of the metaphysics of gift. Rather than giving partial responses to the crises of

---

273. Balthasar, *Glory of the Lord V*, 644–45.
274. Balthasar, *Glory of the Lord V*, 644.
275. López, *Gift and the Unity*, 5–6.
276. Balthasar, *Theo-Logic II*, 255.
277. Professor emeritus and former dean of the John Paul II Institute for Marriage

contemporary culture, in his applications of that metaphysics to a vast array of cultural issues from economics to bioethics and biotechnology, political theory, the nature of liberal society (including the hidden ontological and anthropological presuppositions in both the liberal and conservative forms), and more, he seeks the most comprehensive understanding, for "superficial diagnoses prompt essentially pragmatic solutions, which, as such, are not only bound to fail in the long run but will inevitably breed despair insofar as they neglect one of the greatest of all human needs, namely, the need for truth."[278] He is not alone, of course, and would be the first to acknowledge his reciprocal debt to many others. One of these is Kenneth Schmitz.

Schindler on the Work of Kenneth Schmitz

Schindler was a close friend and colleague of Schmitz and has said of him that his metaphysics, outlined in *The Gift: Creation*, "has been a guiding inspiration . . . and will ever remain so."[279] Balthasar, said Schindler, was "enthusiastic" about the book, because it "represented, for him . . . the Thomism he so appreciated in the writings of Gustav Siewerth and Ferdinand Ulrich: a vision of being open from its core to generosity."[280] Schindler notes three ways in which Schmitz unfolds that generosity. We will briefly mention them here to return to them later:

Dependence

We have noted that philosophers of "emergence" claim to offer "fresh ways" to think about contingency: not as accidental, but rather as signifying a sense of dependency upon something else. An even more profound sense of radical dependency, reaching to the ontological depths, is at the heart of the metaphysics of gift. Schmitz saw that we can be dependent—contingent—and autonomous at the same time, without the "humiliation" often seen in the condition of dependency, because it is dependence on the very generosity that is the original condition of the

---

and the Family, as well the editor of the North American edition of the *Communio: International Catholic Review*.

278. D. C. Schindler and Healy, Introduction, xvii.
279. D. L. Schindler, "In Memoriam," 405.
280. D. L. Schindler, "In Memoriam," 403.

creature's being. If dependence were an imperfection, a negation, then the creature's "very being would be in a totally deprived and absolutely abject state; so that the creature would be *nihil*, rather than *ex nihilo*."[281]

The World

The first corollary follows from seeing all things, Schmitz says, as "constituted by the spirit of creative generosity which takes the world not simply as given (*datum*) but as gift (*donum*)."[282] The giftedness of everything means that "the world" is not an individual, with its own act of being, over against which the person stands; nor is it a "mere collection" of individuals; nor is it "the system," a "self-determining reality" of which individuals are members; instead, "the world is that which is built into its creatures, and they into it. . . . Ontological commonality or universality (as distinct from abstract universality) is inseparable from the fullness of existential act; so that act [as *esse*] is the primal principle of plenitude."[283]

Interiority and Non-human Creatures

The second corollary is that Schmitz's recognition of generosity at the heart of each entity and his interpretation of causality through the metaphysics of gift enable us "to recover an appropriate *interiority* and depth in all being" which is shared by both *conscious and non-conscious beings*.[284] If the gift of being is constitutive of created beings, it is not a merely external relation, and applies to all:

> *It is imperative, therefore, to release interiority from its modern prison in human subjectivity and to restore to natural things* (res) *the appropriate kind of interiority which they have in a metaphysics of being, where they are not mere objects standing before the human subject. . . . And this ontological interiority*

---

281. Schmitz, *The Gift*, 73–74.
282. Schmitz, *The Recovery of Wonder*, 104.
283. Schmitz, *The Gift*, 111, 118.
284. D. L. Schindler, "In Memoriam," 405. He continues that we thus move beyond "the divorce between objectivity and subjectivity in their modern and mutually exclusive senses" ("In Memoriam," 405).

lends its character to all interior relations, including the spiritual interiority encountered in personal beings.[285]

In ecological ethics, this will provide a deeper ground for what so many seek to maintain: the "intrinsic value" of natural entities. Rather than set intrinsic and instrumental value against each other, for the metaphysics of gift nothing in nature can be purely instrumental (seen only as an instrument for what is outside of it, or external to it) because nothing is purely extrinsic; everything bears an interior relation via the gift of being to everything else: "All creatures, by virtue of their very *ratio* as creatures, have receptive relation inscribed in their *esse*. All creatures thus bear the dimension of interiority, and hence immateriality, needed to accommodate such a relation."[286] If *nothing is shared* between entities (other than causal physical force) as in the modern science following Galileo, then the things of nature, rather than being embedded in a community of shared being, become merely the interacting parts of a mechanism, and, Michael Hanby says, "the temptation to manipulate these parts to a design of our own inchoate imagining becomes irresistible."[287] If *everything is shared*, as in most versions of ecological "holism"—reduced to temporal nodes in a flux of energy, or successive states of a single material substrate—then the things of nature, the very things that the ecologists want to save, are lost.

The "real distinction" between *esse* and essence establishes a logic of gift at the heart of all entities, living and nonliving, conscious and not conscious; thus, we return to that starting point in David L. Schindler's work.

On Esse *and* Agere

Among the most profound and fruitful contributions Schindler has made is his thinking on *esse* and *agere*, which clarifies the deepest roots of being, gift, love, and action, including ethical action, in a way that is novel and surprising, yet strikes so many as the almost inevitable unfolding of what came before. He looks at the axiom often repeated by Aquinas, *agere*

---

285. Schmitz, *Texture of Being*, 127–28 (emphasis added).

286. D. L. Schindler, *Heart of the World*, 291. He also distinguishes human persons and non-human beings. The latter have "analogically conceived interiority whereby each is open to others," but in human persons "this interiority takes a properly spiritual form" (D. L. Schindler, "Being, Gift [Part Two]," 435n44).

287. Hanby, "Few Words," 78.

sequitur esse (action follows existence; an entity acts as it is), and sees it in the light of the unity-in-distinction we have returned to throughout this study, and Balthasar's understanding that *agere sequitur esse* and *esse sequitur agere* mutually imply each other.[288]

> "*Esse* is simple and complete but not subsistent" (*De potentia* 1, 1), and second, "*esse* is innermost in each thing and most fundamentally present within all things, since it is formal with respect to everything that is in being" (*Summa [Theologiae]* I, 8, 1). *The first principle establishes the foundational claim that being is given to the creature as gift. . . . The second principle affirms that* esse, *in its "formal"-act character with respect to the whole and every "part" of creaturely being, shapes the latter in its inmost depths in (and toward) giftedness and giving. Since* esse *is "formal with respect to everything in being," it follows that all specific acts, principles, and aspects of being are ordered in and toward the generosity implied in* esse.[289]

So Schindler returns to the statement that has been central to our discussion: "*Esse* is simple and complete but not subsistent." *Esse*, as complete, is perfect and *prior to substance*: *esse* is "formal with respect to everything that is in being,"[290] that is, it is "the actuality of every form commonly, whether substantial or accidental,"[291] and "existence must be compared to essence, if the latter is a distinct reality, as actuality to potentiality."[292] *Esse*, then, is the primary locus of a being's perfection: "Being [*esse*] . . . signifies the highest perfection of all,"[293] the perfection of perfections.

On the other hand, *esse* is non-subsistent; substance, the actual being, is what subsists: "For being means something having existence, but it is substance alone that subsists."[294] If *esse* is dependent upon substance, then, in a sense, substance has priority over *esse*. Looking more deeply into substance we find that "every substance exists for the sake of its

---

288. Balthasar, *Theo-Drama II*, 11.
289. D. L. Schindler, "Being, Gift (Part Two)," 474 (emphasis mine).
290. Aquinas, *Summa Theologiae*, I, q. 8, a. 1.
291. Aquinas, *Aristotle's* On Interpretation, I, l. 5, n. 22.
292. Aquinas, *Summa Theologiae*, I, q. 3, a. 4.
293. Aquinas, *De Potentia Dei*, q. 7, a. 2, ad 9.
294. Aquinas, *Aristotle's* Metaphysics, lib. 12, l. 1, n. 2419.

operation,"²⁹⁵ and that operation—action—"is the ultimate perfection of each thing."²⁹⁶

Thus is asserted, says Schindler, "(1) a priority of *esse* over substance/*agere* as source of perfection, simultaneous with (2) a distinct priority of substance/*agere* over *esse* as source of perfection."²⁹⁷

This is the same conundrum that Ulrich faced, and Schindler deepens the response from a slightly different perspective. As D. C. Schindler puts it, the reciprocal tension between irreducible parts "cannot be sustained if we only have the two parts. Instead, it can be sustained only if the two parts are embraced and included within something more than they are."²⁹⁸ The conundrum is resolved when we see the distinction-inside-unity character of *esse*: "The act of being (*esse*) thus bears, *in its unity as esse creatum*, a dual character of *being given or communicated to* the creature, and simultaneously being *exercised by* the creature."²⁹⁹ The gift of *esse* is a form of generosity which "consists precisely in the creature's *being granted a share* in the perfection of existing, which means so far being itself an agent of being and acting, given to itself."³⁰⁰

> *The triplex character is crucial: a "third," which is to say the substantial identity or unity of an entity, is what gives it the stable, enduring center whereby it can serve as both origin and end for its movement from and toward an other. This stable, enduring center is at once the presupposition and the consequence (ontological, not temporal) of each entity's dual-dynamic relation to the other. Without this stable identity, what we are terming the gifted character of being would necessarily dissolve into a purely processive, formless relationality.*³⁰¹

295. Aquinas, *Summa Theologiae*, I, q. 105, a. 5.
296. Aquinas, *Summa Contra Gentiles*, lib. 3, cap. 113, n. 1.
297. D. L. Schindler, "Being, Gift (Part Two)," 415.
298. D. C. Schindler, *Dramatic Structure*, 167–168. He continues, "Parts that are in tension with each other are necessarily members of a greater whole, and conversely, a whole that is truly such involves parts that are not indifferent to each but rather integrated in a permanent tension" (*Dramatic Structure*, 168).
299. D. L. Schindler, "Being, Gift (Part One)," 241.
300. D. L. Schindler, "Being, Gift (Part Two)," 416.
301. D. L. Schindler, *Ordering Love*, 418n49 (emphasis mine). He continues, "As such, [it] would just so far lack the capacity for its own participation as gift in the generosity of creation. The generosity implied in the double movement of giving and receiving can be sustained only in terms of a 'third' principle, a 'substantial in-itselfness' in and through which giving and receiving are brought into original-final unity" (*Ordering Love*, 418n49).

So Schindler's proposal is that each being has an ontologically "triplex character"—the substantial "in-itselfness (*esse in*) that at once receives from the other (*esse ab*) and gives to the other (*esse ad*)."[302] This proposal neither rejects the fundamental distinction between *esse* and essence or substance, nor does this triform relationality (*in, ad, ab*) dissolve substantive identity into a "process," for an act that "determines substance in the way *esse* does" can at the same time "inherently and dynamically open substance to the other."[303]

After Schindler's grounding of *substantiality* comes the opening up of *relationality* and *receptivity*. Aquinas implied that relationality is a primordial dimension of every being, inseparable from substantiality, just as action is inseparable from existence. This was a radical departure from Aristotelian metaphysics, for which substance was essentially real and relation was accidental or circumstantial.[304] Keeping in mind that *esse* and *agere* constitute an asymmetrical unity-in-distinction, such that *esse* is ontologically prior to *agere*, what Schindler wants to clarify is that receptivity is not passive, or a deficiency, or secondary to being and only arising in being's second act. *Agere*, in truth, is inscribed in *esse* and signifies the first meaning of relation in creation. Thus, relationality and receptivity complement each other; receptivity is ontologically prior and is both active and a perfection.

> Not only is activity, active self-communication, the natural consequence of possessing an act of existence (*esse*); St. Thomas goes further to maintain that self-expression through action is actually the whole point, the natural perfection or flowering of being itself.... Relationality is a primordial dimension of every real being, inseparable from its substantiality, just as action is from existence. But since "every substance exists for the sake of its operations,"... being as substance, as existing in itself, naturally flows over into being as relational, turned towards others by its self-communicating action.[305]

---

302. D. L. Schindler, *Heart of the World*, 287.

303. D. L. Schindler, *Heart of the World*, 289. This trinity-in-unity and unity-in-trinity neither confounds the diversity nor divides the unity.

304. It is important to note, however, that "Aristotle's substance is simply not static in the way that, say, the Lockean substance is" (D. L. Schindler, *Ordering Love*, 354).

305. Clarke, *Explorations in Metaphysics*, 604, 607.

RECEPTIVITY

Recall the position that holds that a gift cannot "assume any return or even reception."[306] Among those who *do* accept the importance of receptivity, some propose that it begins in *agere,* not *esse*—that it is *subsequent* first to substantiality, and then to relationality or communicativity. In other words, that it must first *be,* and only then can it receive. Schindler disagrees with both camps; like Schmitz, he insists that a gift, to be complete, must be received.[307] This is essential to metaphysics of gift on the whole, because if we cannot conceive of the reception of being in these terms, *esse* cannot truly be a gift at all. For this reason Schindler insists on the original simultaneity of giving and receiving "inside" *esse.* To recap Schindler's proposal, *esse* does not simply ground the substantiality ("in-itselfness") that causes the thing to be; *esse* is also the original "home" of receptivity. And receptivity, that is, being-given (*esse-ab*), is ontologically prior to being-for-others (*esse-ad*), giving, communicativity. The capacity to give follows from first *having been given. Agere,* then, recapitulates the triplex character of *esse:* "I am never the origin or source of generosity but always a participant in generosity: I am the origin of generosity only-always *qua* recipient of generosity, a generous giver but only-always *qua* receiver of generous giving."[308] This brings to light the consequence that receptivity is *not passive,* and indeed is *perfect,* for, as Schmitz said, "there is more than passivity in reception; there is also self-possession and ordination to the good."[309]

In classical metaphysics, receptivity had generally been identified "with the deficiency side of being, i.e. with poverty, potentiality, a prior lack that is later filled up,"[310] hence as an imperfection. Receptivity was a passive potentiality that could only become perfect by being actualized. In modernism, Schindler says, if *agere* as human agency is conceived the way Bacon and Descartes saw it, characterized by a primacy of power rather than a primacy of receptivity, then "on this dominant post-Enlightenment understanding, an original receptivity in the agent would

---

306. See Milbank, "Foreword," ix.

307. "Now reception is integral to the very character of a gift, for a gift refused is an unfinished gift. . . . The acceptance completes the gift, fulfills it" (Schmitz, *Texture of Being,* 126).

308. D. L. Schindler, "Embodied Person," 405.

309. Schmitz, *Texture of Being,* 127.

310. Clarke, *Person and Being,* 83.

indicate a passivity that is *eo ipso* defective."[311] That "primacy of power," as so many writers on the genealogy of modernity have shown, led directly to the technological paradigm.[312] And as freedom became a "purely formal exercise of choice," so receptivity was reduced to "dehumanizing passivity."[313] Perhaps even more so today, there is a sense that receptivity epitomizes passivity and even immaturity, both in the American concept of "the self-made man" and the equivalent Marxist claim that a man can only become independent and thus authentic through his own labor.[314]

The work of Ulrich and Balthasar, who integrated "the receptive" (in terms of the ontological meaning of "poverty" and "child" respectively) into the proper meaning of act or activity, Schindler says, was needed to understand the "active" dimension of receptivity, through conceiving of the meaning of act in terms of love. Once the co-incidence of being and love was opened up by Ulrich and Balthasar, then receptivity could be revealed as a perfection, for it is necessary to complete the act of love. Love recapitulates the triplex nature of *esse*: "Love consists not only in giving, but in receiving and turning back. . . . Act (*esse*) in all its purity includes the dimension of receptivity."[315] Receptivity, then, is *essential*, not merely *potential*, as *activity*, not simply as "*passivity*."[316]

Schindler says that since analogy is intrinsic to *esse* and present wherever *esse* is instantiated, then what he says about receptivity applies not only to persons but to *all* entities, in a manner *proportionate to each thing's being*. For persons, receptivity involves freedom and consciousness, while nonhuman entities must have something analogous, which he takes to be "some minimum level of immanent activity, order, and transitive activity."[317] In light of Schmitz's "interiority," this allows us to recover

---

311. D. L. Schindler, "Embodied Person," 412.

312. See Guardini, *Letters from Lake Como*.

313. D. L. Schindler, "Embodied Person," 415.

314. "A *being* only considers himself independent when he stands on his own feet; and he only stands on his own feet when he owes his *existence* to himself. A man who lives by the grace of another regards himself as a dependent being . . . [but for] the socialist man the *entire so-called history of the world* is nothing but the creation of man through human labour" (Marx, *Economic and Philosophic Manuscripts*, 112).

315. D. L. Schindler, *Heart of the World*, 241.

316. Schindler does not reject passivity but sees it in a new light: "To see the unity within distinction of the so-called passive and active virtues, and to understand (thus) that 'passivity' and 'activity' each give primitive form to the other in each's most basic meaning as such" (D. L. Schindler, "The Embodied Person," 426).

317. D. L. Schindler, "The Person," 175.

a far more adequate apprehension of natural entities than is allowed for in either a technological or holistic understanding, one that is both more comprehensive, including "both the mechanical manifestations of nature and those formal and qualitative features which mechanistic ontology regards as epiphenomenal"; and less reductive: in refusing "to make the world less than the mystery it is by insisting that its reality conform to a defective concept of knowledge, allowing the forms of natural things to show forth of their own inner logic that the mystery of love constitutes them in their naturality."[318]

Relationality

According to Walker, one of "the golden threads" of Schindler's thinking is the "constitutive relation thesis," which "brings to the fore Schindler's genius for overcoming dualism without leaving behind duality."[319] It opposes *extrinsic relationality*, in which things are related only subsequently to their standing within themselves. If things are only connected at the "outer edges," so to speak, then "each has merely a negative, regulatory role in the other, each determines the limits of the other from outside, rather than playing a positive role of *in-forming* that content that properly belongs to the other."[320] As D. C. Schindler explains, if the relations between things stopped at the edges,

> then not only must relation be trivialized as failing to touch the core of being (relation, thus, as "merely accidental")—which of course would imply that the core of being is an opaque and impenetrable (and ultimately unreal, because abstracted from the essentially synthetic character of real being) "nugget," an "atom"—but indeed *by the same token all entities of whatever sort would stand in what one might call ontological competition with one another. The presence of one thing would precisely require the absence of the other, the insistence on "intrinsic" presence would then be the violent imposition of the other.*[321]

318. Hanby, "Beyond Mechanism," 189.
319. Walker, "'Constitutive Relations,'" 124.
320. D. C. Schindler, *Catholicity of Reason*, 308.
321. D. C. Schindler, "Beauty and the Holiness," 9–10 (emphasis mine). He adds, "a synthetic view of being does not in the least intend to remove the distinction between substance and accidents, but rather to relativize both, within their abiding asymmetrical difference, to a more fundamental actuality of being" ("Beauty and the Holiness," 10n11).

Thus the logic of relation necessitates the rejection of the principle of simple identity: that an entity has its identity solely in itself, outside of any relation to anything else. In this, he echoes Heidegger's critique of Cartesian rationality, a critique that has been taken up by postmodern scholars, though Schindler does not reject substantiality, as postmoderns frequently do.

The problem with the presupposition of the principle of simple identity as a first principle is that it "forces inclusion by way of dualistic addition, whereas the presupposition of the principle of relation leads to inclusion by way of integration."[322] "Addition" creates not *real relation or unity*, but a mere juxtaposition of entities; one thinks of sociologist Diane Vaughan's definition of divorce as an "uncoupling,"[323] a term drawn from the hooking up and releasing of train cars. This is purely extrinsic and mechanical, and remember that for Schindler, even a postmodernism that ostensibly rejects mechanism is still unconsciously mechanistic, in that relations do not reach to the ontological level:

> In a mechanical relation . . . x and y each retain their integrity only from outside each other, in a state of what we have called juxtaposition. X remains truly distinct from y only by virtue of something like abstract-spatialized lines drawn between them, establishing as it were the boundaries of perfectly separate spheres. *On the one hand, any unity between entities so distinguished can be established only "additively," insofar as the elements remain extrinsic (after the manner of a collection or sum). On the other hand, any attempt to make the unity between such entities internal now necessarily takes the form of reduction or confusion (a mixing together that violates the integrity of one or the other, or both).* In a relation of love, things are quite different. Here we find a relation wherein the unity of the partners and the rightful distinctness of partners grow directly-intrinsically and not inversely-extrinsically in relation to each other.[324]

For Schindler, true relations are *constitutive*, first given in the *esse*-essence constitution of each being. Relations and the original communities implicit in these relations are "*gifts* 'before' they are *constructions*,"[325]

---

322. Rowland, *Culture and the Thomist Tradition*, 96.
323. See Vaughan, *Uncoupling*.
324. D. L. Schindler, "'God and the End of Intelligence,'" 517 (emphasis mine).
325. D. L. Schindler, "'Homelessness,'" 354.

and a community of beings that is *constitutively (intrinsically) related* is distinguished from one in which beings are related by *extrinsic interaction*:

> An inter-active community logically presupposes multiple subjects, each of which is first constituted as an existing subject (*ens*) in itself, which realizes relation to the other . . . first-simply through its activity (*agere*) . . . constitutive relationality, on the contrary, indicates a community that is given to creatures in their original constitution as being (*esse commune*), even as this initially given community is—in the very act of creation—handed over to each creature as simultaneously its own task (*agere*).[326]

To summarize, the beings of the world do not first "possess themselves" through a primordial act of existence, *esse*, and only then are able to enter into relations, in a second act (*agere*). Receptivity and relationality are inscribed into the original gift of being, ontologically prior not only to self-communication through action but even prior to self-possession; the creature is a being that is "first given to itself." This crucial point that Schindler returns to again and again means that community is prior to "in-itselfness" and has a role in forming and structuring *ens*. *Esse* and *agere* may mutually imply each other in a duality-within-unity, but as with most dualities, it is asymmetrical and *esse* is prior; action follows being, ethics follows metaphysics (not temporally, of course, but ontologically). This is the reason ontology and ethics cannot be separated.

> Each individual substance possesses a substantial unity (*esse in*) while bearing from its beginning and in its depths a dynamic reference from (*esse ab*) and toward (*esse ad*). This dynamic reference . . . indicates the ontological beginning of the receiving-giving that characterizes the primitive meaning of human action and is (thereby) meant to be realized in every human action.[327]

Schindler's metaphysical analysis lies at heart of his life's work on the political-constitutional order, on culture, on communities, on bio-engineering, and more; far from being esoteric or academic, the "real world" implications are endless. Understanding that action is rooted in ontology breaks open the discourse of bioethics and reveals why attempting to provide a foundational "list of virtues" as a consensus on the lowest common denominator of what people will agree on is bound to fail, and

326. D. L. Schindler, "Being, Gift (Part Two)," 434.
327. D. L. Schindler, "Embodied Person," 404.

why even perfectly coherent ethical theories will always face opposition from without, due to conflicts at a more fundamental level.

Freedom and Ethical Action

In terms of the freedom necessary for ethical action, it would appear a person must first fully possess himself (in the first act, *esse*), and only then enter relations in a second act (*agere*). The predominant account of free human action (the freedom to "choose," the freedom of indifference[328]) emphasizes creativity and self-determination, says Schindler, and no one would deny the worth of those features; without them, "human freedom is emptied of its legitimate power."[329] Though relationality is written into the primordial level of being itself, this does not mean that "the relations are not also in some essential way matters of freedom"; it means rather that "these relations are objects of free choice only as already constitutive of the subject of free choice."[330] Schindler too turns to Balthasar's Smile of the Mother to elucidate the insistence on the intrinsic nature of relations, which, according to D. C. Schindler,

> may remain too distant and abstract if we see it as stemming from the supra-formal character of actuality, which implies a synthetic meaning of being that makes difference co-incident with identity, but it is brought immediately close in the reality of love: a child comes to himself, both physically-developmentally and intellectually-personally, not in abstraction from all relations, but precisely as abiding within the presence of the love of his parents, and as being penetrated to the core by that love. This presence, if it is genuinely loving, does not at all compromise the child's identity, but is rather the abiding guardian of its integrity, and indeed its relative "independence" or "autonomy." The relations, then, are not extrinsic to or subsequent upon the substance, but intrinsic to it and constitutive of it in a way that sets it *substantially* free. . . . The general "relationality" of being comes to be seen in the more concrete form of reciprocal

---

328. "A freedom defined in terms of a self-determination that initially excludes being determined by anyone or anything, one that looks on initially determining factors as intrusions upon rather than as intrinsic to the proper and most basic activity of the will" (D. L. Schindler, "America's Technological Ontology," 266).

329. D. L. Schindler, "'Homelessness,'" 371.

330. D. L. Schindler, "'Homelessness,'" 354.

self-gift, and this form penetrates into the very physical roots of things.[331]

The dominant view of freedom emphasizes self-determination over/against the presence of the other. The insight that freedom is not incompatible with community *in its very heart and center* becomes clear once autonomy is re-visioned not simply as self-sufficiency or independence, but as the integrity and wholeness befitting created reality. Freedom as gift both originates and culminates in community (whose etymology reveals one of the Latin words for "gift," *munus*). "Individuality and community in their primary meanings do not oppose but on the contrary presuppose each other. Individuality emerges *from within* community and is always already an expression *of* community, even as individuality itself conditions and is presupposed by the original meaning of community."[332]

Love and the Order of Reality

Reality at root is a matter of love and love is a matter of order. . . . Indeed, modernity's marginalization of love is bound up indissolubly with its technological understanding of order. . . . By technology or "technological" I thus do not refer in the first instance to what is customarily understood as the practical application of knowledge. . . . I refer rather to a particular ordering of being and consciousness.[333]

We close our discussion of Schindler by looking at his book, *Ordering Love: Liberal Society and the Memory of God*, a collection of articles that underscores our thesis that bioethics and biopolitics have been formed by a denial of metaphysics that masks an inadequate metaphysics unconsciously assumed. Schindler claims that "if one denies metaphysics, or thinks one can make claims about this or that aspect of reality without somehow implying metaphysical claims about the nature or logic of reality as a whole, the result will be, not that one successfully avoids such claims, but only that one is now being controlled by presuppositions of which one remains unaware."[334]

---

331. D. C. Schindler, "Beauty and the Holiness," 19–21.
332. D. L. Schindler, "'Homelessness,'" 352.
333. D. L. Schindler, *Ordering Love*, ix–x.
334. D. L. Schindler, *Ordering Love*, 352.

Love is not just one act like all the other acts of any creature, but rather "has its ground in the act of acts (*esse*), and in this sense love itself is the 'form' of forms, also for creaturely being."[335] The history of the metaphysics of gift, begun in Aquinas's "real distinction," culminates here in being-as-love, specified at the very deepest metaphysical level. The order of love or gift (the terms are interchangeable for Schindler) has its origin in the very structure of the creature, and characterizes not only persons but "via an adequately conceived analogy, the meaning of all creaturely being."[336] Schindler expounds upon this by addressing the objections to this position.

The first objection to ordering love as the structure of all reality is that love is *personal* and would not apply to entities lacking human consciousness. The second is that even for humans, love is an act of freedom and will, *not* intelligence and order. Regarding the first, Schindler says the horizon of his discussion is not the human being, but "being in its most radical and comprehensive sense."[337] Love is conceived analogically—not, again, as metaphor or poetry but in the understanding that "all beings share in the unity characteristic of their being created *gifts*... even as each shares in this unity differently, in terms of the evergreater difference (*maior dissimilitudo*) proper to each kind of being, from non-living to living to human."[338] For humans, true giving and receiving (that is, love) are revealed in one way, but as Schmitz noted above when discussing physics, etc., analogically speaking, giving runs throughout all of nature. As for the second objection, Schindler does not deny that in humans love is an act of the will, but says that the question at hand is the *meaning of those acts relative to the primary act*. If, repeating Aquinas, *esse* is "formal with respect to everything that is in being,"[339] then *esse* communicates its gifted-giving "form" of love to all the other acts, including intellectual, rational ones: "Love is (ontologically) prior to and operative within all human acts. It thus cannot but give integrative-dynamic 'form' to these acts, at the most radical level."[340]

335. D. L. Schindler, "Being, Gift (Part Two)," 476.

336. D. L. Schindler, "Embodied Person," 397. Note that Deleuze and others misunderstand analogy as the equivocity of being, the univocity of attributes. Schindler makes it clear that *both* being and attributes are analogical.

337. D. L. Schindler, *Ordering Love*, 4.

338. D. L. Schindler, *Ordering Love*, 4.

339. Aquinas, *Summa Theologiae*, I, q. 8, a. 1.

340. D. L. Schindler, "Being, Gift (Part Two)," 411.

A third objection is that love refers to how persons relate and does not "reach to the *substance*, hence substantial order, of persons or things."[341] In part, we have addressed this above, regarding the constitutive reality of beings. Schindler sums the argument up:

> To secure the substantial identity of persons or things, we do not need to oppose or even simply juxtapose the substantial character of identity and the relationality of love. On the contrary, each in its own way is an inner condition of the other, and each thus enters into the original meaning of the other. For this reason, we can indeed speak of love as the basic meaning of things, of each thing at once in itself and in its receiving from and moving toward all others.[342]

After a fourth, primarily theological objection, which we will not review here, comes the fifth: that love as the order of things flies in the face of all evidence—we need only look around to see that it is "more an ethical wish, or moral value or duty" rather than a fact of reality.[343] Schindler answers that "we do not need to deny this massive evil in order to sustain the claim of a natural participation in and tendency toward generosity that is structured into the original constitution of being. . . . No being, however broken, can ever at its core be indifferent to or wholly forgetful of the call to generosity."[344]

Finally, the language of love might be fine for the private realm but is inappropriate for the state, the economy, or the academy, where suitable language concerns juridical rights, or the mutuality of self-interests, or the methodological language of "mechanism in the physical sciences complemented by self-interested survival mechanisms in the life sciences."[345] However, the point is *not* to substitute the language of private affection or piety. There is, of course, a distinction between language proper to the family or church and to other institutions, but it is a distinction by way of analogy, always "the deeper anterior unity within them, and within the things to which they refer."[346] Nor is the point to simply add on to the legitimate language of each domain some extrinsic

---

341. D. L. Schindler, *Ordering Love*, 2.

342. D. L. Schindler, *Ordering Love*, 6–7.

343. D. L. Schindler, *Ordering Love*, 3.

344. D. L. Schindler, *Ordering Love*, 8. For, "evil in no way has any but an accidental cause" (Aquinas, *Summa Theologiae*, I, q. 49).

345. D. L. Schindler, *Ordering Love*, 3.

346. D. L. Schindler, *Ordering Love*, 10.

"value" statements or ethical judgments. In the end, there is no language that is neutral to the gift-character of persons and other beings:

> There is no language of simple strategic or methodological "purity," no language that is barren of implications, with respect to the meaning of nature as created in love and called to love.... The point is neither simply to *replace* nor simply to *add to* the legitimately autonomous language proper to each domain. It is rather to insert within each a dynamic for transformation rooted in memory. Transformation, rightly understood, involves securing in their integrity the truth and goodness of things *as articulated in the various public or institutionally specialized languages,* all the while *re-forming that truth and goodness from within a deeper and broader framework of integration.* The newness is not only by way of a new context, but enters into the original content of truth itself; otherwise we slip back into so-called "integration" by way of "addition."[347]

This last point is crucial: "integration by addition" leaves intact antagonistic dualities, while integration by analogy *broadens and deepens reason*, allowing the logic of love, for example in science, "to account without reduction for the legitimate mechanical properties of things, even as this will properly entail a new reading of these mechanical properties,"[348] and in ethics, to account without dualism for the mutual implication between, and complementary status of, theory and praxis:[349]

> My participation in love, which takes form as responsive generosity, defines my first and most basic act *as* a creature: love is (ontologically) prior to and operative within all other human acts. This act lies at the heart of all the other acts and aspects of my being, and thus cannot but give integrative-dynamic "form" to these—at the most radical level, even if, to be sure, not always intentionally. Love in this sense is rightly said to be "constitutive" of my being.[350]

---

347. D. L. Schindler, *Ordering Love*, 10–11 (emphasis mine).

348. D. L. Schindler, *Ordering Love*, 12.

349. For example, the demand that people should be ethically consistent by "practicing what they preach" is not simply a moral exhortation to consistency between the (dual) worlds of thought and action, but is rather the metaphysical claim that the one follows from the other. Thus, this is not the cold bond of Kantian moral duty, in which we act well by acting *in spite of* our desires and inclinations; rather we act *in accord with* the deepest meaning of our being.

350. D. L. Schindler, "Being, Gift (Part One)," 250.

Conclusion

> *There is, then, in any particular gift, not only its special character, but also a certain transcendental character by which it bears a universal good and releases the generosity without which life is impossible. This transcendental character is inseparable from every genuine gift and is constitutive of man and his world.*[351]

What Schindler has done is to further illuminate and develop that which Przywara, Ulrich, Balthasar, and Schmitz brought to light as latent in the seed that is Aquinas's "real distinction." Non-subsistent *esse* causes the existence of the essences, while needing those same essences to receive it. In the Przywarian dynamism of the paradoxical interplay of Ulrich's wealth that includes poverty in a mutual embrace ("'rich' in the very 'poverty' of the receptiveness that enables his *full and substantial being* as a creature"),[352] the focus is shifted away from *esse* alone "to the mutual letting be of *esse* and essence, which alone does justice to the order or logos of being as love."[353] The simultaneity of wealth (fullness, completeness, receiving) with poverty (dependence, non-subsistence, giving away) is the paradox of love itself, so that the meaning of being can rightly be called "love." Balthasar's concrete methodology, in which the child's first experience of being is through the loving embrace of his mother's smile, "hence through the radiant presence of the goodness of another," is an experience of existence as generous gift.[354] The mother's smile evokes the child's responsive smile as the sun evokes a flower's blossom. This, then, is "the primitive structure of a creaturely ontology"—gift-from-another and being-as-response, *esse ab* and *esse ad*, the unfolding of the triune character of *esse*, made visible in every creature.

This authentic knowledge of the goodness and beauty of reality generates in the receptive subject the experience of wonder, which is what spurred us on in the first place. Thus, it is only fitting that we end this chapter by returning to that wonder.

---

351. Schmitz, *The Gift*, 56–57. See also Aquinas, *Summa Theologiae*, I, q. 73, a. 3, ob 2.
352. D. L. Schindler, "Embodied Person," 413.
353. Healy, "*Praeambula fidei*," 101.
354. D. L. Schindler, "'Homelessness,'" 355.

Wonder, Beauty, and Gift

> *Wonder is not a univocal concept but a happening making us porous to the intimate strangeness of being. . . . It is a gift.*[355]

While for the Greeks philosophy began in wonder, one need only think of Descartes's method to see, as Desmond notes, that "modern philosophy begins in doubt":

> The difference in doubt and wonder reflects a different sense of the ethos of being, reflected also in the drift toward system and critique in modernity. Wonder is prior to system and beyond system. It enables system but is not part of the system. It opens to engendering origin. Wonder is closer to the generous mother, one of whose prodigal and wayward offspring is doubt. Doubt can become so wayward that it ceases to know it has a mother.[356]

The emphasis on doubt, the hermeneutic of suspicion in philosophy, and the loss of meaning and the sense of "the intimate strangeness of being" in metaphysics grew up together with the rise of the desire for the mastery and control of system in all its manifestations.[357] Modern philosophy abandoned form, finality, and natural teleology (though biology seems to be unable to drop teleological language), and postmodern philosophy continued this trajectory, albeit explicitly rejecting both modernity's dualism and the unity of the Hegelian dialectic. These were replaced with equivocal pluralism, "which is either supremely suspicious of, or outrightly hostile to, any claim for integral unity or wholeness."[358] In the miasmic drift toward nihilism, Cartesian doubt becomes full-blown skepticism about truth, beauty, goodness, reason, and reality itself.[359] There is now a narrative, says Hart, "that makes nihilism—in the technical sense of disbelief in any ultimate meaning or purpose beyond the physical—plausible and powerful."[360]

---

355. Desmond, *The Intimate Strangeness*, xxxii, 34.

356. Desmond, *The Intimate Strangeness*, 105–6.

357. It is necessary to be careful with the language of "mastery" and "control" as well. The mastery of nature in terms of, for example, controlled experiments gave us vaccines for infectious diseases. But a control that aspires to become total leads inevitably to destruction.

358. Desmond, *The Intimate Strangeness*, 47.

359. Desmond, *The Intimate Strangeness*, 112. Nihilism, he says, is the final fruit of skepticism about truth and intelligibility.

360. Hart, "Purpose and Function."

The metaphysics of gift returns to wonder—wonder rooted in the "primitive structure of the human cognitional act," with that act presupposing being as "structurally worthy or evocative of wonder, hence as an order, the causal meaning of which consists most basically in giving and receiving goodness and beauty."[361] Conversely, the "primitive structure of being" has at its heart "*a causal order of goodness and beauty which of its inner logic elicits receptive wonder as the most basic human cognitional act.*"[362]

Thus wonder and beauty are mutually interrelated. For Balthasar, "Beauty is objectively located at the intersection of two moments Thomas calls *species* and *lumen* ('form and splendor'), [and] the encounter of these is characterized by the two moments of beholding and being enraptured."[363] The contemporary use of "wonder" can slide into sentimentality and has become familiar with overuse; for this reason, the word "astonishment" is often used as another translation for the Greek *thaumazein*. Wonder as astonishment arises from an excess or surplus which calls forth a self-transcending movement of the mind: we *behold* something, and though we often think of "beholding" as "taking hold of" or grasping, when we are struck by wonder it is *we ourselves who are taken hold of*, enraptured (etymologically, carried off, transported, with delight). As Desmond explained, "We do not go toward something, but find ourselves going out of ourselves because something has made its way, often in startling communication, into the very depths or roots of our being."[364] If the enrapturing came first, human freedom would be eliminated; but it is at one with the movement of beholding.

Beauty, according Balthasar, "is the last thing which the thinking intellect dares to approach, since only it dances as an uncontained splendour around the double constellation of the true and the good and their inseparable relation to one another."[365] Beauty integrates and orders both the intellect and will, because the object of beauty presents itself both to the mind and to the appetite. That is, of all the transcendentals, it is the only one that is directly sensible, visible, and palpable to us. We may "see" wisdom or goodness, but that sight is metaphorical. Only in true beauty

---

361. D. L. Schindler, *Given as Gift*, 86–87.
362. D. L. Schindler, *Given as Gift*, 87 (emphasis mine).
363. Balthasar, *Glory of the Lord I*, 10.
364. Desmond, *The Intimate Strangeness*, 106.
365. Balthasar, *Glory of the Lord I*, 18.

do we see *both* visible appearance *and* the depths of being, both form and the radiance of being. Beauty lies at the conjunction of transcendence and immanence, subject and object, intellect and sense. For Balthasar, this is a simultaneous event; beauty is what moves us upward and outside of ourselves at the same time that it brings us deeper into the reality of the particular.

In addition, beauty, like wonder, entails *patience*: a receptivity toward, openness to, and appreciation of the object *before* any demands for using, analyzing, or manipulating the object. It lets the object "be" in its own fullness, prior to appropriation. That receptivity is, then, "*a contemplative wonder born of and sustained by the beauty of the other.*"[366] Finally, beauty and gift go hand in hand: "We speak of beauty as 'gratuitous,' meaning it exceeds rational calculation and projects of self-interest even while being luminous with intelligibility and the very meaning of self-fulfillment"; the world should be approached not with calculation or critical distance, but with "the warm and attentive disposition of welcoming wonder."[367]

An Ever-New Gaze

Science and philosophy can both be subject to a loss of astonishment, such that the "intimate strangeness" of being becomes domesticated; they can also both lead to nihilism, "the assertion of the valuelessness of being."[368] The technological paradigm might either assert the same valuelessness of being, or maintain that we can claim nothing about value since it is a "private matter." Much postmodern philosophy also devalues meaning and being in such a way as to open the possibility of nihilism, as many have pointed out.[369] If the world is taken for granted as a given fact and not a gift, "the being there of what is arouses no ontological astonishment, or metaphysical nausea, or aesthetic jubilation, or religious celebration."[370]

The difference between doubt and wonder reveals crucial differences in metaphysical outlook. That difference becomes dazzlingly

---

366. D. L. Schindler, "'Homelessness,'" 356 (emphasis mine).
367. D. C. Schindler, "Beauty and the Holiness," 27.
368. Desmond, *Perplexity and Ultimacy*, 39.
369. See Cunningham, *Genealogy of Nihilism*.
370. Desmond, *Perplexity and Ultimacy*, 39.

evident when we examine carefully the metaphysics of gift, resting on Aquinas's real distinction, unfolded by Przywara to reveal the beauty of its rhythm, unveiled by Ulrich and Balthasar as an obligation ultimately "to understand Being in its ontological difference as pointing to love,"[371] and further opened up in David L. Schindler's triune heart of being that establishes a communion between receiver and giver in a place where wonder and gift are ontologically inseparable.

Metaphysics of gift is not a new philosophical proposal, much less an all-encompassing system. What it does provide is an ever-new way of seeing the world that is capable of transforming all things by integrating their unique truth and goodness into a more profound context: the whole of being. Both the desired "consilience" of those marked by the technocratic paradigm and the holism of postmodern ecological sensibilities seek a unification that they impede by their chosen relationship to being.

Balthasar said that truth is *symphonic* and that we must take the prodigious multiplicity seriously. From a multitude of voices, we seek to form a choir. This is what the metaphysics of gift does. Mechanism truly describes one aspect of reality that is good; identity philosophies address another. If either is absolutized, the consequences are disastrous, but if each can be harmonized relative to the truth of Being, their goodness and beauty will shine through. The lost key to this harmony is *analogy*, which "names the unity-in-difference characteristic of the gift of being."[372] Only by understanding reality analogically can we comprehend that something always remains strange and "other" even while being intimate and close. This analogical gaze upon the world has its epiphany in the moment of wonder and in every apparent paradox:

> For the polarity of essence and appearance, universality and particularity, reveals *each time more* of the being than the knower expects. We can be aware that there are two movements: the movement from the essence to the appearance and the movement from the appearance to the essence. . . . It is impossible, however, really to actuate both movements simultaneously. Thus, one pole always and essentially escapes us, and the movement of thought never comes to an end. In revealing itself, a being demonstrates its ever greater fullness and thus its ineliminable mystery.[373]

---

371. Balthasar, *Glory of the Lord V*, 646.
372. Hanby, "Creation as Aesthetic Analogy," 366.
373. Balthasar, *Theo-Logic I*, 158.

The history of philosophy oscillates between privileging unity or difference, with most postmoderns championing either difference or a very uneasy tension. Analogy reveals not only *how* things can be unified while still being many, but that this unity-in-distinction is the true form of reality despite the apparent contradiction. How is it that things become more themselves the more deeply they are unified? Here our human experience is truly a microcosm by which we can understand that love both glorifies the uniqueness of the other at the very same time that it binds us together.[374] Communion-in-love is very different from a mere absence of distinction, and "difference is inscribed in the heart of the unity of being as something fundamentally positive."[375]

Metaphysics of gift is also a metaphysics of love, when love is conceived of in this way and not misconstrued. Desmond and others use the Christian term *agape* to describe many aspects of reality that conform to this ordering structure. True wonder, *thaumazein*, must be the essential attitude and starting place of the metaphysician, and it too is *agapeic*: "I do not go out from myself toward the other to appropriate the other.... I go toward the other because the other is for itself and always irreducible to what it is for me. It is its being for itself that is affirmed, celebrated in this movement of going beyond itself."[376]

Only a metaphysics of gift can be the true "guardian of metaphysical wonderment,"[377] which includes and goes beyond mere natural wonder. Only a metaphysics that leaves room for mystery can both start and end in astonished wonder. Essence and existence, being and appearance, universality and particularity, can be observed by thought in "eternal movement" around the mystery, which is not unintelligible darkness, but Aquinas's excess of light, an "inexhaustible well of knowledge and contemplation."[378]

---

374. Caldecott, *Radiance of Being*, 95.
375. Healy, *Eschatology*, 52.
376. Desmond, *The Intimate Strangeness*, 11.
377. Balthasar, *Glory of the Lord V*, 646.
378. Balthasar, *Theo-Logic I*, 158.

5

Metaphysics of Gift in Action

> *Gift is the form of action in that it gathers the different elements that constitute human action into a dynamic unity. Acting, at its core, is the reception and the reciprocation of the gift of being.*[1]

WE HAVE NOW EXAMINED gift and action at the deepest ontological levels; gift is not simply something handed over to another in the same manner as a birthday present, but as the permanent underlying principle, the *arche*. The relation of *esse* (being) and *agere* (operation, action) is analogical, constituting an asymmetrical unity-in-distinction: the human person's capacity to act is a revelation of the original gift of being, and as Antonio López notes above, the ontological structure of gift is present in each concrete thing both as form and content. For the metaphysics of gift, the highest good is both good in itself and good in its effects, action "is the ultimate perfection of each thing,"[2] and, as *esse* gives itself away in concrete, substantial beings, so those beings give themselves away through their actions.

The discussion of the technological paradigm in bioethics in chapter 3 continued our preliminary examinations of the central topics of the openness of reason, of the good, and of freedom. We saw that because *reason* is open, it points beyond itself, revealing that reality cannot be fully captured by an ideological rationalism. It is an impoverished vision

---

1. López, *Gift and the Unity*, 128.
2. Aquinas, *Summa Contra Gentiles*, lib. 3, cap. 113, n. 1.

of the common *good* that equates it solely with fulfilling the necessities of the members of a political order—a pursuit of needs, even a broad one like "happiness," resulting in the mere co-incidence of private goods—rather than seeing it as "a way of being, specifically, a paradoxical unity of giving and receiving."[3] Finally, without gift, without the connection to others in the interplay of giving and receiving, *freedom* too falls, becoming reduced to the abstraction of a negative independence from coercion, or autonomy in the face of an infinite array of neutral "choices."

This last point on freedom brings us to the topic of this chapter. It is an attenuated notion of work and of human action to conceive of freedom only under the rubric of individual autonomy. For Aristotle, any action had the character of a gift, a contribution in the present that extended from one's immediate circle outward to both others and to the future. If being political (participating in a *polis*) is a necessary part of what it means to be human, and the creation of that *polis* depends on bonds of friendship and reciprocity, then "the defining human action is donation ... [which] lies between modern individual action on one hand and modern political/economic structure on the other."[4] Rather than being merely an expression of personal liberty or the isolated individual's autonomous will, every act is part of a public domain characterized by relationality and modified by that domain.

The metaphysics of gift and its understanding of reason, the good, freedom, and work presents us with a very different vision of bioethics than that of the biotechnological paradigm. Remembering that the paradigm cannot avoid the dualism that is an essential feature of liberalism, we must first turn to a preliminary point. It appears that the dominant paradigm today in the popular culture tends not toward dualism but toward a holistic identity philosophy, inextricably linked with ecological awareness. While scientists and modern philosophers look at popular holism skeptically, ecological holism looms large in public discourse. So before looking at "gift in action" in terms of *work* and *dialogue*, it is first beneficial to briefly recount the history and consequences of these ideas that identify themselves in opposition to the technological paradigm. The existing tension between these two philosophical positions will help us illustrate the partiality of both and the "symphonic" nature of truth that

---

3. D. C. Schindler, "Enriching the Good," 657.
4. Milbank, "Paul against Biopolitics," 38.

can only be achieved through the openness to reality that animates the metaphysics of gift.

Is Holism the Answer?

Holism is not a new philosophy, and though it has many permutations, it essentially sees all things in terms of the whole, not merely as an aggregation of parts. The term applies in many fields, from agriculture and architecture to neurology and psychology, and has helped to overcome some of the negative effects of the disconnected worldview inherent in the technological paradigm. The most familiar form of holism derives from Arne Naess's well-known "Deep Ecology," originating in James Lovelock's "Gaia" hypothesis that the earth is a single self-regulating system or even a single organism,[5] which is also the most extreme manifestation of holistic eco-philosophy. A specific ethic follows from this, one that often pits the human against the nonhuman in favor of the latter.

Of course, much good has come from the realization that we hold a deep and abiding community with the natural world, but when pressed, as Dubo points out, the result is another defective pole, the other side of the same coin:

> The identification of holists with nature, rather than the mark of a radical paradigm shift, is no less a characteristically modern move than [the] dichotomisation of humans and nature. Both essentialise, fixing nature's meaning in order to create the distinct categories that they need in order to fulfil their identification with one pole or the other.[6]

Both dichotomization (dualism between humans and nature) and identification (their fusion) are deficient tools that do not resolve the ambivalences. The former, following the Enlightenment, sees nature as a neutral resource for the benefit of humans; its utilitarianism reduces goodness itself to a variable in a cost-benefit analysis, easily changeable according to the current political climate. The latter asks us to eliminate the ontological differences between persons and nature, "since the biosphere is considered a biotic unity of undifferentiated value."[7] The

---

5. See Lovelock, *Gaia*. The book was received with almost religious fervor by those inclined to a kind of environmental mysticism that has little to do with science.

6. Dubo, "'Saving' 'Nature,'" 30.

7. John Paul II, "Conference on Environment."

biotechnological paradigm reflects the former; early environmental writers developed the latter as a critique, calling for humans to pass "from conqueror of the land-community to plain member and citizen of it."[8] However, this philosophical expression became extreme, dissolving all distinctions and therefore, all points of reference.

Criticisms quickly arose in response to the lack of differentiation in holism:

1) Early eco-feminists saw the "wider identity" with nature sought by holists as the "echo of patriarchal modernity's totalizing attitude,"[9] and this political point emanates from a metaphysical one. Val Plumwood noted that if for holists humans are just one strand in the biotic web, then what is proposed is "an indistinguishability metaphysics of unbroken wholeness in the whole of reality . . . the obliteration of all distinction."[10]

2) Around the same time, others noted the loss not only of the uniqueness of persons but also *the loss of the uniqueness of the things of nature*, the very things holism was meant to save. For holistic schools of ecological philosophy, the "web of equivalent relationality" (e.g., Naess's "rejection of the man-in-environment image in favor of the relational, total-field image"[11]) among all forms of life, and even non-life in the case of geographical features, is problematic:

> In a field theory of ecology, individual organisms are conceived as momentary formations of energy rather than enduring material objects. . . . The study of nature by analysis of isolated objects becomes untenable not only because isolation alters their sense but because, as fixed forms, their existence is too transient to bear study. "The reality of individuals is problematic because they do not exist per se."[12]

If all being is dissolved into what is essentially the Heraclitean Flux, how do we maintain the substantial unity and integrity of natural entities? How do we salvage persons and the things of nature? Indeed,

---

8. Leopold, *Sand County Almanac*, 240.
9. Zimmerman, *Contesting Earth's Future*, 10.
10. Plumwood, "Nature, Self, and Gender," 10.
11. Naess, "Shallow and the Deep," 95.
12. Gadow, "Existential Ecology," 600, quoting Morowitz, "Biology as a Cosmological Science," 156.

how do we even salvage "relations," since not only is it true that "a process which is its own end or necessity cannot account for the singular things which are ends in themselves within it," but "relationships unsustained by substantial persons [or other entities] bear no analogy to anything we could conceive of as relations"?[13] Real relationships require real being.

3) For others, relying on insights offered by phenomenology,[14] the problem was that holism continued the false dilemmas of dualism. Dualists observed nature in a detached manner, as if through a window; the presumption of dualism removes all subjectivity *from* nature, which becomes a mere research project, a view in which "an intrinsically-meaningless objective realm ('nature') is separated epistemically from—and so needs to be mastered through the activities of—isolated, self-certain subjects."[15] Holists attempted to overcome dualism and mechanism by drawing humans *into* nature, eliminating the subject/object split altogether, but this is clearly problematic in itself. There can be relational, non-holistic responses to dualism; Neil Evernden, who first brought the work of Martin Heidegger to bear on environmental discussions, said that it was necessary to *encounter* nature *precisely as other*.[16]

The post-phenomenological rejection of holism extends over a wide and complex network. To browse through various academic journals is to see every possible postmodern philosophy—phenomenology, post-structuralism, hermeneutics, post-constructivism, bioculturalism, ecosemiotics, and many more—recycled into various environmental ethics. As we have said, for the metaphysics of gift, postmodernity is essentially "a continuation and intensification of the 'logic' of modernity,"[17] and postmodern attempts to resolve the tensions between holistic relationships and unique persons or natural entities to somehow "shore up" substantial being fall short. The standard postmodern response to dualities is the

---

13. Murphy, *God Is Not a Story*, 224.

14. Phenomenological eco-philosophers include Erazim Kohak, who drew on Husserlian phenomenology in his *The Embers and the Stars* (1984); David Seamon; Edward Casey; Bruce Foltz; Ingrid Leman-Stefanovic; and David Abram, whose *The Spell of the Sensuous* (1997) brought an eco-phenomenology that owed a great deal to Husserl and Merleau-Ponty into the public domain.

15. Thomson, "Ontology and Ethics," 382.

16. Evernden, *The Social Creation of Nature*, 108.

17. Caldecott, "New Sins," 491.

tension of "irreducible ambiguity,"[18] which does not bode well either for dialogue or for working together in the "friendship/polis" Aristotle had in mind:

> Rather than a universal *physis* or nature to which the material world conforms, postmodernism turns to the diverse and unique traits of distinctive cultures. Since truth is seen as merely a product of human culture, *physis* is fundamentally malleable and constructed by the dominant cultural ethos. Because language is believed to have no connection to the external world, the truth of *physis* remains concealed from human knowing. The purpose of language therefore is not to arrive at the truth of things, but to persuade or attract persons in solidarity to a particular movement or worldview.... Postmodernism is less a school of thought and more a political activist strategy wherein power is held in greater esteem. In this postmodern world of foundationless "truths" composed of an endless multiplicity of cultural narratives, no overarching truth is available to set a single nuanced idea above any particular tribal rhetoric. Intellectual discourse devolves into an all-or-nothing shouting match that excludes any attempts at a synthesis through analysis or dialogue.[19]

"Woodcraft Ethic" vs. "Leave No Trace"

Consider the practical applications of the two views of a person's relation to nature and a typical postmodern response. On the one hand, the "Woodcraft Ethic," which involved living off the land by *using* nature, saw the public wilderness areas as a "means for allowing the more virile and primitive forms of outdoor recreation to survive," where American men could test themselves by "living in the open" and "killing game."[20] In the early twentieth century, Horace Kephart described woodcraft as "the art of getting along well in the wilderness by utilizing nature's storehouse."[21] The Boy Scouts of America especially adopted this ethos from their inception.

However, as increased numbers of people began entering wilderness areas and national parks, it appeared that the "greatest threat to wilderness

---

18. Dubo, "'Saving' 'Nature,'" 82.
19. Steele, *Postmodern Metaphysics*.
20. Leopold, "Wilderness," 404.
21. Kephart, *The Book of Camping*, xi.

is from the wilderness lovers themselves."[22] The Sierra Club stressed the notion that the primary human benefit of wilderness is ecological and appreciative; hence the wilderness should remain unchanged. Rather than cutting down trees for shelter or fires, or foraging for plants and animals to eat (which supposedly evinced an anthropocentric and dualist approach), the outdoor ethic called "Leave No Trace" sought to have minimal impact—or better, no impact at all—on the land, using nothing in the wilderness.

When managing a popular wilderness area, this makes sense pragmatically, but the problem arises when this attitude is universalized. This ostensibly holistic approach mirrors dualism, as Dubo and others said it would: one assumes "that there is a [separate] thing called nature that needs our help"[23] and that we should relate with it minimally. The most extreme version of this vision is perhaps E. O. Wilson's "Half-Earth" proposal, which insists that we must leave half the earth untouched by man.[24] First, this proposal reinforces a dualistic vision in which there is an inherent conflict between the well-being of nature and the well-being of humans. Michael Northcott argues that this perspective came about through the emphasis on competition over symbiosis in Darwin's theory of evolution.[25] Wilson's proposal is also ambiguous and self-defeating. If nothing in the wilderness can be used, then our use of "non-wilderness" is seemingly of no consequence but it will inevitably affect the whole: bees do not respect the boundaries between pesticide-free wilderness preserves and toxic non-wilderness. Hikers and campers who want to enjoy the wilderness may do so only by importing resources from far away, usually China. James Morton Turner was particularly hard on this aspect of Leave No Trace as a form of consumerism:

> The exchange of external resources (such as petroleum-fired stoves) for wilderness resources (such as wood-depleting camp fires) . . . helped ally the modern backpacker with the wilderness recreation industry—encouraging backpackers to practice Leave No Trace in the wilderness and keep an eye out for the Leave No Trace logo in the shopping mall. Only in the convoluted logic of modern consumer culture did it make sense

22. Brower, "Wilderness Is for People, Too!," 3.
23. Evernden, *Social Creation of Nature*, 99.
24. See Wilson, *Half-Earth*.
25. Northcott, "Indigenous Peoples."

that those actions in the shopping mall were the best way to save wilderness beyond.[26]

Of course, the products of the consumer culture must be manufactured, leaving significant traces on nature in other parts of the world.

Should wilderness be treated as a recreational resource or a pristine preserve? Dogsledder Blair Braverman reflects on the tension between these two views:

> One of the things I love about dogsledding is how it forces me to engage with nature on a deep level. I think the Leave No Trace ethos is vital, I'm glad it exists, I practice it when I go camping—but I'm also grateful that I came of age as an outdoorsperson in northern Norway, where I was taught to build fires and improvise shelters and otherwise interact with the landscape in slightly messier ways. All of our stories about nature are shaped by the ways in which we encounter it. Leave No Trace practices teach us to pass through landscapes like ghosts, rather than become a part of those landscapes. We're already so many steps removed from nature, and Leave No Trace is another veil of separation.[27]

The two views stand in uneasy opposition; like Braverman, some people use one at one time, one at another, or maybe try to juxtapose them or combine them. While we can appreciate "Leave No Trace" when limited to small, ecologically fragile areas, when its underlying attitude becomes incorporated into one's worldview, it brings unintended consequences.

Holism and Gift

The very notion of the physical-as-gift . . . bears within it a necessary and legitimate sense of the physical-as-instrument: of the latter, however, as now situated inside and subordinate to, and thus containing and expressing, the physical-as-gift.[28]

The tension between these two views arises because of a lack of ontological clarity and results in a hidden, subtle form of reductionism. In holism, the "whole" is considered as a dynamic *network*, a *system* (an "ecosystem," or the "system" of patient-doctor-hospital relations). Bioethics recognizes

---

26. Turner, "From Woodcraft," 479.
27. Blair Braverman, interviewed in Wortman-Wunder, "The West."
28. D. L. Schindler, *Ordering Love*, 231–32.

the interrelationships that go into making this system a unity, but "to the extent that this unity results from and is exhausted by this interrelation, it is doubly reducible—to the sum of its component parts and to its antecedent causes. *It therefore remains classically mechanical.*"²⁹ The "whole" of holism might be seen as more than the sum of its parts, but systems theory cannot say what the "more" consists in. The reason it cannot is that insofar as it is empirically based, it cannot acknowledge any trans-empirical ontological value.³⁰ Analogy provides clarity to what D. C. Schindler calls this "murky night of ambiguity."³¹ It is capable of grasping the "more" that neither system's holism nor the uneasy juxtaposition can adequately characterize.

The key, as always, is to see the asymmetrical polar relationship in which gift is prior: the things of the physical world can have instrumental value without being reduced to that value, just as contractual relations can be embraced within the richness of a covenant. For a metaphysics of gift and its analogical community between the natural world and the human world, the mechanical properties of physical things are not denied, but are integrated while remaining distinct. Physical things have an interior order (form and finality) and therefore value, which "indicates an initial, *proportionately-analogically conceived*, participation in the giftedness proper to all being" that makes it possible for us to relate to them.³² There is a similarity between orders of being that ecological holism wants us to recognize, but at the same time we can affirm the proper differences between persons and nature, differences that appear even more wondrous in the light of those very similarities. Proper differences are "simultaneous with a real unity coincident with these differences."³³

Again, analogy leaves us with a kind of irreducible tension, but it is important to recall that a polar relationship is one in which each side "contains" the other—though asymmetrically—and each can be understood only with respect to the other. Thus, analogy reveals not a negative antagonistic opposition but a *generative integration*. In a sense,

29. Hanby, "Beyond Mechanism," 182–83 (emphasis mine).

30. Schindler holds that form follows organization such that different organizational structure equals a different ontology, which may not be apparent until after development. He calls this "ontological consequentialism" (Hanby, "Beyond Mechanism," 183).

31. D. C. Schindler, *Dramatic Structure*, 6.

32. D. L. Schindler, *Ordering Love*, 231.

33. D. L. Schindler, *Ordering Love*, 231.

analogous relationships are mirrored in the symbiotic relationships found in nature, where each aspect or participant is more itself yet also *more than itself* because of the relationships it participates in. What would bees be without flowers, or flowers without bees? We can uphold the giftedness and intrinsic value of nature and its usefulness, but always from within that larger context. These exist in a symbiotic tension, not a competitive one. D. C. Schindler provides an illuminating example that transcends the duality between "instrumental value" and "intrinsic value," between the Woodcraft Ethic and Leave No Trace:

> There are two ways a tree can be good. There is first its immediate, natural goodness, as when it displays itself in a forest or a park, in the magnificence of its stature, manifesting the beauty of its color, filling the air with its scent, perhaps offering food to squirrels or a home to birds. Then there is a second, "artificial" goodness, when it becomes wood for a fire, for a chair, for a door of a cathedral. These are radically different kinds of goodness, even to the point of being mutually exclusive in any particular case (to enjoy the goodness of the tree qua firewood requires the elimination of the tree qua living organism), and *yet there is no contradiction in affirming both.* Indeed, there is a deep connection between the two, which allows one—in fact, ultimately compels one, if one is to love properly—to love trees in both ways. To love a wooden chair does not oblige me to hate the tree in the forest. To the contrary, the more deeply I love a wooden chair, the more interested I become in the kind of tree out of which it is made, the quality of this sort of wood in comparison to the wood of other types of trees, where such trees grow, what they look like—and feel like, and smell like, as trees.[34]

As we said in chapter 4, the highest good is neither simply good in itself nor good in its use but both, if the "law of the gift" is that something becomes more itself, more perfect, to the extent that it gives itself away. (This too is the law of nature, the nature of nature, in which individual organisms "give themselves away"—their time, energy, resources, and

---

34. D. C. Schindler, "Quaerere Deum." "To be sure, one works, not simply to enjoy a special sort of intimacy with creation and thus to commune with God, but perhaps most obviously in order to produce things that are useful for human existence; moreover, even such production for the most part serves a yet more extrinsic end in providing wages for the laborer, and profits for the merchant. *But these further ends do not in principle require the elimination of the fruitful encounter we just described. Instead, these more extrinsic ends can be affirmed as implications, necessary but subordinate, of the principal good that is the work itself*" ("Quaerere Deum," emphasis mine).

very lives—to create progeny, the next generation). In the end neither holism nor dualism nor ambivalence without resolution is the answer; only analogy can provide an adequate understanding of reality in its many dimensions. In the next section we return to the "Woodcraft Ethic" vs. "Leave No Trace," this time from another perspective. Richard White has said that *work* is central, and that some environmentalists are notorious for failing to grasp that persons historically know nature through work; they distance humans from nature and "call for human connections with nature while disparaging all those who claim to have known and appreciated nature through work and labor."[35]

To Do Good Work

The name of our proper connection to the earth is "good work," for good work involves much giving of honor. It honors the source of its materials; it honors the place where it is done; it honors the art by which it is done; it honors the thing that it makes and the user of the made thing.[36]

So far, we have been discussing the various ontological visions of nature that exist hidden in the presuppositions held about the world. While this discussion might appear abstract and academic, these ideas "reveal themselves to be extremely concrete and indeed relevant to every one of us to the extent that we *work*, that is, to the extent that we are human and so carry out the mission implanted in our nature from the beginning."[37] As D. C. Schindler points out, reflecting on the meaning of work "brings us face to face with the question of the modern transformation of existence; it sets into relief the difference between the classical and contemporary worldviews, and requires us to assess the implications of this difference."[38]

Of course, like everything related to modern man, work can often be subsumed into the technological paradigm such that it "does not reach to the inner reality of man and the world, does not penetrate to the core of human existence in the world, but remains instead a kind of overlay of subjective intentionality, or at most a mere external regulation."[39] In

---

35. White, *Organic Machine*, x.
36. Berry, *Sex, Economy, Freedom & Community*, 35.
37. D. C. Schindler, "Redeeming Work," 259.
38. D. C. Schindler, "Redeeming Work," 259.
39. D. C. Schindler, "Redeeming Work," 261.

fact, the way we understand work has suffered many transformations over time. For Max Weber, this debasement began with the Reformation and the rise of the view that accumulated wealth, quantitatively assessed, was a sign of one's virtue.[40] However it originated, the end result is visible in everything from industrial farming to the numberless and abstract subdivisions of the global financial market. We have created an oppositional duality between the active and contemplative life, so that the former becomes the servility of work, forced upon us as means to various ends. Josef Pieper's *Leisure: The Basis of Culture* is a corrective to the twentieth century's vision of man as essentially a worker in this negative sense: one "who was ready to suffer and sacrifice everything in order to be productive and to contribute to humanity's technological domination of nature."[41] The obsession with productivity techniques and "life hacks" shows that little has changed. This materialistic vision of man reflects a similar vision of reality—the world is "just stuff, formless matter to be worked on, and otherwise meaningless . . . . lacking any *intrinsic* goodness, truth, and beauty."[42]

However, let us consider D. C. Schindler's discussion of work from the perspective of gift. The worker—specifically, the carpenter—involves himself in the reality of trees and wood "in a genuinely corporeal way, and in a way that makes a claim on a significant part of my existence—or perhaps better on the whole of my existence in a certain respect."[43] As we will see, the way one works and relates to the world encapsulates an assessment of what the world is and what it means to one personally. Schindler continues with the example of the carpenter:

---

40. See Weber, *The Protestant Ethic*. Weber believed that with the loss of the assurance of salvation through the Catholic sacraments, it was necessary for people to look for other forms of self-confidence, hence the quantitative rationalization dominating the new order, "now bound to the technical and economic conditions of machine production which today determine the lives of all the individuals who are born into this mechanism, not only those directly concerned with economic acquisition, with irresistible force" (*The Protestant Ethic*, 129).

41. D. C. Schindler, "Work as Contemplation," 598.

42. D. C. Schindler, "Work as Contemplation," 598. "Josef Pieper defines the *ethos* of modernity effectively as the replacement of a sense of the world as gift—a gift that invites praise, thanksgiving, and celebration: all essentially *contemplative activities*—with the 'workaday world,' the world of 'total work,' in which the value of all things arises exclusively from the human effort put into them" ("Redeeming Work," 259).

43. D. C. Schindler, "Quaerere Deum."

> Mastering this craft requires a great deal of time and a discipline, or in other words a learning that is at the same time a training of energies, an inscribing of certain practices, so to speak, into my very flesh. I have to come out of myself, in what can be a toilsome and even painful activity, in order to work with the wood.... The work is thus a joining together of two movements of self-transcendence: man the worker spends himself in a form-giving activity, and the tree is thereby taken up and made into something new. The chair, which results, is more than man and more than tree. It is a new reality that bears the traces, as it were, of its two sources.[44]

The significance of work—in addition to its giving us the means to make a living—is found in how it provides a unique way of knowing things beyond mere conceptual knowledge, in "the generative encounter between man and the world under the sign of beauty, goodness, and truth."[45]

The man who has thought most practically about this in terms of ecological ethics is Wendell Berry, who sees work as the way in which we relate to the world *par excellence*. In fact, he points out, "we are connected by work even to the places where we don't work, for all places are connected."[46] And so his main effort in much of his writing is to insist that we learn to work well, that we learn to do "good work."

Berry, too, rejects the intrinsic/instrumental value dichotomy. He rejects the terminology that arises from dualism, such as the term "environment" (as in something separate from persons that surrounds them), which he said was chosen as "more scientific," since *creation* was too religious and *world* too mundane. At the same time, he is skeptical about holists whose focus is preserving the wilderness, which is normally far from where people live and work, and who set up an opposition between state-preserved and non-preserved areas, the latter of which are simply subject to exploitation. He specifically says that their terms are *still dualistic*; he rejects the terms "biocentrism" (if life is at the center, he asks, what is at the periphery, and *where* is it?) and "deep ecology" (no one has ever thought of their home as "ecological," whether deep or shallow). Instead of such abstract and sterile notions which displace, disembody, and disconnect us, he reminds us that real names are those of the individual

---

44. D. C. Schindler, "Quaerere Deum."
45. D. C. Schindler, "Quaerere Deum."
46. Berry, *Sex, Economy, Freedom & Community*, 35

"rivers and river valleys; creeks, ridges, and mountains; towns and cities; lakes, woodlands, lanes, roads, creatures, and people," and that "the real name of our connection to this everywhere different and differently named earth is '*work*.'"[47]

Specifically, what connects us to the world is *good* work. This work is modestly scaled and known only by its particularity, which is defined differently for each place, job, and worker. Eschewing abstractions, Berry sees "good work" not necessarily as enjoyable, not necessarily as satisfying, or necessarily as fulfilling one's "passion," but as *useful*, a word that, as David Cloutier notes, is "vastly different from the technical focus on *utility*."[48] Usefulness, says Berry, "stands in opposition to the frivolous," and he maintains that useful work, like useful language, is work "that enables seeing, makes clarity," whereas bad work, "instead of asking a man what he can do well, . . . asks him what he can do fast and cheap."[49]

The community is the proper home of good work because it is more of a covenant than the state or the market, which depend on contractual relations. Both private life and public life gravitate toward exploitation, competition, and insatiability, but the disciplines of community are what knit them together. A community is an arrangement of persons that includes marriages, family structures, divisions of work, the relationship with the natural world, etc., not merely the atomized individual against the state, not the mere co-incidence of private interests when people temporarily unite to achieve their own individual goals. Community is central for Berry and indeed most, if not all, conservationists.

> The indispensable form that can intervene between public and private interests is that of the community. The concerns of public and private, republic and citizen, necessary as they are, are not adequate for the shaping of human life. Community alone, as principal and as fact, can raise the standards of local health (ecological, economic, social, and spiritual) without which the other two interests will destroy one another. By community, I mean the commonwealth and common interests, commonly understood, of people living together in a place and wishing to continue to do so. To put it another way, community is a locally

---

47. Berry, *Sex, Economy, Freedom & Community*, 35.
48. Cloutier, "Working with the Grammar," 616.
49. Berry, *Continuous Harmony*, 90.

understood interdependence of local people, local culture, local economy, and local nature.[50]

The solution to the plundering of nature is beyond the standard dichotomy of the market and the state, of public and private. As Cloutier says, "The practice of the grammar of creation can never go on alone, but must be mediated, and its mediation occurs first and foremost in communities."[51] This is why Berry's very first two affirmations in his 1993 book of essays on conservation are simply:

> I. Land that is used will be ruined unless it is properly cared for.
>
> II. Land cannot be properly cared for by people who do not know it intimately, who do not know how to care for it, who are not strongly motivated to care for it, and who cannot afford to care for it.[52]

The law of supply and demand, he says, proposes no limits on either supply or demand. An apparent "consensus" can be "ginned up" against the excesses of the private sector, increasing pressure on the government to "do something," but then we are faced with the coercive and ultimately even totalitarian nature of large-scale political policies based only on such a reactive consensus:

> A government undertaking to protect all of nature that is now abused or threatened would have to take total control of the country. Police and bureaucrats—and opportunities for malfeasance—would be everywhere. To wish only for a public or a political solution to the problem of conservation may be to wish for a solution as bad as the problem and still be unable to solve it.[53]

---

50. Berry, *Sex, Economy, Freedom & Community*, 119–20. "All the plagues of our time are symptoms of a general disintegration. We are capable, really, only of the forcible integration of centralization—economic, political, military, and educational—and always at the cost of social and cultural disintegration.... That we prefer to deal piecemeal with the problems of disintegration keeps them 'newsworthy' and profitable to the sellers of cures. To see them as . . . the symptoms of a greater problem would require hard thought, a change of heart, and a search for the fundamental causes" (Berry, *The Hidden Wound*, 131–32).

51. Cloutier, "Working with the Grammar," 623.

52. Berry, *Sex, Economy, Freedom & Community*, 3.

53. Berry, *Sex, Economy, Freedom & Community*, 38.

A market economy without discipline or limits is matched by state solutions that are misguided at best because they cannot possibly be locally minded, "for 'saving the planet' calls for abstract purposes and central powers that cannot know—and thus will destroy—the integrity of local nature and local community. . . . You *can't* act locally by thinking globally."[54]

Economy of Gift

> *The best, most central paradigm for understanding free economic exchange is not contract among self-interested strangers, but gift-giving among neighbors.*[55]

Our current economic model is flawed and the way in which our natural environment is often pillaged for economic gain is a clear sign of it. One of the most serious consequences of the so-called "Free Market" has been

> the cutting loose of the economy from its roots in nature, which would provide organic limits and keep the production, exchange, and consumption of goods anchored in local communities. . . . The provision of work to otherwise destitute regions of the world represents a mitigation of poverty only in the crudest sense of the term; at a deeper level, in relation to the quality of human existence, outsourcing is actually an exportation of poverty.[56]

People often see things that arise from human desire—greed, consumerism, etc.—as strictly moral issues, as if the solution is simply to learn to share, or to be less avaricious or less driven by conspicuous consumption. But to echo an observation made by Berry, "how we take our lives from this world, how we work" speaks to our religious beliefs, certainly, but to our anthropology and ontology as well.[57] Though metaphysics might seem like an unlikely place to find sound economic advice, being aware of it is indispensable, especially when we consider that everything we do and think is already implicitly rooted in our ontological assumptions, whether we acknowledge them or not.

54. Berry, *Sex, Economy, Freedom & Community*, 23.
55. Walker, "The Poverty," 23.
56. D. C. Schindler, "Redeeming Work," 265–66.
57. Berry, *Sex, Economy, Freedom & Community*, 39.

In economics, ontology is ignored because the "Free Market" is construed as essentially *neutral*, as unlimited and unbound, based on a common denominator: that is, *profit*. According to the current paradigm, profit is the language that every inhabitant of Babel can still speak. When we do recognize that the market occasionally fails to capture something of value, it is taken more as an opportunity to expand the reach of the market rather than to recognize the limited nature of the system. One such example is how carbon markets have sprung up in response to concerns over greenhouse gas emissions.

The truth is that this system is not neutral at all, for it contains its own ontological vision, unacknowledged but there nonetheless. Because relationality is not built into its understanding of being, it privileges extrinsic exchanges between atomistic individuals, indifferent to the objective good. It demands free exchanges but has only a negative vision of freedom, that is, the *freedom from coercion* discussed previously, which often subverts itself by becoming a new kind of coercion, disallowing any rival notions of the good and making its own worldview exclusive. We catch glimpses of it when we see tags or stickers that read "fair trade," "organic," or "rainforest alliance certified," because an economy run on the coinage of profit attempts to convert any type of value—ecological, moral, social, sentimental—into numbers in the black. However, the moment we step out of a multinational department store and into an artisan's shop, the veil of the free market's "neutral" pretensions slips. In the joy of meeting the artisan and learning about his craft and his community, one comes in contact with what Ulrich would call an "ontological wealth" that cannot be quantified.

All work, whether done for financial gain, for self-fulfillment, or for community, is a confrontation of the person with the reality of an "other" and is characterized by *exchange*, though conceived in different ways. Ulrich's particular contribution to a different understanding of exchange through a metaphysics of gift both helps to unveil the deficiencies in the world of economics, technology, politics, and ethics (for example, when bioethics operates under a calculus of risk/benefit) and saves, through transformation, what is good in them. As Adrian Walker explains,

> The gift-giving paradigm can contain all that is of value in the liberal understanding of the market, even while reconfiguring the latter's logic in a profound way within a nonliberal context. This reconfiguration is necessary both to protect human freedom

and to secure economic good sense—a double desideratum that liberal economics, if consistently applied, cannot fulfill.[58]

As we saw earlier, Ulrich adopts Aquinas's "*Esse significat aliquid completum et simplex sed non subsistens*,"[59] which holds surprising possibilities for an ontological understanding of a *good* model of exchange that reverberates throughout all human endeavors, not merely as a moral "extra" or sociological analysis. Recall that the paradox of being—its simultaneous perfection and imperfection—is resolved when we see that *its perfection lies precisely in giving itself away*. Thus, one is ontologically wealthy *in his very being*, before and apart from anything he produces, and his wealth overflows in what Ulrich calls the "poverty" of giving himself away in communion with others. The simultaneity of wealth (fullness, completeness, receiving) with poverty (dependence, non-subsistence, giving away) is the paradox of love itself, such that we can say that, truly, *the meaning of being is love.*

In this way, true wealth is ontological, as "richness in the relations that are integral to man's original meaning."[60] This assessment recognizes that the human person is, first and foremost, a gift to him or herself; the person's freedom is likewise oriented towards the giving of him or herself in relation to others in order to form communion and community. This conception of wealth implies the relative importance of quantitative wealth and is not at all juxtaposed to it, but it also helps clarify the primary importance of non-quantifiable values.

What does any of this have to do with the "real world"? Walker explains that what looks like something perfectly quantitative—the notion of profit—is just a qualitative standard in disguise: privileging the quantitative does not eliminate the priority of ontological wealth, "but simply shifts the burden of ontological wealth onto its quantitative aspects. The result, then, is not really a non-ontological, purely quantitative sense of wealth at all, but rather a reduced form of ontological wealth masquerading as pure quantity."[61] At the same time, "what liberal economics means by self-interest is a drastically reduced form of the enjoyment of one's existence that characterizes ontological wealth."[62]

58. Walker, "Poverty of Liberal Economics," 24.
59. Aquinas, *De Potentia Dei*, q. 1, a. 1, co.
60. D. L. Schindler, "America's Technological Ontology," 270.
61. Walker, "Poverty of Liberal Economics," 35.
62. Walker, "Poverty of Liberal Economics," 35.

Ontological wealth is *prior to* anything the person makes or creates; it is his very being as a gift from another and to others. The ontological truth about persons is that they exist in community. The ontological wealth of the gift of being is self-diffusive: substantial being is structured as generous in the manner of gift, of what gives only as first given, and then it is able to participate in this generosity by passing it along, replaying the free exchange that characterizes being as love. Walker says, "Moreover, just as the person lays hold of his objective good as a person within communion, here too he enters into the possession, and enjoyment, of his ontological wealth within a communion consisting in mutual giving and receiving in love."[63]

In order to flesh out the economic worldview that a metaphysics of gift can offer, we can draw a useful contrast between the artisan or craftsman and what we can call "the technician":

> What distinguishes the craftsman from the technician is . . . the craftsman's openness to experiencing his work as a form of participation in "ontological wealth." This openness to ontological wealth is not, however, an optional extra, a moral icing on the cake. Ontological wealth is what enables the craftsman to achieve a better economic efficiency than the technician—and so to generate a real economic wealth that is not predicated on the concealment of the economic disvalue tied up with the technician's brand of "efficiency."[64]

This explanation contrasts workers in any field who operate under *distinctly different presuppositions*.[65] The technician represents the worldview of Western liberalism's technological paradigm, with its purely pragmatic interpretation of knowing and making, in which self-interested "free agents" enter into mutually beneficial contractual exchanges in a market that is ostensibly neutral to any good and profit is quantified through monetization.

The craftsman, by contrast, lives within a metaphysics of gift, *doing* true *technê* which, as the Greeks conceived it, while being transformative and creative, always maintains an essential connection to what is given naturally in reality. This preserves the giftedness of reality and the

---

63. Walker, "Poverty of Liberal Economics," 33.

64. Walker, "Poverty of Liberal Economics," 48.

65. Socrates says, for example, "No one in any position of rule, insofar as he is a ruler, seeks or orders what is advantageous to himself, but what is advantageous to his subject, that on which he practices his craft" (Plato, "The Republic," 342e [987]).

gratitude that is its appropriate response. In this sense, to echo Guardini's example, it is more natural—in more ways than one—to give thanks for the wind while traveling in a sailboat than for the gasoline while traveling in a motorboat.[66]

It is important to see that these are not in dialectical opposition but represent another polar relation; the craftsman integrates all of the skills and activity of the technician but not vice versa. For the craftsman, ontological wealth includes monetary wealth but goes well beyond it, deeper into the realm of the real; it is the manifestation of his relationship with others and the world. On the other hand, for the technician *as technician* (that is, as ruled by the technological paradigm), the richness of ontological wealth—the connection to a community, the value of relationships, the reality of truth, goodness, and beauty—are fundamentally extrinsic or "added on." They are for him "moral icing on the cake" and his concentration on quantitative wealth results in an ontological impoverishment. This is not a condemnation of the technician himself, who is often trapped within social and economic circumstances far from his own desires, who can even find a certain joy by joining in community with his fellow workers, and who can achieve a certain fulfillment in knowing that he had a part to play in producing the final products at the end of the assembly line. But we *can* critique the thinking that has created this system.

And what about ontological poverty: what does this have to do with real economics and real poverty? Whether one's "craft" is art, politics, or business, when viewed solely within the technological paradigm, bad models of exchange result. The welfare state redistributes wealth without "expecting and enabling the beneficiaries . . . to become responsible economic agents in their own right";[67] they are passive recipients of a "gift from nowhere."[68] The "free market" sees contracts among self-interested strangers as the primary instance of freedom, thus "contract without gift,"[69] which imposes its vision of the debased freedom of *homo economicus* not only in the economic sphere, but also in the marketization of every aspect of life. Only the priority of ontological wealth, of true

---

66. See Guardini, *Letters from Lake Como*, 11–13. There is no Luddite suggestion here that we abandon motorboats or gasoline, or that we shouldn't be grateful for them.

67. Walker, "Poverty of Liberal Economics," 20.

68. Milbank and Pabst, *Politics of Virtue*, 3.

69. Milbank and Pabst, *Politics of Virtue*, 3.

community and solidarity, can have any hope of truly alleviating even material poverty.

For many, especially in places where the technocratic economy has had limited influence, the giftedness of reality, the primacy of relation and community, and the dignity of work are still recognized intuitively because these things are simply true, good, and beautiful human realities. But especially for those submerged in the formalizing logic and reductive ontology of contemporary Western culture, understanding Ulrich's interpretation of being as love and wealth as a fundamentally ontological value is illuminating. First, it shows that there is a real problem with the market itself because of the ontological presuppositions it inherently contains. Thus the problem capitalism faces is not merely at a moral level; in fact, moralism as a response to the errors of the liberal worldview only seems to compound its errors because it does not address the nucleus of the problem. Meanwhile, socialism faces a loss of freedom through disingenuous, bureaucratic gift giving in exchange for power.

The two most prominent economic theories that shape our world—liberal economics and socialism—represent forms of exchange that are ontologically deficient because they reduce and make superfluous the truth about the human person and community. They do not alleviate true poverty but, as they seek to end material poverty, tend to create broader ontological poverty and a material well-being that is more fragile. Ontological wealth describes the abundant overflowing of the richness of "Being itself," which is present and active in all beings in the measure that they are able to live according to their true nature. With the help of Ulrich's conception of ontological wealth, we can recognize the truest desires of human nature, which are founded upon the encounters that build communities, on a "going out" from ourselves, and a reception of the other with openness. For Berry and others, strengthening our communities and shifting our economic activity within this network of relationships that we can see and that we care about is necessary, for "living as we now do in almost complete dependence on a global economy, we are put inevitably into a position of ignorance and irresponsibility.... We cannot connect ourselves to the globe as a whole only by means of a global economy that, without knowing the earth, plunders it for us."[70] Naturally, this brings us to a closer examination of the encounter of dialogue.

---

70. Berry, *Sex, Economy, Freedom & Community*, 37.

Solidarity through Dialogue

We are not talking about a mere external or formal exchange, or a purely dialectical encounter that attempts to impose a set of ideas on the adversary but rather, a reciprocal openness that brings about a deeper relationship with the other. Every encounter worthy of this name produces a change in its participants. And this change culminates in an experience of unity. . . . This "testimonial" form of communication . . . does not give way to any form of relativism, but rather, it exhibits a more radical ambition than a mere "agreement" or "consensus" about a cultural or social diagnosis.[71]

Dialogue is primarily a form of encounter and a mode of building community. A fruit of the modern ethos is an ever-increasing fragmentation and specialization in the professional and academic realms and a more bureaucratic, less participative government. We have already addressed each of these barriers to a certain extent in our critique of bioethical proceduralism, but let us add a few notes here before entering into a broader discussion of dialogue as a path to unity.

Bioethicist Tadeusz Pacholczyk comments on the obvious dissonance we feel when dialogue is summarily dismissed or bypassed. He gives the example of a family requesting medical treatment for a relative that the insurance company, hospital, or doctors see as excessive:

> The question when that happens is: What's the proper response? Should the response be that we start passing laws that allow hospitals to basically shut down the dialogue with the family, then unilaterally, on their own, take matters into their own hands and determine the outcome? Is that the best way to do this? . . . Health care [should not] become something that is carried out by ethics committees, hospital administrators and government officials.[72]

But what *kind* of dialogue are we talking about, based on what? In chapter 3 we discussed the ways that dialogue could fail, that consensus could be overridden by coercion. From a sociopolitical perspective, the freedom and unity purportedly sought was diminished, if not destroyed, whether one's livelihood depended upon being part of the "right" decision, or whether one's "informed consent" was constrained by one's

---

71. Prades and Cantos, "Postsecularism."

72. Tadeusz Pacholczyk, the director of education for the National Catholic Bioethics Center, quoted in Fraga, "The US 'Futile-Care' Debate."

dependence on the doctors. From the perspective of the metaphysics of gift, the problem of finding a true unity is not simply the power struggles involved in reaching an uneasy, fragile, or compelled consensus but what the ontology and anthropology behind such "agreements" say about reason, the good, the human person, and his or her relation to others.

To review: with regard to reason, formal rationality splits content from form, expressed in the notions of private content and public formal procedures. But the idea that one can have "pure form" without content is already a metaphysical decision. Content and form are inextricably related; there is a distinction but not a separation between appearance and being, between the form something takes and the content it expresses. There is an analogical unity between content and form while, at the same time, an irreducible distinction.

With regard to the good, for biotechnological proceduralism, one must appear as holding a neutral position toward any proposed good in favor of what essentially constitutes utility. There are ultimately only arbitrary grounds for non-utilitarian goods, at best only appeals to "moral intuition," which, as David L. Schindler says, "remains locked within the very horizon that exposes the content of that moral intuition for what it now is," namely a capricious value imposed on scientific/technological facts.[73] Any search for consensus within this inner logic will not bring about genuine community sustained by true dialogue, but only a constructed community based on the externals of "managerial techniques and procedural politics."[74]

With regard to relationality, concrete goods become pure choice abstracted from the concrete reality of previously existing relationships. An extrinsic understanding of relationships—when others are viewed primarily as contractual parties—often leads to a functional, utilitarian regard towards others and, finally, to alienation. And there is something more ominous that happens to our relationships under this paradigm: paradoxically, the attempt to identify a common rational core between belief systems upon which to base dialogue—the hallmark of procedural debate—actually foments divisions. Milbank points out that putting rationality and belief into separate, impermeable compartments, confining the public realm to that which is procedural or pragmatically measurable, can create a vacuum or backlash; it leaves "the field free

---

73. D. L. Schindler, "Biotechnology and Givenness," 620.
74. D. L. Schindler, "Biotechnology and Givenness," 620.

for the voices of religious fanatics, whose rival claims a plural fideism is powerless to adjudicate."[75] This anti-metaphysical stance—that there can be only "consensus as to formal procedures which promote narrowly-defined utilitarian benefit combined with negative freedom of choice"[76]—can encourage its own backlash on the other side. The more anti-metaphysical modernity encourages a chasm between public and private, between what it decides is acceptable and what is not,

> the more it must perforce generate a new sort of liberal totalitarianism involving constant surveillance and ever-more exhaustive indexing and categorizing of all citizens and all their activities. There are, therefore, some good reasons for now being concerned about a style of philosophy which eschews the business of trying to determine the ultimate categories of being (or of reality) and the fundamental ways in which they may be said—to put it in Aristotelian terms.[77]

If true unity-in-diversity is sought, and not merely extrinsic consensus, Milbank raises an important question: "Do we not after all need a public rational discourse about substantive truth, goodness and beauty which will rescue these universal and necessary concerns from the hands of fanaticism,"[78] whether that fanaticism stems from excessive fideism or excessive rationalism, whether it is religious terrorism or political totalitarianism?

Once again, it is important to note that it is not the case that everyone must become an expert in metaphysics, or that every discussion must take on absolute questions about the nature of being and the universe. Though the open dialogue championed by bioethics practitioners is indeed necessary, what is needed is *complete* dialogue, a "genuine listening of each to the other, in accord with the other's proper-inner reasonings and practices,"[79] the recognition that, no matter what field we are competent in or what viewpoint we intend to present, we are all talking about the same thing: "not a part, but the (transcendent) *whole*, though from a

---

75. Milbank, "Only Theology Saves," 455.
76. Milbank, "Only Theology Saves," 455.
77. Milbank, "Only Theology Saves," 456.
78. Milbank, "Only Theology Saves," 456.
79. D. L. Schindler, "Biotechnology and Givenness," 642.

particular perspective, under a particular aspect."[80] Once again, analogy is central:

> Truth, understood specifically in its ontological dimension, opens up what we might call a "depth dimension" inside of the different disciplines that allows us to think of their relation to each other in a manner quite different from the conventional one. ... This means that, understood as true in the ontological sense, the different disciplines will bear an *analogical* relationship to each other, that what differentiates them does not compromise their unity.[81]

Through this recovery we can understand that, in a sense, every field is indeed philosophical and every discipline, in addition to doing the work it currently does under the "conventional" model, ought also to ask its own fundamentally "philosophical questions concerning purpose and essence—the 'why?' and the 'what is . . .?' questions—belong to each of the disciplines . . . according to their own particularity."[82] Is it not the case that, as human beings, professionals of diverse disciplines already do this to a certain extent? Are not the wonder and astonishment at being that Plato attributed to the philosophers accessible to everyone? Certainly Plato was not describing the limited experience of one discipline of elite thinkers, but a profoundly human experience.

On the side of the scientists, such dialogue works best if they are able, precisely *as* scientists, to be at least *open to* "a cosmological order—in terms, variously, of physical, biological, and human behavior, and of practices and technical interventions with respect to each behavior—consistent with a view of being as (analogically conceived) gift and wonder."[83] Too often these are dismissed out of hand. Philosophers, theologians, and ethicists of course have their own responsibilities—on their side, there should be no "imperialistic intrusion on science and medicine in their rightfully empirical dimensions," but rather a deep understanding of the nature and methods of science and technology in their particularity.[84]

---

80. D. C. Schindler, "On the Universality," 85.
81. D. C. Schindler, "On the Universality," 85.
82. D. C. Schindler, "On the Universality," 86.
83. D. L. Schindler, "Biotechnology and Givenness," 642.
84. D. L. Schindler, "Biotechnology and Givenness," 641.

Gift and Dialogue

"Receptivity" . . . is arguably the indispensable key to objectivity. . . . The most appropriate relation the subject can . . . engage with respect to the object is a welcoming "taking in" before it is a spontaneous creative or constructive "acting upon."[85]

Typically debates consist in the confrontation of ideas, which tends towards reducing the contribution of the other in the encounter to its mere content, but "when form bears an intrinsic relation to content . . . an argument turns into a more comprehensive kind of encounter."[86] Form bears an intrinsic relation to content when the message and the medium—the person and all his or her concrete circumstances—are conceived of as an indivisible whole. Encounters that begin with a true receptivity that gives priority to the other culminate in a unity far deeper and more long-lasting than that produced by procedural consensus.

Consider, for example, the case of Dr. Rana Adwish. In her 2017 memoir she recounts her own life-threatening illness, one that affected every aspect of her life, causing her to lose an unborn child and to face multiple organ failure. From her new perspective as a patient rather than a doctor, she realized that she had been "trained to value efficiency over cultivating a relationship through trust and disclosure."[87] She had not been trained to listen, but to say things and ask questions that would steer people towards a manageable answer that represented an underlying attitude of control:

> To listen to our patients with a generous ear does require a willingness to relinquish control of the narrative. And like all loss of control, there is an element of risk involved. And risk carries with it an inherent degree of vulnerability. Our questions allow for the possibility that we do not already know the answers. By not dominating the flow of information, we allow the actual history to emerge.[88]

As a further departure from procedural debates, she realized that what was needed were open questions resulting in "listening for not

---

85. D. C. Schindler, "Beauty and the Holiness," 23.
86. D. C. Schindler, *Plato's Critique*, 78.
87. Awdish, *In Shock*, 51.
88. Awdish, *In Shock*, 52.

just what is *said*, but what may be *true*,"[89] not leading, antecedently constrained, or limited questions:

> This kind of humility in listening requires that we abandon our assumptions to make room for truth. A truth that could be messier, but that will allow us to see the patient in the context of their values and their life. It requires that we value the question in a culture that values answers. The real secret, though, is that the honesty elicited from genuine, reflective questions is also a reprieve for the physician.[90]

Returning to our considerations of "work," it is one thing to dialogue one's way to an agreement; it is another to perform the work implied by that agreement. Community requires building, sustaining, and participating in *networks* of good work rather than living "an individual life maximally conformed to perfect work."[91] Genuine consensus arises from a genuine encounter on all levels and requires working with others on all levels: technical, economic, political, ethical—none of which, alone, are adequate. As for "dialogue," the end goal of bioethical or ecological dialogue is not consensus as the lowest common denominator among adversaries trying to avoid lawsuits; nor conformity to the most popular position that is only a "semblance of participation, a superficial compliance with others";[92] nor an uneasy "truce" that leaves open the possibility of contention and anger further down the line, perhaps reached by silencing some perspectives or not even allowing them to sit at the table. All of these violate "the law of the gift": that being (and hence community) *increases* in the measure that we give it away. As Martin Luther King Jr. said, "The end is reconciliation; the end is redemption; the end is the creation of the beloved community. It is this type of spirit and this type of love that can transform opposers into friends."[93]

---

89. Awdish, *In Shock*, 52.

90. Awdish, *In Shock*, 52.

91. Cloutier, "Working with the Grammar," 632.

92. Wojtyla, *The Acting Person*, 290–91. He continues, "The problem of conformism . . . . consists in a definite renunciation of seeking the fulfillment of oneself in and through acting 'together with others'. . . . Hence conformism brings uniformity rather than unity" (*The Acting Person*, 291).

93. King, *A Testament of Hope*, 140.

The Concentric-Spheres Model for Ecological Management

Solidarity is inconceivable without a sense of respect for the integrity of reality.... Finding common and stable environmental solutions based on the available information requires accepting a common and meaningful reality that requires us to not omit any of its given parts, that is to say, it requires its integrity.[94]

The purpose of this study is to suggest a new and more adequate metaphysical light under which to view the ecological and bioethical crises of our times, one that can guide us to an integral resolution. This is not an exercise in idealism, but a practical path that can be transformative for all those involved. The clearest expression of this approach concerning the solution of environmental conflicts is the decision-making model developed by Pablo Martínez de Anguita based on the solidarity possible when a non-reductive path that is open to the reality of the other is chosen. In this model, work and dialogue converge, and through these it is possible for opponents to become, not self-interested temporary allies, but friends. It illustrates why ecological ethics needs metaphysics and provides a captivating demonstration of the "openness to all reality" which has been a hallmark of the metaphysics of gift, over and against every form of reductionism that would bracket out any aspect of true human experience. Most importantly, it provides a response to the problematic ideal of consensus and aims instead at solidarity: "the need to create and maintain ties of collaboration with other beings in light of our common destiny."[95]

Martínez de Anguita systematically describes the practical process of ecological conflict resolution through the ever-widening spheres of human concern: technical, economic, political, ethical, philosophical and ontological.[96] Though some might conceive of these as separate issues, to be resolved in different forums, his concentric-spheres model illustrates that they are all intrinsic to each other. Each upper sphere resolves an aspect left out by the methodology of the sphere just below it, such that all human concerns and perspectives can be addressed within one integral analysis of reality. This is a refreshing perspective from the usual division

---

94. Martínez de Anguita et al., "Environmental Economic," 160–61.
95. Martínez de Anguita, *Environmental Solidarity*, 146.
96. Martínez de Anguita et al., "Environmental Economic," 162.

of fragmented disciplines we find in the contemporary academy, as it accounts for the many relations and connections of the acting person.

The technical sphere is that in which technological solutions are proposed. One aspect, however, that falls outside of the consideration of the technical is the scarcity of resources, and so the economic sphere must encompass it. Proper analysis within these two spheres assures that a solution will be both effective and efficient. Martínez de Anguita points out that there are those who argue that these are the only two spheres we need to concern ourselves with because of their "Scientific Technical Optimism" which "proposes that the inconveniences of scientific progress will always be surpassed by better scientific and technical applications."[97] This is the technological paradigm, which, among other things, assumes "that any environmental problem can be traded off" through the reduction of all factors to a single monetary one that, in turn, is subject to a simple cost–benefit analysis. Of course, the very nature of "value incommensurability" flies in the face of this assumption, as they "are likely to be operative when a good is essential or has a moral or other irreducible form of value."[98] And so we must move to the political sphere within which environmental policy seeks social acceptability to avoid injustices and conflict. This is not always possible, however, as political arbitration breaks down when different parties cannot see eye to eye. Neither does appealing to the political sphere free us from the domination of the technical, as the technological paradigm simply morphs into a technocratic one, where political interests serve economic and technical ones and not the other way around. We must move to a higher paradigm, to the ethical sphere.

Ethical considerations, in and of themselves, appear to be mere limitations on economic and political overreach but, when reality is considered as a unity and not as a fractured and competitive backdrop to human action, it becomes evident that pursuing what is *good* is not only beneficial to all, but essential to the community. However, conflicting visions of reality, as we have seen for example between the two extremes of the biocentric–anthropocentric spectrum, carry with them contradictions in values that cannot be resolved without raising the discussion to a broader philosophical one and, ultimately, to the level of ontology, where finally a unity can be rediscovered through solidarity,

---

97. Martínez de Anguita et al., "Environmental Economic," 156.
98. Martínez de Anguita et al., "Environmental Economic," 155.

which "cannot be reached unless there is a place that can be approached jointly."[99] Martínez de Anguita notes that an essential requirement of solidarity is "a sense of respect for the integrity of reality" which moves us "towards a common destiny."[100] Thus an essential element to this entire process, despite our technical prowess, our economic mastery, and our political power is the humility capable of recognizing and respecting mystery. "Only the consideration of nature as a mystery," Martínez de Anguita says, "permits the possibility of advancement in knowledge and, even more importantly, to be able to detect in it a meaning not given by man."[101]

The concentric-spheres model conforms to the observations and convictions of the five metaphysicians previously discussed on the unity of being, which is the unity of reality, especially Balthasar's description of truth as symphonic: from the diversity of voices, a harmony can be awakened. While each perspective offers an accurate account of its own competence and is capable of seeing (and willing to accept) that the other perspectives are also valid to their own extent, a solidarity can be generated that does not produce winners and losers (as in a negotiation), but members of a community. This model, because it is truly open, can also be truly holistic, which means that it is also practical; it was designed as a tool for environmental managers that can be used in a number of different ways. However, the ideal use, as seen through the life and work of Martínez de Anguita, is to start by building solidarity and community and work towards a solution together. He describes his experience after working as a forestry expert and rural development consultant in the poor and politically volatile, yet naturally beautiful, village of San Marcos de Colón in Honduras, which is tucked away in the northern forests:

> The future of the forest of San Marcos depends now on this change of attitude born among people who have looked into nature with love and respect, with wonder, and whose perception of beauty has joined [them] in an association that, even if it seeks economic alternatives, has its deepest origin in the human heart, in a desire similar to the one I felt a few years ago, a desire that appears as the answer to a provocative beauty,

---

99. Martínez de Anguita et al., "Environmental Economic," 160.

100. Martínez de Anguita et al., "Environmental Economic," 160–61.

101. Martínez de Anguita et al., "Environmental Economic," 161n16. Mystery refers to the superabundance of intelligibility present in reality that, through contemplation and discursive reason, we can come to know truly but never exhaustively.

> to the mystery of life that asks to be penetrated and shared. This is the secret of conservation: to correspond to that vital mystery that makes claims upon the human heart and from which a friendship among the members of this association has been born as they embark upon an exciting adventure, one that will overwhelm them as it did me. This is also the reason my hope does not finally depend on them, but on the Mystery that has motivated through its beauty. I think this is what defines environmental solidarity: It is to recognize in one way or another that the Mystery is acting, and its deepest manifestation is to ask us to correspond to this call, to this vocation to save the beauty that claims us, and in some way save us from loss of heart, from discouragement.[102]

Here "mystery" expresses the surplus of reality that brings about the experience of wonder in those who are receptive to it. Its recognition is also the sign of a healthy and humble use of human reason. The beauty of the concentric-spheres model is that, in a deeply practical way, it reminds us of the constant need to look to a higher sphere of understanding when faced with conflict and gives us the hope that there exists a point of encounter where truth can be discovered and from which community can be built. Bioethics so easily and so often degrades into a political battle. This is not a hopeful path to pursue, as Caldecott once explained so poignantly, from his personal experience: many in the environmental movement "will try to get their hands on the relevant levers of power and will be increasingly, and everlastingly frustrated, to discover that all their attempts come to nothing or even make things worse."[103] This model provides the motivation and the path to build hope for the future.

To Live in the World

Throughout this study we have chronicled the perpetual pendulum swings from dichotomization to fusion, from dualism to identity and back again, from the ancient ponderings of Heraclitus and Parmenides to the biocentrism vs. anthropocentrism of recent ecological debates. Unity and difference seem to have been perpetually at odds, but it does not have to be this way. Metaphysics of gift, founded in a fully-fledged openness to reality, is capable of holding both in balance through the

---

102. Martínez de Anguita, *Environmental Solidarity*, 114.
103. Caldecott, *Radiance of Being*, 89.

unity-in-diversity expressed in analogy. This means, as Martínez de Anguita so clearly points out, that not only are the values held by the diverse constituents involved in an ecological conflict not at odds, but they enhance the ability to build the solidarity that pertains to "the greatest possible paradigm."[104]

What these practical applications call us to is a sincere openness to and connection with the natural world and the people around us, caring for the natural and social communities we are a part of and building new ones. They call us to reconceive human flourishing according to a deeper set of values that escapes the grasp of every cost–benefit analysis. Though the metaphysics of gift shows us that our connection to others is perhaps more intimate and more real than we could have imagined, we can choose to reject it and fail to let it bear fruit in our lives. If we do not live properly, according to the common destiny we have been born into, we will ultimately lose it, and ourselves, in the process.

The logic of gift brings together valuable truths that, if left untethered, devolve into various, seemingly oppositional positions. The romantic sentimentalism and technological utilitarianism born from the biocentric and anthropocentric visions and their language of ambiguous holism and mechanistic pragmatism can be harmonized, but only in a higher sphere of thinking. This must occur through the action of *good work* in order for it to take root in reality. Metaphysics of gift shows us that we are unfulfilled as isolated individuals, and that

> the change that human work is called to bring about in the world is a participation in a deeper change that was neither begun nor will be completed by man alone. That beings are, that they exist in a communion of beings, and that each of them can neither become itself nor bear fruit without the others, means that human work is a participation in a far deeper working.[105]

Inscribed in everything we do is a deeper collaboration within the community of beings with which we share this world. The carpenter who grows to love the trees and the land he lives on is a perfect example, and the work of his hands, as D. C. Schindler said, "is a new reality that bears the traces, as it were, of its two sources."[106] However, the more our work is bound within the confines of the technological paradigm,

---

104. Martínez de Anguita et al., "Environmental Economic," 160–61.
105. López, *Gift and the Unity*, 133.
106. D. C. Schindler, "Quaerere Deum."

the more that connection is forgotten and the more easily it is abused. Through a recognition of what constitutes good work, true value, and real dialogue that respects the other as a member of a community and whose perspective is valid in the measure that it is open to reality, we can live out the giftedness of our lives in service to those with whom we share it. Only in this way can we truly "begin to protect the world not just by conserving it but also by living in it."[107]

---

107. Berry, *Sex, Economy, Freedom & Community*, 43.

EPILOGUE:
IMAGINATION AND OUR
ONTOLOGICAL COVENANT

> *To speak frivolously, to shirk the duty to come to a deep understanding of the real nature of things and give that meaning a genuinely careful articulation, to technologize speech and instrumentalize it altogether for merely practical purposes, to distort the meaning of words through political manipulation and ideology . . . . is to bring dis-order into the cosmos.*[1]

THE MUSIC OF TOLKIEN'S Ainur from the *Silmarillion* echoes throughout the world of Middle-earth represented in *The Lord of the Rings*. The harmonious beauty of music accompanies the characters on the side of the good, while a loud and vain clamor accompanies those who bring disorder to Middle-earth, like the evil wizard Saruman, who is described as having "a mind of metal and wheels" and who is rebuked by Gandalf for his loss of hope, as one who "breaks a thing to find out what it is."[2] On the side of the Ainur is Tom Bombadil, who fills his days with harmonious song and who is "the Master of wood, water, and hill."[3] When Frodo asks if that meant that all the surrounding land belonged to him, the response is a further indication of the metaphysics Tolkien sought to salvage "from the wreck of history"[4] through his stories: "No indeed! . . . That would indeed be a burden. . . . The trees and the grasses and all things growing or living in the land belong each to themselves."[5]

---

1. D. C. Schindler, *A Companion*, 87.
2. Tolkien, *The Lord of the Rings*, II, 76; I, 272.
3. Tolkien, *The Lord of the Rings*, I, 153.
4. Garth, *Tolkien and the Great War*, xv.
5. Tolkien, *The Lord of the Rings*, I, 153.

We have endeavored to show that, in one way or another, anyone who attempts to understand the nature of reality is indeed doing metaphysics. As Paul Tyson says, "Everyone does metaphysics.... Every time we plan or perform any activity in what we take to be a realistic manner, we do so by putting our confidence in a set of deeply held beliefs about the nature of reality itself."[6] But neither a mechanistic metaphysics, nor one based in emergence, is capable of describing the simple reality that all things belong to themselves because they are recipients of the gift of being. And this is necessarily a reflection of how we see our place in the world, the truth about how we are related to all the beings around us, and, thus, what we ultimately decide is good for us.

As author Michael Pollan has noted, "Humankind has become the most powerful evolutionary force ... even the wild now depends on civilization for its survival."[7] This is true in more ways than one. Perhaps the label of Anthropocene for the period we are now living in is fitting when we consider the immense responsibility we have towards each other and the whole of the natural world, but it seems that most of those who apply it do so in a cynical tone of despair and reproach. As Caldecott prophetically pointed out, the modern and the postmodern mindsets alike encourage us to place all our hope solely in technological solutions and political power. Without a metaphysical appreciation for all things, the inevitable result is that those who pursue this path, as we noted earlier, will actually make things worse.[8] As it was for the Sophist Thrasymachus, without an appreciation for one's intrinsic relation to the good of the whole, beliefs devolve into authoritarianism and depend on an "ontology of violence," which is not without its irony when done so in the name of "saving the earth."

According to Pollan, part of the problem is that we always view ourselves as outside of nature, and thus, inevitably in opposition to it:

> This is simply another failure of imagination: ... Nature is not only to be found "out there," it is also "in here." ... My wager is that when we can find nature in these sorts of places as readily

6. Tyson, *Returning to Reality*, 1.
7. Pollan, *Botany of Desire*, xxiii.
8. Caldecott, *Radiance of Being*, 89.

as we now find it in the wild, we'll have travelled a considerable distance toward understanding our place in the world in the fullness of its complexity and ambiguity.[9]

The "failure of imagination," however, runs far deeper, into the realm of being where our most profound beliefs about reality take root, and so this failure is first and foremost a metaphysical one.[10] D. C. Schindler argues that "a starved imagination represents a crisis indeed," especially when we consider that

> the imagination is, if not the center of the human being, then nevertheless that without which there can be no center, for it marks the point of convergence at which the soul and body meet; it is the place where . . . reason becomes concrete, and the bodily life of the senses rises to meet the spirit. It lies more deeply than the sphere of our discrete thoughts and choices because it is the ordered space within which we in fact think and choose.[11]

Caldecott elaborates, "The healing of the world therefore cannot be envisaged without a reordering and a healing of the inner world of the imagination, intelligence, and will."[12] For it is imagination that gives meaning to the world; in other words, it is in the imaginative intellect where metaphysics is born, not because it is an invention of the mind, but rather a discovery of the subtle truth of reality, "'joining the dots,' discovering the otherwise invisible connection between things, events, [and] qualities."[13]

Perhaps the most profound example of such imaginative power is when Aquinas radically renewed and transformed an ancient philosophical tradition by conceiving of the real distinction between being and essence. It was by imagining the twofold character of being, the simultaneity of immanence and transcendence, the One and the Many, that we may come to see being as a gift that we both participate in and possess uniquely. We must continue to cultivate this imaginative capacity to see

---

9. Pollan, *Botany of Desire*, xxiv.

10. Mary Taylor has said that "what we call the 'ecological crisis,' despite its many proximate causes, is not so much a problem to be solved by recycling or remediation—though they must be dealt with—but is ultimately rooted in a failure of the imagination" ("Ecology on One's Knees," 132).

11. D. C. Schindler, "Truth and Christian Imagination," 522.

12. Caldecott, *Beauty for Truth's Sake*, 108.

13. Caldecott, *Beauty in the Word*, 122.

what Aquinas saw, to renew and transform the ontology that marks our time, lest we fall into the metaphysical blindness that mars modernism and postmodernism alike.

Those of a mechanistic bent would have us divide the world too radically, disconnecting us from living things (persons included) which inevitably, if inadvertently, leads to treating them as objects to be manipulated. Eco-philosophies, on the other hand, have relinquished the intellectual distinctions necessary to see anything as separate from anything else, losing persons in the flux of the universe and the process of cosmic evolution. But in the end the two amount to the same thing, as organisms cannot be conceived of as anything more than the chance manifestation of energy condensed in a particular time and space. Only a metaphysics that sees all beings, human and non-human organisms alike, as the recipients of the gift of being is capable of truly valuing them, recognizing their own being beyond their ecological services and the emotional value they provide us. "To be in act as a living organism is to be *existentially* indivisible, to have a certain share in the simplicity of being. . . . Only by granting the organism this unity of being, only by acknowledging its transcendent wholeness, is it possible to conceive of the organism as a *per se unum*."[14]

It is only in this way that we can understand Tolkien's intuition, in all its simplicity and beauty, that all things "belong each to themselves." Without an imaginative intellect, the constitutive relationships inherent in reality, analogous to the myriad ecological interconnections we share with other creatures, are lost to us in skepticism and a forgetfulness of being that confuses egocentrism for the Good; intellectual activity, when taken up seriously as an attempt to discern the nature of reality, is never morally neutral.

This neutrality is perhaps the most pervasive of contemporary myths. Without the perception of intrinsic relation between truth and goodness, between the intellect and will, and therefore between what we think and what we do, we witness profound impacts not only on bioethics, which was one of the focal points of this study, but on the entirety of our relations with reality and with each other. D. C. Schindler traces the effects of this divorce, which are worth quoting at length:

---

14. Hanby, *No God, No Science?*, 359. As Gilson puts it, "existence belongs to each and every thing in a truly unique manner, as its own existence, which can be shared by nothing else" (Gilson, *Unity of Philosophical Experience*, 315).

If, indeed, the intellect and will are extrinsically related, if we are led to think of the mind as operating in a space that is "neutral" with respect to the good,

- then we take for granted an instrumentalist, formalist, notion of intelligence;
- we separate subjectivity and objectivity;
- we associate scientific objectivity with impersonal detachment;
- we believe passionate involvement—and thus also things like the "pre-critical" commitments of faith—intrude on vision and so compromise the free integrity of reason;
- we isolate public reason from what then becomes the private, subjective adherence of the will;
- we raise up the methods of modern science as a paradigm of rational universality and believe the realm of science is neutral with respect to metaphysical and religious questions;
- we claim that technology is "neutral" in itself, and becomes good or bad only in reference to the uses to which it is put;
- we become accustomed to a fragmented view of the academic curriculum—which is, incidentally, itself a reflection of the way a culture conceives of the "shape" of the mind—in the sense that we see the disciplines as isolated pieces of skills and information that can be "mastered" only by experts, even though they all share generally the same academic "method," mechanically applied;
- and, finally, along similar lines, we negotiate relations in the public order principally according to putatively "neutral" procedures, and we allow dialogue and engagement with the "other" only on the terms set by these procedures.[15]

Ultimately, the dualism between the intellect and the will that is necessitated by the demand for an ostensibly neutral zone of morality gives way to the type of bureaucratic proceduralism we analyzed in chapter 3, which signifies the replacement of human intellectual activity by a technique. It is this division, among others, that Martínez de Anguita seeks to overcome with his concentric-spheres model for decision-making. It is an invaluable tool for the recognition of the bond between truth and goodness and the compliance of technical and political efficacy with the order of reality. To act from a metaphysics of gift, whether it be to

15. D. C. Schindler, "Beauty and the Holiness," 23–24 (bullet points mine).

conserve a forest or make a bioethical decision for the care of a loved one, does not mean merely adding a measure of gratitude and gratuity to one's actions, but transforming them from within. In all of the levels of Martínez de Anguita's framework, it is not that gift comes only at the end but rather it is incorporated into every dimension.

In the *technological sphere*, there is no denial from the perspective of the metaphysics of gift that organisms and ecosystems can behave in mechanistic ways and respond to mechanistic manipulation. What we *do* contest is that mechanism serves as a tool for the diagnosis of a problem that is always ultimately far more complex. As proponents of emergence properly point out, the whole is indeed greater than the sum of its parts, but not in the way that eco-philosophies argue. As Hanby says, "The priority of form to matter and whole to parts invokes the constitutive role of mystery . . . as the essentially *gifted* and excessive character of things to themselves that is 'woven into the fabric of organic reality, into the very nature of an organism.'"[16]

In the *economic sphere*, while it would be good if economic transactions in the free market were accompanied by feelings of gratitude and reciprocity, this is not what metaphysics of gift proposes. Rather, it allows us to appreciate the deeper nature of our exchanges: "the things produced, exchanged, and possessed will themselves differ in their very character as things, depending on the extent to which their production, exchange, and possession are integrated into a grateful sense of reality as gift—that is, such that the things themselves take on the nature of gift."[17] Consider again Gandhi's example of the way a wristwatch changes in meaning based on the relationships it creates in its exchange. It should be clear, however, that these relationships are more easily lived in communities invested in and connected to the land, as Berry points out.

In the *political sphere*, metaphysics of gift critiques the organization of society around promises of freedom and peace based on a neutral stance towards any particular notion of the good, as these will inevitably devolve into an ontology of violence and coercive state control. Instead, it points to the need for a public forum based on true dialogue, mutual respect, and a striving towards "symphonic" truth born from the recognition of common human values within the lived human traditions of the communities that make up a society.[18] From there, the political

16. Hanby, "Beyond Mechanism," 197.
17. D. L. Schindler, *Ordering Love*, 175.
18. See Prades and Cantos, *Postsecularism*.

sphere ought to operate under the principle of subsidiarity in order to promote solidarity, participation, and adherence while protecting citizens from the binary logic of the market-state.

In the *ethical sphere*, the truth of the relatedness of all things, first and foremost through their mutual yet graduated participation in being, is understood as the primary normative factor. The dichotomy of intrinsic vs. instrumental value is abandoned for a greater comprehension of the shared covenant of all things in being and consensus is abandoned in favor of the solidarity that is born from the widest possible framework, the *ontological sphere*.

Under the current paradigm, we fail to recognize the ontological covenant that we are all born into, which predates and surpasses our own existence. Understanding that we are part of nature implies "a rediscovery of Being, of metaphysics . . . a rediscovery of love. The civilization of love that we hope and long for would be one in which the metaphysical dimension of all things has been recovered."[19]

The love we have referred to throughout is much more than a mere sentiment of good will; conceived analogically, it is the very meaning of being-as-gift. The primordial generosity of being gives form and order to all of creation such that we can say with David L. Schindler, "Reality at root is a matter of love and love is a matter of order."[20] And it is this order that we must seek to correspond to on every level of existence: "This love, which is the principle of the micro-relationships of family, friends, and small groups, is meant to be the principle also of the macro-relationships proper to the social, economic, and political order."[21]

Ultimately, an integral ecological ethic must be illuminated and transformed by a deeper knowledge of being as love. It must seek to do right by the persons and all other living things on this earth, who always "belong each to themselves," when they are most vulnerable, when they depend on us to uphold their dignity. In this task, the gift of being calls us to imitate its own generosity. This is what it means to uphold the order of the cosmos in gratitude to *"the Love that moves the sun and the other stars."*[22]

19. Caldecott, *Beauty in the Word*, 135.

20. D. L. Schindler, *Ordering Love*, ix–x.

21. Mary G. Taylor, "Ecology on One's Knees," 172, citing Benedict XVI, *Charity in Truth*, §2.

22. Alighieri, *Paradise*, 351 (33, 145).

Bibliography

Abram, David. *The Spell of the Sensuous: Perception and Language in a More-Than-Human World*. New York: Vintage, 1997.
Alighieri, Dante. *Paradise*. Translated by Anthony Esolen. New York: Modern Library, 2007.
Allodi, Leonardo. "Persona e Società Post-Secolare." In *Verso una società post-secolare?*, edited by Sergio Belardinelli et al., 21–56. Soveria Mannelli: Rubbettino, 2009.
Amrine, Frederick, et al., eds. *Goethe and the Sciences: A Reappraisal*. Dordrecht: Reidel, 1987.
Aquinas, Thomas. *A Commentary on Aristotle's* De Anima. Translated by Kenelm Foster and Sylvester Humphries. New Haven: Yale University Press, 1951.
———. *Commentary on Aristotle's* On Interpretation. Translated by Jean Oesterle. Milwaukee: Marquette University Press, 1962.
———. *Commentary on Aristotle's* Physics. Translated by Richard J. Blackwell et al. New Haven: Yale University Press, 1963.
———. *Commentary on the* Metaphysics of Aristotle. Translated by John P. Rowan. Chicago: Regnery, 1961.
———. *De Unitate Intellectus Contra Averroistas*. Translated by Beatrice H. Zedler. Milwaukee: Marquette University Press, 1968.
———. *Quæstiones Disputatæ de Potentia Dei*. Translated by the English Dominican Fathers. Westminster, MD: Newman, 1952.
———. *Quæstiones Disputatæ de Veritate*. Translated by Robert W. Mulligan. Chicago: Regnery, 1952.
———. *Summa contra Gentiles*. Translated by Vernon J. Bourke. Notre Dame: University of Notre Dame Press, 1975.
———. *Summa Theologica*. Translated by the Fathers of the English Dominican Province. Westminster, MD: Christian Classics, 1981.
Aristotle. "De Anima." In *The Basic Works of Aristotle*, edited by Richard McKeon, 535–603. New York: Random House, 1941.
———. "Metaphysics." In *The Basic Works of Aristotle*, edited by Richard McKeon, 689–926. New York: Random House, 1941.
———. "Physics." In *The Basic Works of Aristotle*, edited by Richard McKeon, 218–394. New York: Random House, 1941.
Awdish, Rana. *In Shock: My Journey from Death to Recovery and the Redemptive Power of Hope*. New York: St. Martin's, 2017.
Bacon, Francis. *The Major Works*. Edited by Brian Vickers. Oxford: Oxford University Press, 2008.

———. *The New Organon*. Edited by Lisa Jardine and Michael Silverthorne. Cambridge: Cambridge University Press, 2000.
Badiou, Alain. *Being and Event*. Translated by Oliver Feltham. London: Continuum, 2006.
———. *Manifesto for Philosophy*. Translated by Norman Madarasz. Albany: SUNY Press, 1999.
———. "Preface." In *After Finitude: An Essay on the Necessity of Contingency*, by Quentin Meillassoux, vi–viii. Translated by Ray Brassier. London: Continuum, 2009.
Balthasar, Hans Urs von. *Explorations in Theology III: Creator Spirit*. Translated by Brian McNeil. San Francisco: Ignatius, 1993.
———. *The Glory of the Lord I: Seeing the Form*. Edited by Joseph Fessio and John Riches, translated by Erasmo Leiva-Merikakis. San Francisco: Ignatius, 1983.
———. *The Glory of the Lord II: Studies in Theological Style: Clerical Styles*. Edited by John Riches, translated by Andrew Louth et al. San Francisco: Ignatius, 2006.
———. *The Glory of the Lord V: The Realm of Metaphysics in the Modern Age*. Edited by Brian McNeil and John Riches, translated by Oliver Davies et al. San Francisco: Ignatius, 1991.
———. *Love Alone Is Credible*. Translated by D. C. Schindler. San Francisco: Ignatius, 2004.
———. *Man in History: A Theological Study*. London: Sheed & Ward, 1972.
———. *My Work: In Retrospect*. San Francisco: Ignatius, 1993.
———. "On the Tasks of Catholic Philosophy in Our Time." Translated by Brian McNeil. *Communio* 20.1 (1993) 147–87.
———. *Our Task: A Report and a Plan*. Translated by John Saward. San Francisco: Ignatius, 1994.
———. *Theo-Drama II: The Dramatis Personae; Man in God*. Translated by Graham Harrison. San Francisco: Ignatius, 2000.
———. *Theo-Logic I: Truth of the World*. Translated by Adrian J. Walker. San Francisco: Ignatius, 2000.
———. *Theo-Logic II: Truth of God*. Translated by Adrian J. Walker. San Francisco: Ignatius, 2004.
———. *A Theology of History*. San Francisco: Ignatius, 1994.
———. *Unless You Become Like This Child*. Translated by Erasmo Leiva-Merikakis. San Francisco: Ignatius, 1991.
Beauchamp, Tom L. "A Defense of the Common Morality." *Kennedy Institute of Ethics Journal* 13 (2003) 259–74.
———. "Principlism and Its Alleged Competitors." *Kennedy Institute of Ethics Journal* 5 (1995) 181–98.
Beauchamp, Tom L., and James F. Childress. *Principles of Biomedical Ethics*. 5th ed. Oxford: Oxford University Press, 2001.
The Belmont Report: Ethical Principles and Guidelines for the Protection of Human Subjects of Research. US Department of Health, Education, and Welfare, 1979.
Benedict XVI. *Charity in Truth—Caritas in Veritate*. San Francisco: Ignatius, 2009.
———. "Faith, Reason and the University: Memories and Reflections." http://www.vatican.va/content/benedict-xvi/en/speeches/2006/september/documents/hf_ben-xvi_spe_20060912_university-regensburg.html.

———. "Homily for the Solemn Inauguration of the Petrine Ministry April 24, 2005." http://www.vatican.va/content/benedict-xvi/en/homilies/2005/documents/hf_ben-xvi_hom_20050424_inizio-pontificato.html.

———. *Saved in Hope—Spe Salvi*. San Francisco: Ignatius, 2008.

Berry, Wendell. *A Continuous Harmony: Essays Cultural and Agricultural*. New York: Counterpoint, 2012.

———. *The Hidden Wound*. Berkeley, CA: Counterpoint, 2010.

———. *Sex, Economy, Freedom & Community: Eight Essays*. New York: Pantheon, 1994.

Betz, John. R. "After Barth: A New Introduction to Erich Przywara's *Analogia Entis*." In *The Analogy of Being: Invention of the Antichrist or Wisdom of God?*, edited by Thomas Joseph White, 35–87. Grand Rapids: Eerdmans, 2011.

———. "Translator's Introduction." In *Analogia Entis: Metaphysics: Original Structure and Universal Rhythm*, by Erich Przywara, translated by John R. Betz and David Bentley Hart, 1–116. Grand Rapids: Eerdmans, 2014.

Beuchot, Mauricio. "The Limits of Cultural Relativism: Metaphysics in Latin America." In *Cultural Relativism and Philosophy: North and Latin American Perspectives*, edited by Marcelo Dascal, 159–73. Leiden: E. J. Brill, 1991.

Bieler, Martin. "*Analogia Entis* as an Expression of Love according to Ferdinand Ulrich." In *The Analogy of Being: Invention of the Antichrist or the Wisdom of God?*, edited by Thomas Joseph White, 314–37. Grand Rapids: Eerdmans, 2011.

———. "Introduction." In *Homo Abyssus: The Drama of the Question of Being*, by Ferdinand Ulrich, xv–lv. Baltimore: Humanum, 2018.

Black, Edwin. *War against the Weak: Eugenics and America's Campaign to Create a Master Race*. Washington, DC: Dialog, 2012.

Brogan, Hugh. "Tolkien's Great War." In *Children and Their Books: A Celebration of the Work of Iona and Peter Opie*, edited by Gillian Avery and Julia Briggs, 351–68. New York: Oxford University Press, 1989.

Brower, David. "Wilderness Is for People, Too!" *Sierra Club Bulletin* (Feb 1962) 3.

Brugger, E. Christian. "The Agonizing Case of Alfie Evans." https://www.ncregister.com/blog/the-agonizing-case-of-alfie-evans.

Caldecott, Stratford. *Beauty for Truth's Sake: On the Re-enchantment of Education*. Grand Rapids: Brazos, 2009.

———. *Beauty in the Word: Rethinking the Foundations of Education*. Tacoma: Angelico, 2012.

———. "The Divine Benefactor and Universal Kinship." https://theimaginativeconservative.org/2018/12/theology-gift-divine-benefactor-kinship-stratford-caldecott.html.

———. "Lost in the Forest? Some Books on Ecology." *Priests and People* 9.2 (1995). Reprinted in *Second Spring*, 2002. https://archive.secondspring.co.uk/articles/scaldecott8.htm.

———. "New Sins: Technology and the Frontiers of Catholic Social Teaching." *Communio* 28.3 (2001) 488–504.

———. *The Radiance of Being: Dimensions of Cosmic Christianity*. Tacoma: Angelico, 2013.

Callahan, Daniel. "The Puzzle of Profound Respect." *The Hastings Center Report* 25.1 (1995) 39–40.

Caputo, John D. *Demythologizing Heidegger*. Bloomington: Indiana University Press, 1993.

———. *More Radical Hermeneutics: On Not Knowing Who We Are*. Bloomington: Indiana University Press, 2000.

———. *Radical Hermeneutics: Repetition, Deconstruction, and the Hermeneutic Project*. Bloomington and Indianapolis: Indiana University Press, 1987.

Carnap, Rudolf. "The Elimination of Metaphysics through Logical Analysis of Language." In *Logical Positivism*, edited by A. J. Ayer, 60–81. New York: Free Press, 1959.

———. "Empiricism, Semantics, and Ontology." In *The Linguistic Turn: Essays in Philosophical Method*, edited by Richard M. Rorty, 72–84. Chicago: University of Chicago Press, 1992.

Casarella, Peter. "Trinity and Creation: D. L. Schindler and the Catholic Tradition." In *Being Holy in the World: Theology and Culture in the Thought of David L. Schindler*, edited by Nicholas J. Healy and D. C. Schindler, 30–54. Grand Rapids: Eerdmans, 2011.

Casarett, David J., et al. "Experts in Ethics? The Authority of the Clinical Ethicist." *The Hastings Center Report* 28.6 (1998) 6–11.

Ceballos, Gerardo, et al. "Biological Annihilation via the Ongoing Sixth Mass Extinction Signaled by Vertebrate Population Losses and Declines." In *Proceedings of the National Academy of Sciences* 114.30 (2017) E6089–E6096. https://www.pnas.org/content/114/30/E6089.

Chivian, Eric, and Aaron Bernstein, eds. *Sustaining Life: How Human Health Depends on Biodiversity*. Oxford: Oxford University Press, 2008.

Clarke, William Norris. *Explorations in Metaphysics: Being, God, Person*. Notre Dame: University of Notre Dame Press, 1994.

———. *Person and Being*. Milwaukee: Marquette University Press, 2008.

Clouser, K. Danner. "Bioethics and Philosophy." *Hastings Center Report* 23.6 (1993) 10–11.

Clouser, K. Danner, and Bernard Gert. "A Critique of Principlism." *The Journal of Medicine and Philosophy: A Forum for Bioethics and Philosophy of Medicine* 15.2 (1990) 219–36.

Cloutier, David. "Working with the Grammar of Creation: Benedict XVI, Wendell Berry, and the Unity of the Catholic Moral Vision." *Communio* 37.4 (2010) 606–33.

Coles, Romand. "Ecotone and Environmental Ethics: Adorno and Lopez." In *In the Nature of Things*, edited by Jane Bennett and William Chaloupka, 226–49. Minneapolis: University of Minnesota Press, 1993.

Cottingham, John. "'A Brute to the Brutes?': Descartes' Treatment of Animals." *Philosophy* 53.206 (1978) 551–59.

Couzin, Iain D., et al. "Effective Leadership and Decision-Making in Animal Groups on the Move." *Nature* 433 (Feb 2005) 513–16.

Crawford, David S. "Recognizing the Roots of Society in the Family, Foundation of Justice." *Communio* 34.3 (2007) 379–412.

Crawford, Matthew. *Shop Class as Soulcraft: An Inquiry into the Value of Work*. New York: Penguin, 2010.

Crutzen, P., and E. Stoermer. "The 'Anthropocene.'" *Global Change Newsletter* 41 (2000) 17–18.

Cunningham, Conor. *Genealogy of Nihilism: Philosophies of Nothing and the Difference of Theology*. London: Routledge, 2002.

Dastidar, Samriddhi. "Stephen Hawking Claims to Know What Happened before the Big Bang." www.techtimes.com/articles/222309/20180303/.
Dawkins, Richard. *The Selfish Gene*. Oxford: Oxford University Press, 2016.
Dell'Oro, Roberto. "Theological Discourse and the Postmodern Condition: The Case of Bioethics." *Medicine, Health Care and Philosophy* 5.2 (2002) 127–36.
Descartes, René. *Principles of Philosophy*. Edited by Valentine R. Miller and Reese P. Miller. Dordrecht: Reidel, 1991.
Desmond, William. *The Intimate Strangeness of Being: Metaphysics after Dialectic*. Washington, DC: Catholic University of America Press, 2012.
———. *Perplexity and Ultimacy: Metaphysical Thoughts from the Middle*. Albany: SUNY Press, 1995.
de Vos, Jurriaan M., et al. "Estimating the Normal Background Rate of Species Extinction." *Conservation Biology* 29.2 (2014) 452–62.
Dewan, Lawrence. *Form and Being: Studies in Thomistic Metaphysics*. Washington, DC: Catholic University of America Press, 2006.
Donaldson, Susan. "Death Drugs Cause Uproar in Oregon." abcnews.go.com/Health/story?id=5517492&page=1.
Dubo, D. Nathan. "'Saving' 'Nature' since Earth Day 1970: Management, Holism, Postmodernism, and Merleau-Ponty." University of Manitoba, National Library of Canada, 1999.
Dummet, Michael. *Origins of Analytic Philosophy*. Cambridge: Harvard University Press, 1994.
Dworkin, Ronald. "Liberalism." In *Public and Private Morality*, edited by Stuart Hampshire, 113–43. Cambridge: Cambridge University Press, 1978.
Edwards, Lucy. "What Is the Anthropocene?" *Eos* 96 (30 Nov 2015). eos.org/opinions/what-is-the-anthropocene.
Emerson, Ralph Waldo. *Essays: First and Second Series*. London: Dent, 1906.
Evans, John H. *Playing God? Human Genetic Engineering and the Rationalization of Public Bioethical Debate, 1959–1995*. Chicago: University of Chicago Press, 2002.
———. "A Sociological Account of the Growth of Principlism." *The Hastings Center Report* 30.5 (2000) 31–38.
Evernden, Neil. *The Social Creation of Nature*. Baltimore: Johns Hopkins University Press, 1992.
Feser, Edward. "Contract Schmontract." web.archive.org/web/20120519182541/http://www.ideasinactiontv.com/tcs_daily/2006/01/contract-schmontract.html.
Finkelstein, Joanne L. "Biomedicine and Technocratic Power." *The Hastings Center Report* 20.4 (1990) 13–16.
Fletcher, John C. "Evolution of Ethical Debate about Human Gene Therapy." *Human Gene Therapy* 1.1 (1990) 55–68.
Foltz, Bruce. *The Noetics of Nature Environmental Philosophy and the Holy Beauty of the Visible*. New York: Fordham University Press, 2014.
Fraga, Brian. "The US 'Futile-Care' Debate: How Are Cases Like Alfie Evans' Handled Here?" www.ncregister.com/daily-news/the-us-futile-care-debate-how-are-cases-like-alfie-evans-handled-here.
Francis. *Praise Be to You—Laudato Si': On Care for Our Common Home*. San Francisco: Ignatius, 2015.
Frum, David. "The Lessons of the Somme." *The Atlantic*. Last modified July 1, 2016. www.theatlantic.com/international/archive/2016/07/somme-centennial/489656/.

Gabriel, Markus. *Fields of Sense: A New Realist Ontology.* Edinburgh: Edinburgh University Press, 2015.
Gadow, Sally. "Existential Ecology: The Human/Natural World." *Social Science and Medicine* 35.4 (1992) 597–602.
Gandhi, Mahatma. *Indian Home Rule.* Auckland: The Floating Press, 2014.
Garth, John. *Tolkien and the Great War: The Threshold of Middle-Earth.* London: HarperCollins, 2011.
Gilson, Étienne. *Being and Some Philosophers.* Toronto: Pontifical Institute of Mediaeval Studies, 1952.
———. *Le Thomisme: Introduction à La Philosophie de Saint Thomas d'Aquin.* 6th ed. Paris: J. Vrin, 1986.
———. *The Unity of Philosophical Experience.* San Francisco: Ignatius, 1999.
Goldstein, Jeffrey. "Emergence as a Construct: History and Issues." *Emergence* 1.1 (1999) 49–72.
Gonzales, Philip. "Why We Need Erich Przywara." *Communio* 44.1 (2017) 144–72.
Goodenough, Ursula. "Vertical and Horizontal Transcendence." *Zygon* 36 (2001) 21–31.
Goodenough, Ursula, and Terrance W. Deacon. "The Sacred Emergence of Nature." In *The Oxford Handbook of Religion and Science*, edited by Philip Clayton and Zachary Simpson, 853–71. Oxford: Oxford University Press, 2006.
Gould, Stephen Jay. *Rocks of Ages: Science and Religion in the Fullness of Life.* Cambridge: International Society for Science and Religion, 2007.
Green, Mitchell S. "Kripke, Saul Aaron." In *Dictionary of Modern American Philosophers*, edited by John R. Shook, 1360–67. Bristol: Thoemmes Continuum, 2005.
Guardini, Romano. *Letters from Lake Como: Explorations in Technology and the Human Race.* Translated by Geoffrey W. Bromiley. Grand Rapids: Eerdmans, 1994.
Guttmacher Institute. "Abortion Incidence and Service Availability in the United States." https://www.guttmacher.org/report/abortion-incidence-service-availability-us-2017.
Habermas, Jürgen. *The Theory of Communicative Action, Vol. II: Lifeworld and System: A Critique of Functionalist Reason.* Translated by Thomas McCarthy, Boston: Beacon, 2005.
Hanby, Michael. "Beyond Mechanism: The Cosmological Significance of David L. Schindler's Communio Ontology." In *Being Holy in the World: Theology and Culture in the Thought of David L. Schindler*, edited by Nicholas J. Healy and D. C. Schindler, 162–91. Grand Rapids: Eerdmans, 2011.
———. "Creation as Aesthetic Analogy." In *The Analogy of Being: Invention of the Antichrist or the Wisdom of God?* edited by Thomas Joseph White, 341–78. Grand Rapids: Eerdmans, 2011.
———. "A Few Words on Balthasar's First Word." In *How Balthasar Changed My Mind: Fifteen Scholars Reflect on the Meaning of Balthasar for Their Own Work*, edited by Rodney A. Howsare and Larry S. Chapp, 74–90. New York: Crossroad, 2008.
———. "The Gospel of Creation and the Technocratic Paradigm: Reflections on a Central Teaching of *Laudato Si'*." *Communio* 42.4 (2015) 724–47.
———. "Medicine after the Death of God." *Humanum* 4 (2014). humanumreview.com/articles/medicine-after-the-death-of-god.
———. "A More Perfect Absolutism." www.firstthings.com/article/2016/10/a-more-perfect-absolutism.

———. *No God, No Science? Theology, Cosmology, Biology.* Malden, MA: Wiley-Blackwell, 2017.
Handler, Philip. "Science's Continuing Role." *BioScience* 20 (1920) 1101–6.
Harman, Graham. *Bells and Whistles: More Speculative Realism.* Winchester, UK: Zero Books, 2013.
———. *Guerrilla Metaphysics: Phenomenology and the Carpentry of Things.* New York: Open Court, 2005.
Harold, Franklin M. *The Way of the Cell: Molecules, Organisms, and the Order of Life.* New York: Oxford University Press, 2003.
Hart, David Bentley. *The Beauty of the Infinite: The Aesthetics of Christian Truth.* Grand Rapids: Eerdmans, 2004.
———. "The Destiny of Christian Metaphysics: Reflections on the Analogia Entis." In *The Analogy of Being: Invention of the Antichrist or Wisdom of God?*, edited by Thomas Joseph White, 395–409. Grand Rapids: Eerdmans, 2011.
———. *Experience of God: Being, Consciousness, Bliss.* New Haven: Yale University Press, 2013.
———. "The Illusionist." *The New Atlantis*, no. 53 (2007) 109–21.
———. "Purpose and Function." www.firstthings.com/article/2013/08/purpose-and-function.
———. *A Splendid Wickedness and Other Essays.* Grand Rapids: Eerdmans, 2016.
Hawking, Stephen, and Leonard Mlodinow. *The Grand Design.* London: Bantam, 2010.
Healy, Nicholas J. *The Eschatology of Hans Urs von Balthasar: Being as Communion.* New York: Oxford University Press, 2005.
———. "*Praeambula fidei*: David L. Schindler and the Debate over 'Christian Philosophy.'" In *Being Holy in the World: Theology and Culture in the Thought of David L. Schindler*, edited by Nicholas J. Healy and D. C. Schindler, 89–121. Grand Rapids: Eerdmans, 2011.
Heidegger, Martin. *Identity and Difference.* Translated by Joan Stambaugh. Chicago: University of Chicago Press, 1969.
———. *The Question Concerning Technology, and Other Essays.* Translated by William Lovitt. New York: Harper Perennial, 2013.
Hütter, Reinhard. "Attending to the Wisdom of God." In *The Analogy of Being: Invention of the Antichrist or the Wisdom of God?*, edited by Thomas Joseph White, 209–45. Grand Rapids: Eerdmans, 2011.
International Theological Commission. "In Search of a Universal Ethic: A New Look at the Natural Law." www.vatican.va/roman_curia/congregations/cfaith/cti_documents/rc_con_cfaith_doc_20090520_legge-naturale_en.html#.
Jackson, Peter, dir. *They Shall Not Grow Old.* 1 hr, 39 min. WingNut Films, 2018.
James, William. *Pragmatism: A New Name for Some Old Ways of Thinking.* Mineola, NY: Dover, 1995.
John Paul II, Pope. "Address to the Conference on Environment and Health." https://w2.vatican.va/content/john-paul-ii/en/speeches/1997/march/documents/hf_jp-ii_spe_19970324_ambiente-salute.html.
Johnston, Adrian. *Adventures in Transcendental Materialism: Dialogues with Contemporary Thinkers.* Edinburgh: Edinburgh University Press, 2014.
———. "Points of Forced Freedom: Eleven (More) Theses on Materialism." In *Speculations IV: Speculations: A Journal of Speculative Realism*, edited by Michael Austin et al., 91–98. Brooklyn: Punctum, 2013.

Jonas, Hans. *Philosophical Essays: From Ancient Creed to Technological Man*. Englewood Cliffs, NJ: Prentice-Hall, 1974.

———. "The Practical Uses of Theory." *Social Research* 51.1 (1984) 65–90.

Juengst, Eric T. "Germ-Line Gene Therapy: Back to Basics." *Journal of Medicine and Philosophy* 16.6 (1991) 587–92.

Kalton, Michael. "Green Spirituality: Horizontal Transcendence." In *Paths of Integrity, Wisdom, and Transcendence: Spiritual Development in the Mature Self*, edited by Melvin E. Miller, 187–200. London: Routledge, 2000.

Kass, Leon R. "New Beginnings in Life." In *The New Genetics and the Future of Man*, edited by Michael P. Hamilton, 15–63. Grand Rapids: Eerdmans, 1972.

Kauffman, Stuart A. *Reinventing the Sacred: A New View of Science, Reason, and Religion*. New York: Basic Books, 2008.

Kephart, Horace. *The Book of Camping and Woodcraft: A Guidebook for Those Who Travel in the Wilderness*. New York: Outing Publishing Company, 1906.

Kevles, Daniel J. *In the Name of Eugenics: Genetics and the Uses of Human Heredity*. New York: Knopf, 1985.

King, Martin Luther, Jr. *A Testament of Hope: The Essential Writings and Speeches of Martin Luther King, Jr*. Edited by James Melvin Washington. New York: Harper Collins, 1986.

Kohák, Erazim V. *The Embers and the Stars: A Philosophical Inquiry into the Moral Sense of Nature*. Chicago: University of Chicago Press, 1984.

Kühl, Stefan. *The Nazi Connection: Eugenics, American Racism, and German National Socialism*. New York: Oxford University Press, 2014.

Ladyman, James, et al. *Every Thing Must Go: Metaphysics Naturalized*. Oxford: Oxford University Press, 2014.

Lancellotti, Carlo. "Augusto Del Noce on the New Totalitarianism." *Communio* 44.2 (2017) 323–33.

———. "Science, Contemplation, and Ideology." The World and Christian Imagination Conference, 9 Nov 2006, Waco, TX, Baylor University.

Lehrs, Ernst. *Man or Matter: Introduction to a Spiritual Understanding of Nature on the Basis of Goethe's Method of Training and Observation*. 3rd ed. London: Rudolf Steiner, 1985.

Leibniz, Gottfried Wilhelm. *Philosophical Essays*. Edited and translated by Roger Ariew and Daniel Garber. Cambridge: Hackett, 1989.

Leopold, Aldo. *A Sand County Almanac: With Essays on Conservation from Round River*. New York: Ballantine, 1990.

———. "Wilderness as a Form of Land Use." *The Journal of Land and Public Utility Economics* 1.4 (1925) 398–404.

Lewis, C. S. *An Experiment in Criticism*. Cambridge: Cambridge University Press, 1961.

Lindberg, David C. *Science in the Middle Ages*. Chicago: University of Chicago Press, 2007.

López, Antonio. "Eternal Happening: God as an Event of Love." *Communio* 32.2 (2005) 214–45.

———. *Gift and the Unity of Being*. Cambridge: James Clarke, 2014.

Lovelock, James. *The Ages of Gaia*. New York: Norton, 1988.

———. *Gaia: A New Look at Life on Earth*. Oxford: Oxford University Press, 1979.

Lowe, E. J. *A Survey of Metaphysics*. Oxford: Oxford University Press, 2002.

Luke, Timothy W. *Ecocritique: Contesting the Politics of Nature, Economy, and Culture.* Minneapolis: University of Minnesota Press, 1997.

Lyotard, Jean-Francois. *The Postmodern Condition: A Report on Knowledge.* Translated by Geoff Bennington and Brian Massumi. Minneapolis: University of Minnesota Press, 1994.

Lysaught, M. Therese. "And Power Corrupts . . . : Religion and the Disciplinary Matrix of Bioethics." In *Handbook of Bioethics and Religion,* edited by David E. Guinn, 93–128. Oxford: Oxford University Press, 2006.

———. "Respect: Or, How Respect for Persons Became Respect for Autonomy." *The Journal of Medicine and Philosophy* 29.6 (2004) 665–80.

MacIntyre, Alasdair. *Dependent Rational Animals: Why Human Beings Need the Virtues.* Chicago: Open Court, 2001.

Mallia, Pierre. *The Nature of the Doctor–Patient Relationship: Health Care Principles Through the Phenomenology of Relationships with Patients.* Dordrecht: Springer, 2013.

Malone, Ruth E. "Policy as Product: Morality and Metaphor in Health Policy Discourse." *The Hastings Center Report* 29.3 (1999) 16–22.

Martínez de Anguita, Pablo. *Environmental Solidarity: How Religions Can Sustain Sustainability.* New York: Routledge, 2012.

Martínez de Anguita, Pablo, et al. "Environmental Economic, Political and Ethical Integration in a Common Decision-Making Framework." *Journal of Environmental Management* 88 (2008) 154–64.

Marx, Karl. *The Economic and Philosophic Manuscripts of 1844.* Translated by Martin Milligan. Amherst, NY: Prometheus, 2009.

Mathewes-Green, Frederica. "When Abortion Suddenly Stopped Making Sense." www.nationalreview.com/2016/01/abortion-roe-v-wade-unborn-children-women-feminism-march-life/.

McGrath, Sean J. *The Early Heidegger and Medieval Philosophy: Phenomenology for the Godforsaken.* Washington, DC: Catholic University of America Press, 2006.

McIntosh, Jonathan S. *The Flame Imperishable: Tolkien, St. Thomas, and the Metaphysics of Faërie.* Kettering, OH: Angelico, 2017.

McLuhan, Marshall, and Quentin Fiore. *The Medium Is the Massage: An Inventory of the Effects.* New York: Bantam, 1967.

Merchant, Carolyn. *Reinventing Eden: The Fate of Nature in Western Culture.* 2nd ed. New York: Routledge, 2013.

Milbank, John. "Foreword." In *Gift and the Unity of Being,* by Antonio López, ix–xiv. Eugene, OR: Cascade, 2014.

———. "The Franciscan Conundrum." *Communio* 42.2 (2015) 466–92.

———. "Only Theology Saves Metaphysics: On the Modalities of Terror." www.theologyphilosophycentre.co.uk/papers/Milbank_OnlyTheologySavesMetaphysics.pdf.

———. "Paul against Biopolitics." In *Paul's New Moment: Continental Philosophy and the Future of Christian Theology,* by John Milbank et al., 21–73. Grand Rapids: Brazos, 2010.

———. "The Shares of Being or Gift, Relation and Participation: An Essay on the Metaphysics of Emmanuel Levinas and Alain Badiou." www.theologyphilosophycentre.co.uk/papers/Milbank_Metaphysics-LevinasBadiou.pdf.

———. "Stanton Lecture 1: The Return of Metaphysics in the 21st Century." www.theologyphilosophycentre.co.uk/papers/Milbank_StantonLecture1.pdf.
———. "Stanton Lecture 2: Immanence and Life." www.theologyphilosophycentre.co.uk/papers/Milbank_StantonLecture2.pdf.
———. "Stanton Lecture 3: Immanence and Number." www.theologyphilosophycentre.co.uk/papers/Milbank_StantonLecture3.pdf.
———. "Stanton Lecture 8: The Surprise of the Imagined." www.theologyphilosophycentre.co.uk/papers/Milbank_StantonLecture8.pdf.
———. *Theology and Social Theory: Beyond Secular Reason*. 2nd ed. Malden, MA: Blackwell, 2006.
Milbank, John, and Adrian Pabst. *The Politics of Virtue: Post-Liberalism and the Human Future*. London: Rowman & Littlefield International, 2016.
Milbank, John, and Catherine Pickstock. *Truth in Aquinas*. London: Routledge, 2001.
Montagnes, Bernard. *The Doctrine of the Analogy of Being according to Thomas Aquinas*. Translated by E. M. Macierowski. Mikwaukee: Marquette University Press, 2004.
Moreno, Jonathan D. *The Body Politic: The Battle over Science in America*. New York: Bellevue, 2011.
———. "Can Ethics Consultation Be Saved? Ethics Consultation and Moral Consensus in a Democratic Society." In *Ethics Consultation: From Theory to Practice*, edited by Mark P. Aulisio et al., 23–35. Baltimore: Johns Hopkins University Press, 2003.
Morowitz, H. J. "Biology as a Cosmological Science." *Main Currents in Modern Thought* 28 (1972) 151–57.
Murphy, Francesca Aran. *God Is Not a Story: Realism Revisited*. Oxford: Oxford University Press, 2007.
Naess, Arne. "The Shallow and the Deep, Long-Range Ecology Movement. A Summary." *Inquiry* 16 (1973) 95–100.
Nagel, Thomas. *Mind and Cosmos: Why the Materialist Neo-Darwinian Conception of Nature Is Almost Certainly False*. Oxford: Oxford University Press, 2012.
Neuhaus, Richard John. *America against Itself: Moral Vision and the Public Order*. Notre Dame: University of Notre Dame Press, 1992.
Nichols, Aidan. "Balthasar's Aims in the 'Theological Aesthetics.'" In *Glory, Grace and Culture: The Works of Hans Urs von Balthasar*, edited by Ed Block, 107–26. Mahwah, NJ: Paulist, 2005.
Nietzsche, Friedrich. *The Will to Power*. Translated by Walter Kaufmann and R. J. Hollingdale. New York: Vintage, 1968.
Nordhaus, Ted, and Michael Shellenberger. *Break Through: From the Death of Environmentalism to the Politics of Possibility*. Boston: Houghton Mifflin, 2007.
Norris, Christopher. "Speculative Realism: Interim Report with Just a Few Caveats." In *Speculations IV: Speculations: A Journal of Speculative Realism*, edited by Michael Austin et al., 38–47. Brooklyn: Punctum, 2013.
Northcott, Michael S. "Indigenous Peoples, Land Rights, and Care for Creatures." Radical Ecological Conversion after Laudato Si': Discovering the Intrinsic Value of All Creatures, Human and Non-Human (conference), 8 Mar 2018, Rome, Pontifical Gregorian University.
Oakes, Edward T. "The Achievement of Alasdair MacIntyre." www.firstthings.com/article/1996/08/the-achievement-of-alasdair-macintyre.
———. *Pattern of Redemption: The Theology of Hans Urs von Balthasar*. New York: Continuum, 1997.

O'Connor, Tim. "Do We Have Souls?" https://web.archive.org/web/20170608005805/www.bigquestionsonline.com/2013/01/08/have-souls/.

O'Meara, Thomas F. *Erich Przywara, S.J.: His Theology and His World*. Notre Dame: University of Notre Dame Press, 2002.

Oster, Stefan. "Thinking Love at the Heart of Things: The Metaphysics of Being as Love in the Work of Ferdinand Ulrich." *Communio* 37.4 (2010) 661–700.

Pabst, Adrian. *Metaphysics: The Creation of Hierarchy*. Grand Rapids: Eerdmans, 2012.

Palmer, John. *Parmenides and Presocratic Philosophy*. Oxford: Oxford University Press, 2012.

Parmenides. *Parmenides of Elea: Fragments*. Edited by David Gallop. Toronto: University of Toronto Press, 1984.

Pellegrino, Edmund D. *The Philosophy of Medicine Reborn: A Pellegrino Reader*. Edited by H. Tristram Engelhardt and Fabrice Jotterand. Notre Dame: University of Notre Dame Press, 2011.

Pellegrino, Edmund D., and David C. Thomasma. *For the Patient's Good: The Restoration of Beneficence in Health Care*. New York: Oxford University Press, 1988.

Peters, Francis Edwards. *Greek Philosophical Terms: A Historical Lexicon*. New York: New York University Press, 1967.

Pieper, Josef. *Leisure: The Basis of Culture*. San Francisco: Ignatius, 2009.

———. *The Silence of St. Thomas: Three Essays*. South Bend, IN: St. Augustine's, 1999.

Pimm, S. L., et al. "The Biodiversity of Species and Their Rates of Extinction, Distribution, and Protection." *Science* 344.6187 (2014) 987, 1246752-1-10.

Plato. "Phaedrus." In *Complete Works*, edited by John M. Cooper, 506–56. Indianapolis: Hackett, 1997.

———. "The Republic." In *Complete Works*, edited by John M. Cooper, 971–1223. Indianapolis: Hackett, 1997.

———. "The Sophist." In *Complete Works*, edited by John M. Cooper, 235–93. Indianapolis: Hackett, 1997.

Plumwood, Val. "Nature, Self, and Gender: Feminism, Environmental Philosophy, and the Critique of Rationalism." *Hypathia* 6.1 (1991) 3–27.

Pollan, Michael. *The Botany of Desire: A Plant's-Eye View of the World*. New York: Random House, 2002.

Prades, Javier, and Marcos Cantos. "Postsecularism, Postmodernism and Pluralism. The Contribution of Christian Witness to the 'Good Life' in Contemporary Society." Translated by Michael D. Taylor. The Center for Ethics and Culture Fall Conference, 3 Nov. 2018, Notre Dame, IN, University of Notre Dame.

Prum, Richard O. *The Evolution of Beauty: How Darwin's Forgotten Theory of Mate Choice Shapes the Animal World—and Us*. New York: Anchor, 2018.

Przywara, Erich. *Analogia Entis: Metaphysics: Original Structure and Universal Rhythm*. Translated by John R. Betz and David Bentley Hart. Grand Rapids: Eerdmans, 2014.

Putnam, Hilary. *Ethics without Ontology*. Cambridge: Harvard University Press, 2004.

Quine, Willard Van Orman. *From a Logical Point of View: Nine Logico-Philosophical Essays*. Cambridge: Harvard University Press, 1980.

———. "Two Dogmas of Empiricism." *Philosophical Review* 60 (1951) 20–46.

———. *Word and Object*. Cambridge: MIT Press, 2013.

Ramsey, Paul. *Fabricated Man: The Ethics of Genetic Control*. New Haven: Yale University Press, 1970.

Ratzinger, Joseph. *Dogma and Preaching*. Translated by Michael J. Miller and Matthew J. O'Connell. San Francisco: Ignatius, 2011.
———. *Introduction to Christianity*. San Francisco: Ignatius, 2004.
Rawls, John. *Political Liberalism: Expanded Edition*. New York: Columbia University Press, 2005.
Ricoeur, Paul. *The Rule of Metaphor: Multi-Disciplinary Studies of the Creation of Meaning in Language*. Translated by Robert Czerny. Toronto: University of Toronto Press, 2008.
Rolston, Holmes. "Environmental Virtue Ethics: Half Truth but Dangerous as a Whole." In *Environmental Virtue Ethics*, edited by Ronald Sandler and Philip Cafaro, 61–78. Lanham: Rowman & Littlefield International, 2005.
Rorty, Richard. *Philosophy and the Mirror of Nature*. Princeton: Princeton University Press, 2018.
———. *Truth and Progress*. Philosophical Papers 3. Cambridge: Cambridge University Press, 1998.
Rothfork, John. "Postmodern Ethics: Richard Rorty and Michael Polanyi." *Southern Humanities Review* 29.1 (1995) 15–48.
Rowland, Tracey. *Benedict XVI: A Guide for the Perplexed*. London: T. & T. Clark International, 2010.
———. *Culture and the Thomist Tradition: After Vatican II*. London: Routledge, 2003.
Russell, Bertrand. "Knowledge by Acquaintance and Knowledge by Description." *Proceedings of the Aristotelian Society* 11 (1910) 108–28.
———. "On Denoting." *Mind* 14.56 (1905) 479–93.
Sachs, Carl B. "What Is to Be Overcome? Nietzsche, Carnap, and Modernism as the Overcoming of Metaphysics." *History of Philosophy Quarterly* 28 (2011) 303–18.
Schindler, D. C. "Beauty and the Holiness of Mind." In *Being Holy in the World: Theology and Culture in the Thought of David L. Schindler*, edited by Nicholas J. Healy and D. C. Schindler, 3–29. Grand Rapids: Eerdmans, 2011.
———. *The Catholicity of Reason*. Grand Rapids: Eerdmans, 2013.
———. *A Companion to Ferdinand Ulrich's* Homo Abyssus. Washington, DC: Humanum, 2019.
———. "Enriching the Good: Toward the Development of a Relational Anthropology." *Communio* 37.1 (2010) 643–59.
———. "'Ever Ancient, Ever New': Jesus Christ as the Concrete Analogy of Being." *Communio* 39.1 (2012) 33–48.
———. *Freedom from Reality: The Diabolical Character of Modern Liberty*. Notre Dame: Notre Dame University Press, 2017.
———. "The Grace of Being: Ferdinand Ulrich and the Task of a Faithful Metaphysics in the Face of Modernity." In *Christian Wisdom Meets Modernity*, edited by Kenneth Oakes, 149–64. London: Bloomsbury, 2016.
———. *Hans Urs von Balthasar and the Dramatic Structure of Truth: A Philosophical Investigation*. New York: Fordham University Press, 2004.
———. "Hans Urs von Balthasar, Metaphysics, and the Problem of Onto-Theology." *Analecta Hermeneutica* no. 1 (2009) 102–13.
———. "On Experience and Reason." *Communio* 37.2 (2010) 255–65.
———. "On the Universality of the University: A Response to Jean-Luc Marion." *Communio* 40.1 (2013) 77–99.

———. *Perfection of Freedom: Schiller, Schelling, and Hegel between the Ancients and the Moderns*. Cambridge: James Clarke, 2017.

———. *Plato's Critique of Impure Reason: On Goodness and Truth in the Republic*. Washington, DC: Catholic University of America Press, 2011.

———. "Quaerere Deum: Work as Love of God and World." *Humanum* no. 1 (2017). humanumreview.com/articles/quaerere-deum-work-as-love-of-god-and-world.

———. "Redeeming Work: On Technê as an Encounter Between God, Man, and the World." In *Enlightening the Mystery of Man: Gaudium et spes Fifty Years Later*, edited by Antonio López, 256–74. Washington, DC: Humanum Academic, 2018.

———. "Surprised by Truth: The Drama of Reason in Fundamental Theology." *Communio* 31.4 (2004) 587–611.

———. "Truth and the Christian Imagination: The Reformation of Causality and the Iconoclasm of the Spirit." *Communio* 33.4 (2006) 521–39.

———. "'Unless You Become a Philosopher . . .': On God, Being, and Reason's Role in Faith." *Communio* 43.1 (2016) 83–103.

———. "What's the Difference? On the Metaphysics of Participation in a Christian Context." *Saint Anselm Journal* 3.1 (2005) 1–27.

———. "Why Socrates Didn't Charge: Plato and the Metaphysics of Money." *Communio* 36.3 (2009) 394–426.

———. "'Wie kommt der Mensch in die Theologie?': Heidegger, Hegel, and the Stakes of Onto-Theo-Logy." *Communio* 32.4 (2005) 637–68.

———. "Work as Contemplation: On the Platonic Notion of Technê." *Communio* 42.4 (2015) 594–617.

Schindler, D. C., and Nicholas J. Healy, Jr. "Introduction." In *Being Holy in the World: Theology and Culture in the Thought of David L. Schindler*, edited by Nicholas J. Healy and D. C. Schindler, xi–xvii. Grand Rapids: Eerdmans, 2011.

Schindler, David L. "America's Technological Ontology and the Gift of the Given: Benedict XVI on the Cultural Significance of the Quaerere Deum." *Communio* 38.2 (2011) 237–78.

———. "Being, Gift, Self-Gift: A Reply to Waldstein on Relationality and John Paul II's Theology of the Body (Part One)." *Communio* 42.2 (2015) 221–51.

———. "Being, Gift, Self-Gift (Part Two)." *Communio* 43.3 (2016) 409–83.

———. "Biotechnology and the Givenness of the Good: Posing Properly the Moral Question Regarding Human Dignity." *Communio* 31.4 (2004) 612–45.

———. "The Embodied Person as Gift and the Cultural Task in America: Status Quaestionis." *Communio* 35.3 (2008) 397–431.

———. "The Given as Gift: Creation and Disciplinary Abstraction in Science." *Communio* 38.1 (2011) 52–102.

———. "'God and the End of Intelligence: Knowledge as Relationship." *Communio* 26.3 (1999) 510–40.

———. *Heart of the World, Center of the Church: "Communio" Ecclesiology, Liberalism, and Liberation*. Grand Rapids: Eerdmans, 1996.

———. "'Homelessness' and Market Liberalism: Toward an Economic Culture of Gift and Gratitude." In *Wealth, Poverty, and Human Destiny*, edited by Doug Bandow and David L. Schindler, 347–413. Wilmington, DE: ISI, 2003.

———. "In Memoriam: Kenneth L. Schmitz." *Communio* 44.2 (2017) 401–5.

———. "Introduction: The Problem of Mechanism." In *Beyond Mechanism*, edited by David L. Schindler, 1–12. Lanham, MD: University Press of America, 1986.

———. *Ordering Love: Liberal Societies and the Memory of God.* Grand Rapids: Eerdmans, 2011.

———. "The Person: Theology, Philosophy, and Receptivity." *Communio* 21.2 (1994) 172–90.

———. "The Significance of Hans Urs von Balthasar in the Contemporary Cultural Situation." In *Glory, Grace, and Culture: The Work of Hans Urs von Balthasar,* edited by Ed Block, 16–36. New York: Paulist, 2005.

Schmitz, Kenneth L. *The Gift: Creation.* Milwaukee: Marquette University Press, 1982.

———. *The Recovery of Wonder: The New Freedom and the Asceticism of Power.* Montreal: McGill-Queens University Press, 2005.

———. *Texture of Being: Essays in First Philosophy.* Edited by Paul O'Herron. Washington, DC: Catholic University of America Press, 2007.

Schöne-Seifert, Bettina. "Danger and Merits of Principlism: Meta-Theoretical Reflections on the Beauchamp/Childress-Approach to Biomedical Ethics." In *Bioethics in Cultural Contexts: Reflections on Methods and Finitude,* edited by Christoph Rehmann-Sutter et al., 110–19. Dordrecht: Springer, 2006.

Sherrard, Philip. *Human Image, World Image: The Death and Resurrection of Sacred Cosmology.* Limni, Evia, Greece: Denise Harvey, 2004.

Seeley, T. D. *Honeybee Ecology: a Study of Adaptation in Social Life.* Princeton: Princeton University Press, 1985.

Simpson, Christopher Ben. *Religion, Metaphysics, and the Postmodern: William Desmond and John D. Caputo.* Bloomington: Indiana University Press, 2009.

Smith, Christian. *What Is a Person? Rethinking Humanity, Social Life, and the Moral Good from the Person Up.* Chicago: University of Chicago Press, 2011.

Smith, Mick. *Against Ecological Sovereignty: Ethics, Biopolitics, and Saving the Natural World.* Minneapolis: University of Minnesota Press, 2011.

Soames, Scott. "Ontology, Analyticity and Meaning: The Quine-Carnap Dispute." University of Southern California, 2008. www.dornsife.usc.edu/assets/sites/678/docs/Selected_Publication/Quine_Carnap.pdf.

Sokolowski, Robert. *Introduction to Phenomenology.* Cambridge: Cambridge University Press, 2000.

Spaemann, Robert. *Happiness and Benevolence.* Edinburgh: T. & T. Clark, 2005.

Spitzer, Robert J. *New Proofs for the Existence of God: Contributions of Contemporary Physics and Philosophy.* Grand Rapids: Eerdmans, 2010.

Stahl, Ronit Y., and Ezekiel J. Emanuel. "Physicians, Not Conscripts—Conscientious Objection in Health Care." *New England Journal of Medicine* 376.14 (2017) 1380–85.

Steele, Dan. "Postmodern Metaphysics: Violence vs. Music." www.wordonfire.org/resources/blog/postmodern-metaphysics-violence-vs-music/5925/.

Tahko, Tuomas E. "In Defence of Aristotelian Metaphysics." In *Contemporary Aristotelian Metaphysics,* edited by Tuomas E. Tahko, 26–43. Cambridge: Cambridge University Press, 2012.

Taylor, Jameson. "A Defense of Moral Praxis: Karol Wojtyla's Acting Person." PhD diss., University of Dallas, 2007.

Taylor, Mary G. "Deeper Ecology: A Catholic Vision of the Person in Nature." *Communio* 38.4 (2011) 583–620.

———. "Ecology on One's Knees: Reading *Laudato Si'*." *Communio* 42.4 (2015) 618–51.

———. "Healing the Rift? Christians and Ecology." *Second Spring* 14 (2011) 17–23.

ten Have, Henk A. M. J. "Medical Technology Assessment and Ethics: Ambivalent Relations." *The Hastings Center Report* 25.5 (1995) 13–19.

Thomson, Iain. "Ontology and Ethics at the Intersection of Phenomenology and Environmental Philosophy." *Inquiry* 47 (2004) 380–412.

Tolkien, J. R. R. *The Letters of J. R. R. Tolkien*. Edited by Humphrey Carpenter. Boston: Houghton Mifflin, 2000.

———. *The Lord of the Rings*. Boston: Houghton Mifflin, 1994.

———. *The Silmarillion*. Edited by Christopher Tolkien. Boston: Houghton Mifflin, 2004.

Trakakis, Nick. "Meta-Philosophy of Religion." *Ars Disputandi* 7.1 (2007) 179–220.

Tunstall, Dwayne. *Doing Philosophy Personally: Thinking about Metaphysics, Theism, and Antiblack Racism*. New York: Fordham University Press, 2013.

Turner, James Morton. "From Woodcraft to Leave No Trace: Wilderness, Consumerism, and Environmentalism in Twentieth-Century America." *Environmental History* 7.3 (2002) 462–84.

Tyson, Paul. *De-fragmenting Modernity: Reintegrating Knowledge with Wisdom, Belief with Truth, and Reality with Being*. Eugene, OR: Cascade, 2017.

———. "A Post-Secular Approach to Understanding Religion and Global Security." In *Faith's Knowledge: Explorations into the Theory and Application of Theological Epistemology*, 130–58. Eugene, OR: Wipf & Stock, 2013.

———. "Reasoning within the Good: An Interview with David C. Schindler." *Radical Orthodoxy: Theology, Philosophy, Politics* 1 (2012) 322–32.

———. *Returning to Reality: Christian Platonism for Our Times*. Eugene, OR: Cascade, 2014.

Ulrich, Ferdinand. *Homo Abyssus: The Drama of the Question of Being*. Translated by D. C. Schindler. Washington, DC: Humanum, 2018.

Vattimo, Gianni, and Carmelo Dotolo. *Dios: La posibilidad buena: Un coloquio en el umbral entre filosofía y teología*. Barcelona: Herder, 2012.

Vaughan, Diane. *Uncoupling: Turning Points in Intimate Relationships*. New York: Vintage, 1990.

Veatch, Robert M. *Hippocratic, Religious, and Secular Medical Ethics: The Points of Conflict*. Washington, DC: Georgetown University Press, 2012.

Vieira, Celso. "Which Is More Fundamental: Processes or Things?" aeon.co/ideas/which-is-more-fundamental-processes-or-things.

Walker, Adrian. "'Constitutive Relations': Toward a Spiritual Reading of Physis." In *Being Holy in the World: Theology and Culture in the Thought of David L. Schindler*, edited by Nicholas J. Healy and D. C. Schindler, 123–61. Grand Rapids: Eerdmans, 2011.

———. "Foreword." In *The Radiance of Being: Dimensions of Cosmic Christianity*, 1–3. Tacoma: Angelico, 2013.

———. "Love Alone: Hans Urs von Balthasar as a Master of Theological Renewal." In *Love Alone Is Credible: Hans Urs von Balthasar as Interpreter of the Catholic Tradition*, edited by David L. Schindler, 16–38. Grand Rapids: Eerdmans, 2008.

———. "Personal Singularity and the Communio Personarum: A Creative Development of Thomas Aquinas' Doctrine of Esse Commune." *Communio* 31.3 (2004) 457–79.

———. "The Poverty of Liberal Economics." In *Wealth, Poverty, and Human Destiny*, edited by Doug Bandow and David L. Schindler, 19–50. Wilmington, DE: ISI, 2003.

Weber, Max. *Economy and Society*. Berkeley: University of California Press, 1968.

———. *The Protestant Ethic and Spirit of Capitalism*. Translated by Stephen Kalberg. New York: Routledge, 2001.

Weigel, George. "Remembering Father Neuhaus." www.newsweek.com/weigel-remembering-father-neuhaus-77699.

Westphal, Merold. *Overcoming Onto-Theology: Toward a Postmodern Christian Faith*. New York: Fordham University Press, 2001.

Wheeler, Samuel C., III. *Neo-Davidsonian Metaphysics: From the True to the Good*. New York: Routledge, 2013.

———. "Saul Kripke." Review of *Saul Kripke*, edited by Alan Berger. *The European Legacy* 19.2 (2014) 284–85.

White, Lynn. "The Historical Roots of Our Ecologic Crisis." *Science* 155.3767 (1967) 1203–7.

White, Richard. *The Organic Machine: The Remaking of the Columbia River*. New York: Hill and Wang, 2001.

Whitman, James Q. *Hitler's American Model: The United States and the Making of Nazi Race Law*. Princeton: Princeton University Press, 2018.

Wilson, Edward O. *Consilience: The Unity of Knowledge*. New York: Vintage, 1999.

———. *Half-Earth: Our Planet's Fight for Life*. New York: Liveright, 2017.

Wippel, John F. *Mediaeval Reactions to the Encounter between Faith and Reason*. Milwaukee: Marquette University Press, 1995.

———. *The Metaphysical Thought of Thomas Aquinas: From Finite Being to Uncreated Being*. Washington, DC: Catholic University of America Press, 2000.

Wojtyła, Karol. *The Acting Person*. Translated by Andrzej Potocki. Dordrecht: D. Reidel, 1979.

World Health Organization. "Mental Health." www.who.int/mental_health/en/.

Wortman-Wunder, Emily. "The West, When Women Are Telling the Story." *High Country News* 49.19 (2017) www.hcn.org/issues/49.19/the-west-when-women-are-telling-the-story.

Zimmerman, Michael E. *Contesting Earth's Future: Radical Ecology and Postmodernity*. Berkeley: University of California Press, 1997.

www.ingramcontent.com/pod-product-compliance
Lightning Source LLC
Chambersburg PA
CBHW022002220426
43663CB00007B/926